Children and television

Since the first edition of *Children and Television: The One-Eyed Monster?* was published in 1990, the home entertainment environment has undergone evolutionary change. There has been an explosion in the number of television channels available and in the range of entertainment media on offer, such as CD-ROM and interactive video games.

This completely revised second edition of *Children and Television* brings the story of children and television right up to date. In addition to presenting the latest research on all of the themes covered in the first edition, it includes a discussion of the new entertainment media now available, and a new chapter which examines the role of television in influencing children's health-related attitudes and behaviour.

Barrie Gunter and Jill McAleer examine the research evidence into the effects of television on children and their responses to it. They conclude that children are more sophisticated viewers than we often give them credit for, and control television far more than it controls them.

Barrie Gunter is Professor of Journalism at the University of Sheffield. His previous publications include *The Anatomy of Adolescence* with Adrian Furnham (Routledge, 1989). **Jill McAleer** is Research and Information Manager for the Royal Borough of Kensington and Chelsea.

Children and television

Second edition

Barrie Gunter and Jill McAleer

London and New York

First edition published 1990; second edition published 1997
by Routledge
11 New Fetter Lane, London EC4P 4EE

Simultaneously published in the USA and Canada
by Routledge
29 West 35th Street, New York, NY 10001

© 1990, 1997 Barrie Gunter and Jill McAleer

Typeset in Times by Routledge
Printed and bound in Great Britain by Redwood Books,
Trowbridge, Wiltshire

British Library Cataloguing in Publication Data
A catalogue record for this book is available from the British Library

Library of Congress Cataloguing in Publication Data
A catalogue record for this book is available from the Library of Congress

ISBN 0–415–14451–5 (hbk)
ISBN 0–415–14452–3 (pbk)

Contents

Preface to the second edition

THE HOME ENTERTAINMENT EVOLUTION

Since the first edition of *Children and Television: The One-Eyed Monster?* was published in 1990, the home entertainment environment has undergone evolutionary change. The standard television set now represents the receptacle for a plethora of information and entertainment channels delivered through a variety of distribution systems. Since the beginning of the current decade, the average household in Britain has acquired a greater range of home entertainment equipment. In 1989, just under 500,000 households had a satellite dish receiver and just over 300,000 were linked to a cable television system. By 1994, nearly 3,000,000 homes had satellite television and over 1,000,000 had cable.[1]

Today, family households use TV sets for a great deal more than simply watching broadcast television. With around one in six homes with children (17 per cent) possessing a video camera, many now increasingly engage in producing their own video material. Young viewers these days want to interact with and actively control events on screen, and approaching half of all homes with children have a home computer linked to a TV monitor (45 per cent), and the same number own video games.[2]

With the profound and rapidly occurring changes that have taken place with television in the past few years, it is timely to take a fresh look at children's involvement with television. The first edition of this book covered research up to the late 1980s. This second edition revisits the topics examined before, bringing each one up to date with a discussion of the latest research evidence to emerge during the 1990s. In addition, a new topic has been added, which examines the role of television in shaping children's health-related knowledge, attitudes and behaviours.

NEW TECHNOLOGY AND PARENTAL CONTROL

Even with the many new technological developments on the home entertainment front, standard television viewing remains a popular pastime for many millions of people, children included. Many of the old, established public concerns about the allegedly harmful side effects of too much telly-watching by young viewers, or of exposure to certain kinds of unsuitable programming, persist to this day. Indeed, with the expansion of subscription-based, satellite and cable television reception through which audiences can gain access to much more adult-oriented material than ever before, public anxieties about the possibility of children watching programmes containing explicit sexual material, graphic depictions of violence or 'adult' language have, if anything, become more acutely focused.

Concerns about violence on television in the United States in the 1990s have placed such political pressures upon broadcasters that, in early 1996, the leading American television networks and cable companies agreed to adopt a voluntary ratings system to warn viewers about levels of violence in programmes. In conjunction with this new policy is a new technological development in the form of a computer chip, nicknamed the 'V-chip', which can be built into the TV set to enable parents to scramble programmes they believe to be unsuitable for their children. The chip works by reading a code transmitted with the programme which identifies whether the programme contains certain categories of material: violence, sex, bad language or possibly an age classification similar to that used for cinema films. This facility is believed by its supporters to offer an important new weapon in the parental armoury, giving them greater control over what their children are able to watch, even when parents themselves are not physically present to control their youngsters' use of the set. Meanwhile, critics have voiced concerns that this device may give broadcasters an excuse to transmit even more salacious material, knowing that parents have the power to block out any programmes they don't want their children to watch. Other observers have pointed out two further problems. First, the coding of all programmes will be expensive and needs careful thought as to the classification criteria to be used. Second, given the lifespan of the average TV set, it could be twenty years or more before everyone has a V-chip set. People are likely to hold on to their old sets, however, and many of them will probably find their way into children's bedrooms.

Of course, even if all these practical issues were resolved, in the end the effectiveness of any new technology always boils down to the willingness of people to use it. The control of children's viewing ultimately rests, as with all other aspects of a child's early socialisation, primarily with parents. Parents generally accept that they share responsibility with broadcasters for what their children might watch on television.[3]

Despite this admission, many parents do not know what their children watch and, indeed, given the growth of sets in children's bedrooms, cannot reasonably be expected to. Even so, as we will show in this book, while children do not accept everything they see on the small screen at face value, when they are young some guidance can be helpful in enabling them to make important distinctions about different kinds of television content, to view television more critically and selectively and to control for themselves how much (and what) they watch. In an evolving home entertainment environment in which more and more choice and control is passing into hands of the consumer, these are the kinds of measures that are likely to work best.

BG and JLM
April 1996

Preface to the first edition

THE 'CHILD' VIEWER: THE MYTH AND THE REALITY

How does today's society perceive children and television and the interaction between the two? Are youngsters really spending a high proportion of their waking hours staring fixedly at a television screen, making little attempt to communicate with the rest of the household? Do they passively absorb all they see and hear irrespective of content or format? And has the continuous bombardment of media 'messages' been a prime factor in increased breakdown of family life or encouraged spates of violent and antisocial behaviour amongst adolescents? If some of the sweeping generalisations quoted regularly in the daily press are to be believed, this and more is the 'true' effect of television – or is it?

Back in the nineteenth century and earlier in this one, concerns were expressed about the harmful effects that the growing avalanche of 'pulp literature' such as 'penny dreadfuls', cheap novelettes and comics would have, both on the young and the less well-educated. Nowadays, although some concern is still expressed about the content and quality of children's literature, notably comics and the ubiquitous Enid Blyton, it is a mere 'drop in the ocean' when compared with the amount of criticism levelled at television. But how much of this criticism is based on 'myth' and therefore unjustified and how much is reality?

THE CONCERNS: WHAT ARE THEY?

In Britain today, 98 per cent of all homes possess at least one television set, the majority of them (particularly those with children) more than one, yet in the early 1950s only a handful of people had the desire or the means to purchase a set. However, from the late 1950s onwards, there was a phenomenal explosion in the number of television households, with a parallel increase in the amount and type of programming. More and more, educationalists, politicians, as well as other authority figures started to voice their fears about the social and educational impact that this new medium might have, fears that continue to be expressed today. For example, it is not uncommon to read stories in the press about individuals committing a violent crime, the idea for which arose from something seen on television. We are told that television can provide examples of bad behaviour which young viewers especially may copy, or that seeing well-known television characters using violence to solve their problems provides some justification for young viewers to emulate their heroes: 'If the members of *The A-Team* can do it, why can't I?'

It is said that television can teach lessons about the world, but that this is a world in which certain types of people predominate, a world in which they behave towards each other in certain ways and play certain types of roles. Television, in other words, is a very stereotyped world. Women, for example, tend to be portrayed in domestic roles more than professional ones and, as opposed to men, are more often the victims of crime. They are also portrayed as more emotional and less independent than men on television. These portrayals, it is claimed by some writers, can cultivate, especially among children who know no better, stereotyped beliefs about the sexes which serve to limit their career aspirations and their attitudes towards men and family life.

Educationalists have been worried that television viewing would displace reading and harm children's school performance. Other critics of television have argued that it is a disruptive influence in the family context both through its presence in the household and through the lessons and values it may teach.

Television is criticised as giving a low priority to family life in that it rarely depicts happy, intact families on screen. It is seen as having a deleterious influence on family interaction – family members no longer talk to each other as they used to – leading to a breakdown in the essential bonds that are so crucial to a stable family environment and to the development of socially responsible children. These then are the concerns, but how justified are they?

In this book, we shall examine evidence for the role television can play in children's intellectual and social development. Despite the emphasis given to possible social ills of television, we believe a more balanced view of the medium's impact on children is warranted. Television can be of general benefit to children. It can bring them into contact with aspects of life they would not otherwise become aware of. It can provide a valuable tool in the home and at school not simply to keep children occupied but also, if used appropriately, as a constructive way to use their time.

There are many myths about television and children. These include misconceptions about how youngsters use it, how actively they respond to it, and how much and in what ways they are changed by it. There is a bias towards thinking ill of television when the medium deserves a fair hearing. Television is not a 'one-eyed monster' lurking impishly in the corner of the living room, kitchen or bedroom waiting to exert an evil influence over young members of the household. It is a channel through which a range of entertainment, drama and learning can be obtained and experienced and increasingly these days is under the control of the viewer.

BG and JLM
April 1990

Chapter 1

What is the nature of children's viewing?

VIEWING PATTERNS

Television may be almost a universal feature on the domestic scene, but it is not used in the same way by everyone who has access to a set. To begin our look at children and television, we shall examine some basic questions about television viewing:

- When do children begin to watch?
- How much viewing goes on?
- What kinds of programmes are watched?
- In what ways does viewing change with age?
- How does viewing interact with other activities?

MEASURING TELEVISION VIEWING

There are various ways of finding out from people how much and what kinds of television they watch. Some researchers draw a distinction between 'on-line' and 'off-line' measurement of television viewing. 'Off-line' techniques include questionnaires, telephone interviews and, arguably, paper and pencil diaries, and are characterised by the fact that they obtain information from viewers about what they have watched when they are not actually watching. 'On-line' techniques, such as people meters and direct observation, obtain viewing measures while individuals are in the process of watching television.[1] The most popular techniques used include traditional data collection via *questionnaires, diaries* and, more recently, *electronic meters* (none of which is able to produce viewing figures of guaranteed accuracy), plus *observation methods.*

Questionnaires, popular with researchers because they are cheap and convenient to produce, invariably require viewers to estimate retrospectively the amount of television they have watched for a given period of time. Diaries, which usually consist of a weekly booklet divided into timed segments or programme listings, have to be completed by a pre-selected panel of viewers as they watch. However, the measuring tools most heavily relied upon by the broadcasting industry to estimate audience ratings (i.e. the number of people who have watched a particular programme) are either the electronic set meters or the more sophisticated people meters. Electronic set meters, commonly used in conjunction with diaries, record when and how long a television set is switched on, and which channel it is tuned to at a particular time. People meters are also set meters, but with an electronic rather than a pencil and paper diary, whereby individuals push buttons on a handset to indicate their presence or absence when the set is switched on.

However, all of these methods are usually dependent on the reliability of viewers themselves. For example, how many people who complete questionnaires really remember the exact number of hours they watched the previous day or week? How many more fail to push the button on their people meter each time they enter or leave the room and, once their viewing presence has been registered, how much of their attention is then directed at the screen?

Observation

On rare occasions researchers have observed television viewing directly. These studies have generally been undertaken – either via participant observation where an observer joins a household, or via direct film or video recording of behaviour in front of the screen – to offer insight into the use of television by families which are, by and large, unattainable by more traditional methods.

Photographic records of a family's viewing behaviour have been made by placing either a time-lapse still camera or video camera in the home. Observers may record activities by using a structural log or by less structural note-taking. These methods can produce a wealth of detailed information about how people watch television; they also raise questions about the accuracy of viewing figures obtained by more traditional methods.[2]

An investigation of the way people watched television in the United States started out with the principal aim of testing the accuracy of viewers' personal questionnaire or diary estimates of how much they watched. Video cameras were installed in the main television viewing rooms at the homes of twenty families who volunteered to take part. One camera was mounted over the TV set and filmed the family while watching; the other camera was aimed directly at the set so as to film the programmes actually being watched. These pictures were then relayed to a video recorder in an equipment truck outside the home.[3]

Participants also filled out a variety of questionnaires designed to estimate viewing behaviour. These consisted of a five-day diary, with each day broken down into fifteen-minute segments. Families had to mark off the intervals during which they watched television. Two questionnaires were also administered. One asked the families to indicate which programmes they had watched on the previous day and how much time they spent with each programme, and a second given at the end of the observation period, asked for an overall estimate of the amount of time spent watching over the five days.

The level of agreement between what people entered into their viewing diaries and what they were observed to watch ranged from 92 per cent agreement in the best case to 54 per cent in the worst case, with an average agreement of 71 per cent. The researchers found that underreporting of viewing time (5.5 per cent) was rare, whereas overreporting was relatively frequent (24.8 per cent).

Questionnaire estimates of viewing produced less agreement with observational evidence than diary measures. When required to produce an estimate for the five-day period, the average level of agreement with camera evidence was only 44 per cent. One complicating feature of this study was the fact that the researchers unfortunately did not determine whether families were basing their reported viewing simply on the amount of time they were present in the viewing room while the TV was switched on or the extent to which they were actually watching the screen. Observational evidence has revealed that people do not always look towards the screen when the set is switched on.

Similar in-home, video-recorded observational studies of viewers' attention to the television screen have been reported by Dan Anderson and his colleagues. They installed time-lapse video cameras in the homes of ninety-nine families and recorded family viewing behaviour and what they were watching for ten full days in each case. The equipment automatically began recording when the set was switched on. In this study, emphasis was placed on children's attention to the screen.[4]

The relative accuracy of diary methods of viewing depended on the precise observational criterion used to corroborate viewers' own estimates. Anderson found, for instance, that families overestimated viewing when the criterion was eyes actually directed towards the TV screen. When diaries were compared with presence in the viewing room, viewers' estimates proved to be much more accurate. The diaries may therefore have been accurate records of what most people consider to be 'watching TV': normally being present in a room with a set in use.

It was found that parents' diary estimates of the children's viewing were accurate when compared with camera evidence of their youngsters' presence in the room when the set was on. Parents were generally better at keeping accurate records for very young children than for their older offspring, who more often viewed independently of parents.

As with all other methods of audience measurement, however, the direct observation technique is not without its problems. Many people are reluctant to be observed in the privacy of their own homes; low acceptance rates are therefore quite common. We must also ask questions about those people who do agree to participate. For example, are they representative of viewers in general? How much of their behaviour is normal, given that participants know they are being observed? Sample sizes are also limited by the expense of producing and controlling equipment and by the time taken to obtain the data. Usually few pieces of equipment exist, and if placements are for a week or longer it may take many months or even years to build up worthwhile samples. Bearing all these problems in mind, what do we know about the time children spend watching television and how it fits in with other activities?

WHEN DO CHILDREN BEGIN TO WATCH?

The television is an integral piece of the household furniture and practically every house has at least one set. Thus, children are born into a world in which television is present from the start. But at what point during early childhood does viewing actually begin?

There are different sources of evidence on this. Parents' reports about their children's viewing have indicated that consistent viewing begins between the age of 2 and 3. Wilbur Schramm and his colleagues reported 2.8 years as the average age of regular television viewing based on the testimony of parents.[5] Following on from Schramm, other published observations have revealed a gradually growing attentiveness from about 2 years old. Under more contrived conditions, researchers have observed a sharp increase in the frequency of looks at a TV screen at the age of 2.5. This increase was correlated with a similar sharp increase in the amount of viewing the same children were reported by parents to do at home.[6]

Even though children are obviously beginning to look at television even as infants, the set by no means commands their constant attention. When 3- to 5-year-olds were monitored while watching *Sesame Street*, the children looked at and away from the TV set about 215 times an hour. Nearly 75 per cent of the looks were under six seconds in length. Lower frequencies of looks have been observed elsewhere, but even those corroborate the rapidly shifting nature of infants' attention to the screen while watching television.[7]

HOW MUCH VIEWING AND WHEN?

It has often been claimed that television can harm children. But anxieties about its undesirable side effects tend to be founded on ill-formed assumptions about the nature of children's television watching. We are told, for instance, that children watch too much television and stay up late to watch programmes that are unsuitable for them.

Another common belief is that children increasingly are exposed to heavy diets of violence-laden programming which can teach them examples of antisocial conduct or condition in them a callous attitude toward violence and its victims in real life. What are the facts of the matter? Are children spending large proportions of their waking hours slumped in front of the box? Are children staying up past what should be their bedtimes, watching programmes they are not ready for? And are children feeding off a television diet of violence, which may only bring out the worst in them? Such worries are understandable, but are they substantiated when we take a careful and considered look at children's viewing figures?

The official viewing figures in the United Kingdom are published by the Broadcasters' Audience Research Board (BARB). Currently, they are drawn from a national panel of some 4,435 households recruited and run by one of Europe's biggest market research companies, Taylor Nelson AGB. Data are collected electronically through a meter system. Each TV set in panel households has an electronic meter attached to it which keeps a record of when the set is switched on and the TV channel it is tuned to. In addition, householders are supplied with a remote control handset, referred to as a 'people meter', with which they indicate their presence in front of the screen when the set is on. All this information is stored in the set meter which is automatically telephoned over night so that the day's viewing data can be pulled off and entered into a central computer. Projections from these data then provide estimates of viewing for the population as a whole or for particular sections of it.

Table 1.1 shows BARB estimates of average amount of viewing per day for a range of age groups, in each of two spells: from 1982 to 1984, and from 1992 to 1994. Focusing on the 4 to 15 years age range, two trends can be highlighted. First, viewing levels rise through ages 4 to 11 and average between two and a half and three hours a day. During the 1980s viewing for the early teenage group exhibited signs of dropping off, but in the 1990s this trend has shown signs of reversing. In the 1982–1984 period, viewing sank to its lowest point during late teens and early twenties but remained largely unchanged for this age group during the 1992–1994 period. At this age, of course, young people tend to go out a lot more. Yet, despite a developing social life outside the home, television viewing in the 1990s has remained a popular pastime among young adults. Second, the average amount of daily viewing carried out by pre-teenage children showed little change from the mid-1980s to mid-1990s, while the average viewing for teenagers and young adults increased over the same period. This trend was also present for most of the adult age groups – the exceptions being the 45–54s. This increase in viewing time probably reflects a response to the expansion of hours of television output through the late 1980s into the 1990s with the growth of satellite and cable TV viewing. A number of the new satellite channels have been especially popular with children and young people. The youngest age groups exhibit the greatest preference for new channels delivered via cable and satellite. In the UK, these channels account for nearly two-thirds of viewing among children up to the age of nine. The channels which are targeted specifically at this age group, such as Cartoon Network, The Disney Channel and The Children's Channel, are favoured the most by young audiences.[8]

Table 1.1   Number of hours of TV watching each day

| | Age groups | | | | | |
	4–11	12–15	16–24	25–34	45–54	55+
1994	2.7	2.7	2.8	3.5	3.6	4.8
1993	2.7	2.8	2.8	3.6	3.6	4.8
1992	2.8	2.6	2.5	3.4	3.5	5.0
1984	2.8	2.6	2.2	3.5	3.8	4.8
1983	2.5	2.1	2.2	3.4	3.5	4.1
1982	2.7	2.5	2.4	3.4	3.6	4.2

Source: IBA/BARB/AGB, 1982–1984; Taylor Nelson AGB/BARB/AGB Television, (1992–1994)
Notes: Channel 4 started 1982
        Breakfast programmes started 1983
        Daytime (BBC, then ITV) from late 1986 onwards
        Late-night services from mid-1987
        BARB measurement system changed December 1984
        Satellite introduced mid-1980s
        1992–1994 figures are for 4–9s and 10–15s

It should also be noted that the BARB measurement system changed its definition of viewership in 1984. A person was classified as a viewer if he/she watched for at least eight minutes out of any quarter-hour segment. This definition was changed to three consecutive minutes in any fifteen, and produced a slight overall increase in apparent viewing levels.

Before leaving Table 1.1, it is worth noting that, despite claims that children are nowadays spending far too much time watching television, they are by no means the heaviest viewers. In the 1980s, every adult age group (except the youngest one) exhibited a greater average number of hours a day watching television than children, while in the 1990s children do the least viewing of any age group.

AND WHEN DO CHILDREN WATCH?

This is an important question and becoming more so as television hours expand. The main worry is about children staying up late at night to watch television. One reason for this worry is that after nine o'clock in the evening, which broadcasters regard as a watershed, programmes may be shown which are suitable for adult viewing, but not necessarily for children.

Viewing figures produced for the television industry in the UK for 1995 show that children aged 4 to 15, watch television throughout the day. Peaks occur twice: first, in the morning and second, mid-evening. The morning peak occurs an hour or two later at weekends than on weekdays, and the weekend peak reaches a much higher level. On Saturday mornings, around one in four children watch television between 9.00 a.m. and 10.00 a.m. Peak viewing for children occurs between 5.00 p.m. and 9.00 p.m., with viewing levels falling off rapidly after 9.00 p.m. on weekdays and Sundays. On Saturday evenings, children's viewing remains at high levels until 11.00 p.m. (see Table 1.2).

Table 1.2   Children's audience level across the day

Time	Monday to Friday %	Saturday %	Sunday %
6.00 am	0	0	0
7.00 am	3	3	1
8.00 am	13	15	11
9.00 am	4	26	11
10.00 am	3	2	20
11.00 am	2	1	13
midday	3	13	9
1.00 pm	4	9	9
2.00 pm	4	8	10
3.00 pm	3	9	11
4.00 pm	22	12	13
5.00 pm	30	17	16
6.00 pm	31	32	19
7.00 pm	26	39	26
8.00 pm	28	37	27
9.00 pm	19	24	21
10.00 pm	11	17	10
11.00 pm	4	12	3
midnight	2	5	1
1.00 am	0	1	0
2.00 am	0	0	0
3.00 am	0	0	0
4.00 am	0	0	0
5.00 am	0	0	0

Source: BARB/AGB Television
Notes: 1 Figures show TVRs (Television Ratings) which represent the percentage of all child viewers, aged 4–15 years, watching terrestrial TV (BBC 1, BBC 2, ITV, Channel 4)
2 Data are averaged for four weeks ending 26 November 1995

WHICH PROGRAMMES DO CHILDREN WATCH?

While concerns have been voiced that children may watch not simply too much television *per se* but also too much of certain types of programmes, a close analysis of children's viewing diet shows that it can be as varied as the television schedules. The rapidly growing number of television channels in most modern industrial societies offer a varied mix of programmes, and children tend to sample liberally from the full range of material that is normally made available. There are certain categories of programmes, however, which stand among children's favourites. One key indicator of popularity is the extent to which programmes are watched. Table 1.3 shows the twenty most watched programmes among children, aged 4 to 15, for the UK in 1994. These programmes comprised movies, drama and light entertainment. There were eight movies among the twenty programmes most watched by children. The next most popular programme type was made-for-TV drama serials or series of which four featured in the top twenty. Clearly the most popular individual series among children were sitcoms, *Mr Bean* and *Gladiators*, each of which made three appearances.

Table 1.3   Top twenty programmes for children aged 4–15 (January–December 1994)

Programme	Channel	Day	Date (1994)	Audience size TVR	'000s	Share
1 Honey, I Shrank the Kids	ITV	Sun	9/1	40.6	3,868	82
2 Gladiators Final	ITV	Sat	17/12	37.7	3,602	76
3 National Lottery Live	BBC 1	Sat	19/11	36.8	3,515	74
4 Gladiators	ITV	Sat	12/11	36.5	3,490	75
5 Do It Yourself, Mr Bean	ITV	Mon	10/1	35.7	3,399	78
6 Neighbours	BBC 1	Wed	23/3	35.5	3,383	79
7 Ghostbusters II	ITV	Sun	27/2	34.4	3,272	76
8 Three Men and a Little Lady	ITV	Sun	6/2	34.2	3,254	78
9 EastEnders	BBC 1	Thurs	27/10	33.4	3,189	88
10 Uncle Buck	BBC 1	Mon	3/1	32.0	3,050	68
11 Gladiators Celebrity Challenge	ITV	Sat	24/12	31.1	2,974	62
12 E.T.	BBC 1	Fri	1/4	31.1	2,961	69
13 Turner and Hooch	ITV	Sun	16/1	31.0	2,955	76
14 Casualty	BBC 1	Sat	19/11	30.5	2,919	75
15 Back to School, Mr Bean	ITV	Wed	26/10	30.5	2,918	63
16 EastEnders	BBC 1	Tues	25/10	29.8	2,847	86
17 Mind the Baby, Mr Bean	ITV	Mon	25/4	29.3	2,790	68
18 Vice Versa	ITV	Sun	23/1	27.9	2,654	70
19 Superman (Film)	ITV	Sun	3/4	27.9	2,654	70
20 Noel's House Party	BBC 1	Sat	15/1	27.8	2,649	64

Source: Taylor Nelson AGB/BARB/AGB Television, 1995 (p. 63)

One of the concerns which parents might have about their children's viewing is the extent to which youngsters are exposed to unsavoury material. Public opinion surveys have consistently shown that people are concerned about the potentially upsetting qualities of programmes which contain violence, sex and bad language.[9] These concerns may, understandably, become heightened where there is a possibility that children may be regularly exposed to such content.

Do children watch too much violence on television? Youngsters may well name certain action adventure series among their favourites. This does not, however, provide an accurate reflection of what their viewing diet contains.

For example, one study in which children kept personal viewing diaries revealed that, on average, children watch two action-adventure programmes and two televised feature films a week. These, however, are interspersed among many other types of programmes. In fact, the programmes most popular with children are comedy and light entertainment made for the family.[10] The programmes listed in Table 1.3 corroborate this last point.

But boys and girls differ in their programme favourites. Boys watch more action-adventure and sport, girls watch more soap operas, while boys tend to watch more children's programmes than girls. With increased age, viewing of programmes made specially for children drops significantly, while viewing of general programming, particularly of feature films and light entertainment, increases substantially.[11]

DOES TELEVISION DISPLACE OTHER ACTIVITIES?

The introduction of television on a widespread scale in Britain in the late 1950s prompted concern among educationalists that viewing would displace reading and harm children's school performance. Although research at the time did not indicate an across-the-board reduction in all kinds of children's reading, once their family had acquired a television set, some displacement was evident.[12]

Thirty years on, the question of displacement of some activities (media-related ones in particular) by others has risen once again. The first half of the 1980s saw an unprecedented growth in availability and use of new electronic media. Increasingly today, homes possess not just one, but two, three, or even more, television sets. Furthermore, the set has acquired a range of accessories and attachments – video recorders, remote controls, personal computers, games consoles – which have significantly modified the way it is used.

Typically, children are more comfortable than their parents with each new medium or gadget as it comes along. They do not have so many hardened media habits to unlearn, they are more receptive to new ideas because they have fewer old ones to abandon and they often take to new gadgets as 'toys', if not for more serious purposes.[13]

Essentially, children are less threatened by new media than are grown-ups. But time is a limited commodity. Greater use of new electronic media or gadgetry must mean that less time is spent doing other things, and this possibly includes using more established media, such as books, magazines, newspapers and radio. Displacement of some activities – particularly something like reading, if it occurs – is as worrisome today as it ever was. To what extent, though, do television viewing and also (these days) the use of television-related equipment result in less time being devoted to other intellectual and social pursuits?

Television viewing uses up time. One observation is that if people spend more time watching television, they must be spending less time doing something else. This is a very simple statement, or at least it appears so on the surface. But in fact it has some very important implications concerning the impact of television. For instance, the displacement effects of television may be a crucial issue when they occur among young viewers during the development years of early cognitive and affective growth. The richness of children's learning environment can be measured in part by the quality and variety of available sources of lessons. Consequently, there is reason for concern about conditions under which a youngster's repertoire of activities may diminish due to a displacement from a competing activity. But which activities among children become squeezed when television viewing increases?

Two principal approaches have been used to ascertain whether or not television viewing displaces other activities. One method has been to monitor the effect on amounts of time devoted to other activities when television is introduced to a community for the first time. As television has become practically universal, however, it has become increasingly difficult for researchers to find virgin territory with totally naïve television audiences on whom such tests can be run. The available evidence obtains from the efforts of far-sighted researchers during the earliest days of television in Britain and the United States, similar investigations conducted in countries to whom television came rather later, and from studies of anomalous cases of communities in otherwise widely penetrated television nations who, because of their geographical location, were unable for many years to receive a television signal.[14]

A second method is to find out relative amounts of time devoted to television, and other media and non-media leisure activities, among current television generations. The critical question is whether heavy users of television spend less time on other activities than do light users of the box.[15] A more interesting question which we shall also examine is whether viewing certain types of television (rather than overall amount of viewing *per se*) is related, either positively or negatively, to time spent with different leisure pursuits.[16]

Early research reported mixed and largely inconclusive evidence that television viewing displaced participation in social, recreational, hobby or work activities among children and families. Studies of early television generations in the United States indicated that children and teenagers soon learned how to accommodate large amounts of television watching without sacrificing other activities. Generations of children reared with television found ways to integrate extensive use of this new medium without finding it necessary to neglect other pursuits.

The basic idea of displacement, however, may take an overly simplistic stance where the dynamic interaction of television and other activities is concerned. The displacement hypothesis, in its simplest form, posits a symmetrical, zero-sum relationship between television and other activities. It states that the amount of time spent viewing television is directly related to the time spent doing other things: the more time spent watching television, the less time spent on various other activities; conversely, the less time spent watching television, the more time a person will devote to other activities. There are some problems with this assumption. For one thing, television, as an activity, is often conducted simultaneously with other things.[17] Another important observation is that television is not invariably the primary activity among those activities simultaneously engaged in. Up to 30 per cent of all television viewing may only be a secondary activity, being carried out at the same time as something else – reading, eating, holding a conversation or, in the case of children particularly, playing.[18]

Following the early introduction of television to a community in the United States, Eleanor Maccoby noted that schoolchildren devoted much more time to television than they took away from other media.[19] Similarly, Thomas Coffin, a few years later, found that a decrease in children's use of other media accounted for only 50 per cent of the additional time spent watching television.[20] Where, then, does the additional time devoted to television come from? Both Maccoby and Coffin believed that it may have derived from non-media activities which went unmeasured in their studies. Even extensive time-budget studies which take into account a wide range of media and non-media activities, have not typically resolved this issue. One review of the literature concluded that, although television viewing did not reduce time spent on most other media, this could not fully account for all the time spent watching the box. There was certainly some evidence that other activities, such as hobbies and interests, might suffer to some extent, but that some of the television viewing time overlapped with the use of other media. Thus children learned to accommodate their reading and viewing by doing both at the same time.[21]

'THE MORE, THE MORE'

It may not simply be a matter of one activity displacing another. An alternative view is that television tends to displace 'functionally equivalent activities'.[22] According to this modified view of displacement, people most readily give up those activities that less effectively satisfy the needs that television serves. Thus, the functional equivalence between television and movies was cited as one reason for the decline in cinema attendance following the introduction of television.[23] Another, slightly different, view is that of functional reorganisation. This notion acknowledges that most mass media can serve a range of functions for individuals. When this is the case, the introduction of a new medium triggers a complex reorganisation of media-related activities such that parts of television might be used in respect of certain functions, while books may still be turned to for other types of gratification.[24] Finally, the marginal-activities hypothesis suggests that children make room for television in their daily activities by sacrificing 'fringe' or 'marginal' activities that are not clearly defined in terms of the functions they serve.[25] Much of the problem in addressing the marginal-activities hypothesis is that the type of activities of concern are by their very nature difficult to measure and most often ignored in the research literature.[26] A number of studies in the past fifteen years have shed further light on these alternative views about television displacement effects.

As television becomes increasingly pervasive throughout the world, it becomes more and more difficult to find people who have no experience of the medium. During the 1970s, however, several natural experiments emerged in which television-naïve communities were introduced to television for the first time. Fortunately, researchers were on the spot to record and measure the impact television had. Broadly, these investigations found that television did not simply replace time devoted to all other leisure activities, but bit into it selectively. Those activities or pursuits most likely to suffer were ones where television could provide the same sort of gratification, but more easily. In one natural experiment in Australia, researchers studied 98 families in a town without television (No-TV), 102 in a town with one year's experience with one government-run channel (Low-TV), and 82 in a town with at least two years' experience of two channels. (High-TV). Parents were interviewed about the amount of time they and their children spent in each of seventeen categories of leisure activities.

Children in the No-TV town spent more time in other leisure activities than did children from the TV towns. The increased presence of television was related to less time spent playing sports, watching sports and other outdoor activities. There was also less cinema attendance, radio listening and record playing among television communities.[27]

A major study conducted in Canada (directed by Tannis Macbeth Williams) examined the impact of television on a community which previously had had no television reception. Once again three towns were compared. These three towns were labelled Notel, Unitel and Multitel. At the start of the study, these towns had no TV, one channel only and four TV channels respectively. By the end of the research, Notel had one channel, Unitel had two channels and Multitel still had four channels. The three towns were compared at the outset and then again two years later, in order to find out what impact television had had on other activities.[28]

Television apparently had little, if any, influence on the number of community activities available to people in each town, but it had a noticeable negative effect on participation in those activities. People, especially children and teenagers, were much more active when there was no television, and became progressively less so as the amount of television available increased. The introduction of television in Notel produced a marked reduction in many community activities and participation in sports. Television decreased attendance at dances, suppers and parties. In other words, in the case of activities which cannot easily be time-shared with television, participation tended to decrease when television was introduced or when the amount of it that was available grew.

One interpretation of the finding which revealed a relatively frequent usage of television along with regular participation in other leisure activities consisted of a notion termed 'the more, the more'. This posits that those motivations which drive an individual to view large amounts of television will similarly compel that person to pursue other leisure activities. In this view, television watching and alternative leisure activities are not seen as competitive but serve rather to reinforce one another – in other words, an interest in one activity stimulates an interest in others.

On the evidence accumulated so far, there are no firm indications that television viewing invariably has a negative impact on how much time is spent doing other things – although, and almost inevitably, not all researchers are in agreement about this. There is mounting evidence that television may replace some alternative activities, though not others, among children and teenagers. Different activities bring different pleasures. Young people today have an unprecedented array of media, media-related gadgetry and in-house entertainment facilities at their disposal. The decision to choose one item or activity over another may depend on which one is judged to give the most satisfaction, given the young person's needs at the time.

Researchers in the United States have considered what they call the 'opportunity costs' of television for young people. Among one group of American adolescents it was found that, among other things, heavy television viewers forfeited taking part in some formal social activities with peers, were less likely to play musical instruments and gave up some sleep.

Interviews were carried out with children and teenagers aged 12 to 14 years who were asked about the television programmes they normally watched; the times they watched; their use of other media such as radio, records or tapes, newspapers and video games; their membership of groups or clubs; and other miscellaneous hobbies, pastimes, sleeping patterns and musical instruments.[29]

Modest support was found for the claims of 'the more, the more' explanations of time use. As television viewing time increased, so did time spent listening to records and tapes, and to a smaller degree listening to the radio and engaging in hobbies. There were some at-home activities which competed with television viewing. The playing of home video games (which may be in competition not only for viewing time, but also for viewing equipment), sleeping and playing musical instruments stood as trade-off activities with television viewing. As involvement with television increased, these activities were seen to decline. Belonging to clubs and the holding of group memberships which take the young person away from the house are in direct competition with watching television. If the child or teenager is out of the home, he/she is unlikely to be in a position to view television. If the amount of television is allowed to increase, therefore, these other activities are likely to be among the first to decline.

In another study which again took advantage of a social environment in which television was introduced for the first time, South African researchers followed a cohort of children over a period which began two years before television transmissions started, and extended over several years after its introduction. The displacement relationship between television and other activities here was found to work in one direction only. As children got into the routine of watching television, certain other activities were observed to decline. However, television viewing did not always remain at the same level. If viewing decreased, though, this did not result in parallel returns to other previously forsaken activities. The redistribution of time caused by the introduction of television primarily affected the use of other media, indicating that it was restricted largely to functionally equivalent activities. Thus, movie-going, radio listening and reading suffered after television became available, and there was also some reduction in time spent on hobbies, sports and club participation. The fact that there was no return to these activities, even if television lost some of its appeal, suggested that time spent with those activities is not the only thing which television displaces, but is accompanied by a displacement of interest in other activities which inhibits participation even when television viewing time declines.[30]

A survey among children in Britain explored which media they have available to them and what use they make of these media. From this research it has become clear that children have access to and make use of a wide range of media – and that the use of older, established ones does not invariably diminish in the face of competition from the new.[31]

Television viewing diaries and questionnaires were completed by a nationwide sample of 468 young people aged between 4 and 12 years. In their diaries, the children logged the programmes they watched on television during the survey week. On the questionnaire they were asked about ownership and use of a range of media and media accessories.

All children surveyed had a television set in their homes, as a condition of being in the panel – national data indicate that 98 per cent of all households have at least one television set. These, then, are the availabilities of seventeen other forms, grouped in terms of their pervasiveness:

- 96 per cent said they had a computer at their school;
- 94 per cent had a shelf of books at home;
- 93 per cent had a cassette player for listening to music tapes;
- 83 per cent had a paintbox or set of colours to make pictures;
- 83 per cent had a record player;
- 70 per cent had a musical instrument to play;
- 68 per cent had a cassette player or radio with earphones;

- 65 percent had their very own radio;
- 62 per cent had a pile of comics;
- 52 per cent had a video recorder at home;
- 52 per cent had a computer at home;
- 49 per cent visited a friend who has a video recorder;
- 43 per cent had their very own television set;
- 41 per cent had a television with a remote control;
- 35 per cent had a toy which operates by remote control;
- 25 per cent had a push button telephone in the home;
- 18 per cent had a teletext receiver at home.

This listing does not exhaust all possible media available to children. For example, questions were not asked about the availability of newspapers and magazines. Nevertheless, it does indicate a media pervasiveness that is on the whole quite extensive; a majority of the children claimed to have most of the items asked about.

How often do children use different media if they have them? If we take a look first of all at what may be called 'TV media' comprising video recorders (VCRs), teletext and remote-control channel changers, then there is clear evidence that VCR usage is fairly extensive. Nearly half the children from VCR households (49 per cent) said they used it regularly. Slightly more claimed a similar level of usage of teletext if they had a set (52 per cent) and a substantial majority of children from homes with remote control claimed to use it often (82 per cent). Frequent use of personal computers was less widespread, but not uncommon either, especially for playing games. One in five children with personal computers at home, however, claimed to use them for non-games purposes.

More than four out of ten said they regularly played records (42 per cent) or listened to music on the radio (44 per cent). Far fewer claimed to play any pop videos, though, and nearly 80 per cent of youngsters from VCR households said they never did.

Despite the obvious use of quite an array of electronic media in the home, there was no indication that print media was being ignored. More than half the children said they read a newspaper at least occasionally. About one in four (26 per cent) claimed to read one fairly often. The same applied to books (32 per cent) and comics (24 per cent).

Even more enlightening were findings which revealed how the use of different media – old and new – fit together. Was there any evidence, for instance, that the most modern media were ousting the traditional ones? The answer is no, with rare exceptions. Not only do the new fit with the new, but so do some of the old.

For example, children who claimed often to watch films and television programmes on their VCR were indeed more likely to have played pop videos, used teletext and a radio/cassette player with earphones, but were also more likely to have been to the cinema recently. Children who said they regularly played computer games were less likely to read comics, but were slightly more likely to read newspapers and magazines. Playing pop videos was also positively associated with reading newspapers and magazines, but made no difference to how often books or comics were read.

More detailed results indicated that there were children who were media-rich – having access to and making use of many media – and there were those (far fewer in number) who were media poor. The latter tended to make do with fewer sources of amusement. Among the media-rich children, however, the new media were not totally replacing the old. Displacement can occur, and does so possibly when a new medium provides the same gratifications as an old one, but in a more attractive package. For instance, although total TV viewing was not significantly related to the use of any reading materials (books, comics, magazines or newspapers), children who watched more TV drama read fewer comics (frequently regarded as being 'bad' for children anyway).

In this multimedia era, today's children may be learning to identify the unique benefits and gratifications that can be derived from different media, and divide their time between the many that are available, according to their personal needs and wants.

But what are these personal needs and wants when it comes to television? This chapter has examined the extent to which children watch television and types of programmes; it is now necessary to investigate the reasons behind children's viewing behaviour.

Chapter 2

Why do children watch TV?

People rarely sit mindlessly watching just anything on their 'box in the corner'; invariably some kind of choice has been made as to which programme they are going to watch. Children, as can be seen from the TV ratings, are no different. They, too, have their likes and dislikes.

As we have seen already, television programmes can be divided up into various categories or types, some of which are watched more often, and by larger numbers of viewers, than others. Furthermore, patterns of television viewing and programme preferences are linked to the demographic and family characteristics of audience members. Thus, some young people exhibit a taste for one type of programme, and other young people show preferences for another sort.[1] Although these relationships are interesting for what they show about the pattern of television-watching behaviour and the character of programme tastes across mass audiences, they do not reveal much about the reasons why people selectively choose to watch one type of programme in preference to another, or why they become 'hooked' on a particular series. Are there psychological reasons why some programmes are preferred by certain people? Do particular programmes satisfy special needs for individual viewers?

There is emerging psychological evidence that both transient and enduring motivations and temporary moods can and do influence the way people use the mass media. Children are no different. In the context of television viewing, their individual personalities and current moods can affect how and why they watch television as well as the specific programmes they select to view.

The study of the major motives which underpin the way people use the mass media has run into trouble with some critics, who have argued that many of the sets of motives identified by media researchers are over-simplistic and fail to get to grips with explaining the fundamental psychological reasons why people have particular media content preferences. Much 'uses and gratifications' research has described fairly generalised motives which predict in very general terms whether a person will prefer one mass medium over another, or one broad type of media content over another. Today's media environment is complex and varied, and offers people opportunities to select entertainment and information from a large number of television channels, radio stations, print publications, and new electronic media accessible through computer technology. In this context, a more advanced model of human behaviour and the forces which affect it is needed.[2] If we really want to understand the psychology of viewers' television programme choices, self-reported reasons for watching television, such as wanting to be entertained or wanting to be informed, cannot explain very much on their own. Deeper-seated psychological factors, such as whether people are sensation seekers, suffer from anxiety, are imaginative and creative, or are aggressive or assertive in their dealings with others, are related to their reasons for watching television and, in turn, to the choices they make. These factors represent fundamental aspects of the human character with a clinically and empirically demonstrated history of influence upon how people behave and why they behave the way they do.[3]

REASONS FOR WATCHING TELEVISION

Researchers have for many years talked about the 'uses and gratifications' served by the media. This means that the media are thought to satisfy various needs of their consumers – to be entertained, to be informed, to have company, to relax, and so on. Such needs may direct people to seek out particular mass media or, in the case of television, to choose to watch particular kinds of programmes. Television viewers are therefore motivated to watch television in order to satisfy their various wants, needs and desires at the time. This does not mean that viewing behaviour is always pushed by strong psychological drives but, for most of the time, that people watch television and, this applies to some extent even to the young, they do so for a reason. This reason may be as simple as 'to pass the time'.

There is a belief among some scholars of media consumption that if the gratifications sought by people are met by watching specific television programmes, listening to particular radio shows and reading certain newspapers or magazines, they will return to those programmes and reading material again when motivated to do so.[4] Thus, viewers may be drawn back to a television series for episode after episode, not simply because they want to see the outcome of the next bit of the story, but also because by watching the series they are gaining some form of satisfaction which is important to them. Viewers may return to the news for information, magazine shows for advice on personal or social problems, soap opera for companionship, drama for excitement and escapism, comedy to be cheered up, or any of these to have something to talk about with others the next day. One early observation, made during the 1940s, was that women who were lonely or socially isolated, or who experienced more anxiety and frustration in their lives, would listen more to radio soap operas. These serials compensated for social or emotional vacuums in their own lives. Women also used radio serials as a source of 'advice' about how to deal with everyday problems.[5]

In the early 1960s, Wilbur Schramm and his colleagues outlined three main uses of television by the child. The first referred to the positive pleasure of being entertained. Television offers a fantasy world in which the child can escape real-life boredom and problems. Schramm observed that children would sit with absorbed faces when watching favourite programmes. Second was information, for example about how to dress, behave, and so on. Third, he identified 'social utility' as a major function. Watching in mixed company, he argued, gave young men and women an excuse to sit close together and often provided topics for conversation.[6]

Several surveys carried out in Britain and the United States have aimed to identify the major reasons children report for watching television. Around six to eight reasons have usually emerged, although there is considerable overlap between them. One survey by Bradley Greenberg was carried out among children in London aged 9, 12 and 15 years. The children were asked to write an essay on the subject 'Why I like to watch television'. An in-depth analysis of the essays yielded eight groups of reasons why children claimed to watch television. These were 'to pass time', 'to forget as a means of diversion', 'learning about things', 'learning about myself', 'for arousal', 'for relaxation', 'for companionship' and 'as a habit'.[7]

A similar survey carried out among young people in the United States identified six reasons why children and adolescents watch television: learning, habit or to pass time, companionship, escape, arousal and relaxation. Viewing to pass time, for relaxation and arousal were the three most salient motives. Thus, children and adolescents report a variety of reasons for watching television.[8] Even those identified above, however, each cover a cluster of needs, motives and gratifications sought by the younger viewer. We turn now to examine what each one means.

VIEWING AS HABIT OR AS TIME FILLER

One of the most prominent reasons for watching television mentioned by most people is simply as a means of passing or filling time. In his work with British children in the early 1970s, Bradley Greenberg found that this was the most important reason given, though its significance weakened with age. Thus, viewing out of habit or because there is nothing better to do is something children are less likely to say they do at age 15 than at 9 or 12.[9]

The particular reasons children give for watching television are related to the types of programmes they watch and what they think about those programmes. Children who say they watch television out of habit or to pass time tend to be less likely to watch news and current affairs and more likely to watch comedy and light entertainment. There is some evidence also that children who claim to watch out of habit are more eager to talk about television.

VIEWING TO LEARN

People may turn to television as a source of learning, but learning motivations do not simply direct viewers towards strictly informational programmes. Certain kinds of learning benefit can also be obtained from drama and entertainment.

Television's dramatic characterisations and plots, for example, may convey lessons about how or how not to deal with other people, solve personal or family problems and disputes, make friends and influence people, and get on in life – professionally and personally. In other words, not only does learning from television consist of improving one's knowledge of what is going on in the world – that is, political, economic, industrial and foreign affairs – but television is also a major source of social learning. This learning may be an incidental by-product of watching ostensibly for entertainment-oriented reasons, though for many people it may be the most significant kind of learning from television.

Most studies of learning motivations and television watching have looked at television in general rather than at specific genres of programming. But, while young people may be able to report their most important reasons for watching television, it is likely that such reports are based upon their reasons for watching specific programmes.

Young viewers, then, may turn to television as a source of various kinds of learning. Through television, children may learn about themselves, about life, about how to behave in different situations, about how to deal with personal and family problems, and so on. In learning about life, television programmes may be selected because they contain information about people, places and the way society operates. They may offer insights into the way people in distant places feel and behave. The child may learn about different social and racial groups, different occupations, lifestyles and events that are happening in the outside world.

Television programmes can sometimes provide helpful suggestions about how to do things that you have not done before. They can provide young viewers with some indications about the appropriate ways to act in certain situations. They may offer hints about current fashions and fads. They may offer advice on how to improve your technique at playing games, give a blueprint for losing weight, information about holidays, cooking tips, getting ahead in a job, and so on.

Television can also be a source of advice for young people. Television programmes may be selected because they can provide useful guidance for decision-making or problem-solving regarding some particular matter a child has to deal with in life. Television may offer some insights which can help young people to make their mind up what to do. Some programmes can offer advice on how to deal with parents and problems within the family. Others may give advice on how to deal with health problems, making and keeping friends, having a romantic relationship, being successful with the opposite sex, and so on.

Research has shown that, where information about how to cope with certain important emotional and social needs is unavailable in their own environment, children will look for alternative means of satisfying these needs. Under these circumstances, television may become particularly significant to youngsters for their schooling in life. Socially disadvantaged youngsters can develop a dependence on television for learning about life, getting to see what people are like, learning how to solve problems. At the same time, youngsters may also depend more on television for excitement and for thrills than their better-off counterparts.[10]

The survey of London children referred to earlier identified and measured two sets of learning reasons: 'learning about things' and 'learning about myself'. Children were asked if they watched to learn about things happening in the world, to learn about things they have done before, to get new ideas, to learn things they do not learn in school, to learn things about themselves, to see how they are supposed to act, to learn about what could happen to them and to see how other people deal with the same problems they have. Practically all these reasons were perceived as pertinent to the viewing experience.[11]

VIEWING FOR COMPANIONSHIP

Watching television can provide a source of companionship both by bringing the family together to share in the enjoyment of programmes and by supplying a collection of fantasy friends with whom the child can vicariously become involved. It is the latter involvement to which most children probably refer when they say that television provides company. Indeed, within the family setting, much use of the television set these days is solitary. Although watching programmes off-air is more often done in the company of others than alone, the opposite is true when the set is used for playing back videos. Furthermore, with the growth of two- and three-set households, there is even more scope for solitary viewing.[12]

TELEVISION AS BABYSITTER

Recognition of the function of television as a source of companionship occurs not simply as a perception of children themselves but also within the family context. One role of television these days is as surrogate babysitter. Although it cannot perform all the usual and expected duties of normal babysitters – it does not break up fights, it cannot tell the child when to go to bed, it may not keep the child from wrecking the house – it may be effective at keeping the kids quiet for a while or at least keeping mischief-making down to a more manageable level.

Television's potential as babysitter was first remarked upon over thirty years ago. Eleanor Maccoby, a prominent TV researcher in the 1950s, found that mothers in one of her surveys mentioned using television as a 'pacifier'. A majority mentioned that television made it easier to care for children in the home. Evidence to substantiate the belief that television can keep children occupied has emerged from the observation that children become more passive while watching, self-absorbed and less likely to misbehave or require constant parental supervision.[13]

How do mothers use television to occupy their child's attention? How widespread is television's use as a babysitter? Do parents talk to their children about television, and in what way? Do mothers rate television highly as a babysitter?

In one American survey, mothers generally believed that television is used quite widely as a babysitter, but they saw it as something which goes on in other families rather than their own.[14] These mothers did not condone habitual television viewing and felt that it is not something they would like their own children to spend all their time doing. Playing with friends was usually seen as preferable to watching television and most of the mothers tended to feel that their kids would rather watch television than play on their own.

When asked what they usually told their children to do when they needed to cook, do some housework or relax, television was mentioned as often as friends, though they claimed to ask their children to help with the chores more often. Many, however, simply told their child to do whatever he or she wanted to do, or to 'get out of mummy's way'.

The majority of these American mothers felt that most other mothers of children aged between 2 and 12 used television as a babysitter. On average, they estimated that other mothers might use television to keep their kids quiet for up to several hours a day. They were much less likely to admit to this amount and kind of use of television in their own homes, however. In other words, mothers are less inclined to admit to using television as a babysitter than they are to estimate its use among other mothers. We do not know how typical this behaviour is, nor do we know how well mothers are aware of how other mothers use television with their children. But it seems likely that, in so far as mothers are prepared to admit to such things at all, television is deliberately used by many to occupy their offspring at times when they cannot be bothered to look after their kids themselves or when they are preoccupied by other matters.

TV PEOPLE AS COMPANIONS

A different aspect of television's role as companion stems from the various relationships which often develop between viewers and the characters and personalities who enter their homes with regularity through the television set. Young viewers may form close associations with certain characters, identifying with these people as desired models whom they aspire to be like.[15] For children who have few friends, TV people may provide substitutes with whom they can engage in what researchers have termed 'parasocial' relationships. In other words, although they cannot really be friends with their TV favourites, they can pretend that they are.

Parasocial interaction is especially likely to occur with those television celebrities who appear frequently and whose performance simulates face-to-face conversation with the viewer at home. One belief is that, in addition to identifying with TV characters, viewers retain their own personas and respond to people on television in the same way they might upon meeting them in the street. A great deal of viewer involvement in television programmes derives from the familiarity viewers develop with television characters. This experience leads viewers to feel that they know the characters and can, as a consequence, predict their likely next actions. This illusion of 'knowing' may be especially likely to develop around those TV personalities who give the impression of talking directly to the viewer; for example, the personality who regularly hosts chat or entertainment shows.

VIEWING AS A SOURCE OF CONVERSATION

Both children and adolescents cite television as a major source of conversation material. Programmes provide a fertile ground of common experience for the next morning's conversations in the classroom. Unless you have watched the most popular programmes of the day, you are likely to be left out. Those children who cannot talk about the latest happenings in the plot of a popular soap are not able to join in the conversation. Thus, a programme may be selectively watched by children to ensure that they will not be left out should it be raised as a topic for discussion the next day (or at some later time).[16]

VIEWING FOR ESCAPE

Television can offer a fantasy world for the vicarious pleasure of viewers into which they can escape from everyday problems or the humdrum of ordinary living. The escapism function of television operates for children as well as adults, and is one of the central mechanisms of television's entertainment functions. Television provides a source of distraction from everyday realities. Through its fantasy material, more than anything else, viewers can become vicariously involved with the characters and events and act out in their minds ways of dealing with their problems. Television's fantasy is also the stuff of dreams which, though unlikely ever to come true, provide some temporary hope and respite from the less desirable everyday realities with which many individuals have to contend.

Various motives have been identified as underlying the need to escape through involvement in the fantasy world television can bring into the home. One idea is that children subjected to harsh parental discipline may use television to escape from an unpleasant home environment. Alternatively, the need to escape may stem from an unhappy experience in school. Early evidence indicated that children of lower intelligence and poorer educational performance sought out programmes through which they could forget about their problems.[17]

Another important factor which seems likely to underlie the use of television as a means of escape is how well children get on with other children. Early observations indicated that children who become addicted to television are found not only to have lower intelligence and come from poorer walks of life, but also to be shy and retiring, to have fewer friends, and to be ill-at-ease with others. Thus, not only might television provide such lonely young people with some form of companionship, but it may also help to take their minds off their loneliness.[18]

And what about children who choose to escape via televised violence? Preferences for media violence have been shown to relate to transient mood states of individuals. People who have been put into an angry mood or aggressive frame of mind have been found to exhibit stronger preferences for violent over non-violent media content when compared with non-angered people.[19] Some researchers have found that, when people have been induced to fantasise about behaving aggressively, this can create a further preference for violent films over non-violent films, especially among male viewers.[20]

Much of the research literature concerning television violence has focused on the impact of violent TV material on viewers' attitudes and behaviours. Much less attention has been paid to whether or not violent programmes are viewed selectively, in particular by individuals whose personalities are already characterised by strong aggressive dispositions;[21] and, if so, whether and to what extent this may account for the relationships so frequently observed in correlational surveys between the viewing of violent programming and personal aggressiveness. A number of surveys carried out in the United States during the early 1970s reported relationships between delinquent aggressiveness and preferences for violence-containing programmes. These results have most commonly been taken as evidence that watching television violence encourages the development of antisocial tendencies among young people. But another way of looking at the findings is that they may reveal a different sort of connection, whereby those youngsters who are already aggressive tend to prefer to watch programmes which contain violence.[22]

Evidence supporting the thesis that aggressive predispositions may underlie the enjoyment of violent television content has emerged from several studies. In one of these, a panel of young people was surveyed twice across a period of one year. Measures of their attitudes towards the use of aggression and their television viewing habits over time were taken. Although general patterns of viewing changed little over the year, some evidence did emerge that individuals who exhibited aggressive attitudes at the beginning of the study expressed particularly strong preferences for violent programming after one year, even when other important variables – such as sex, age and initial viewing patterns – had been statistically controlled. The reverse relationship between viewing television violence initially and the development of aggressive attitudes over time was much smaller.[23]

VIEWING AS AROUSAL

Psychologists have long recognised that human beings have basic needs for stimulation. It is well documented that people have a natural curiosity and that their seeking new and varied experiences reflects these drives. According to some media scholars, television viewing preferences are underpinned and shaped by these stimulation-seeking tendencies.[24] The aim, however, is not to seek endless stimulation, but a sufficient amount to achieve an optimal state of arousal. There is a point at which the individual attains an ideal level of arousal, while to be either above or below that level is less comfortable. In their pioneering study of the role of television in children's lives, Wilbur Schramm and his colleagues reported that television is viewed predominantly for the simple pleasure of being entertained. Entertainment follows from various gratifications being effectively satisfied. Whether or not a programme excites or amuses its viewers in some significant way is a major ingredient in its entertainment value.[25]

Television offers various forms of entertainment – serious drama, science fiction, romantic serials, situation comedy, music and variety shows, game shows among them. The emotions aroused will often differ from one type of programme to the next, as will viewers' tastes in these programmes. General liking for one kind of drama or entertainment may be linked to enduring dispositions which characterise a viewer's personality. At the same time, the extent to which a viewer will want to watch one particular type of programme – even one that is normally liked – may depend on how he/she feels at the time. As moods change, so too does appetite for certain programmes. Thus, television viewing may provide a means for 'mood management'. Programmes are chosen in a selective fashion according to the individual's need to achieve a satisfactory level of arousal.[26]

OVERCOMING BOREDOM

One aspect of the arousal function of television is that it may be used as a means of overcoming boredom, providing a source of stimulation – both mental and emotional – and able to brighten up a dull day or night. Obviously, programmes can vary in their arousal properties. Thus, the choice of what to watch can depend on how much stimulation we need. Bored viewers have been found to select exciting programmes which increase their level of arousal. By contrast, individuals who are already in a state of excitement (or stress) have been found to choose calming or relaxing programmes to watch.

The need for young viewers to seek stimulation or relief from boredom has been linked by some researchers to adolescents' appetites for extreme forms of audiovisual entertainment, such as graphic horror movies. Some young people experience feelings of distress when watching them, while others express delight.[27] These different reactions are often associated with the gender of the viewer, with young male viewers more likely to demonstrate enjoyment, and young females more likely to express distress.

Whether or not young people enjoy horror movies, however, does not simply depend upon what sex they are. The nature of reactions to graphic horror is linked to the original motives for wanting to watch in the first place[28] and also to the psychological characteristics of viewers.[29]

More recent research has identified that adolescents have four main motives for watching horror movies. A study of 13- to 16-year-old American teenagers referred to visceral enjoyment of blood and guts and the ways that people can die ('gore watching'), liking to be scared ('thrill watching'), watching to feel brave and to appear mature to peer groups ('independent watching'), and watching to escape from problems at home or for company when lonely ('problem watching'). The extent to which any of these motives was significant in relation to enjoyment of horror films, however, also depended upon the adolescent's personality makeup. Teenagers, who expressed gore-watching motives exhibited a poorly developed sense of empathy, low generalised levels of fearfulness and a strong sense of adventure seeking. High adventure seeking, a component of sensation seeking and a highly developed sense of empathy were personality characteristics which underpinned thrill-seeking motives for watching horror films.[30]

Gore watchers were also characterised by having the greatest preference for scenes of graphic violence and the strongest tendency to identify with killers in these movies. This motive was more characteristic of boys than girls. Gore-watching motives seemed to reflect a curiosity about physical violence, an interest in methods of killing and an attraction to the grotesque. The measurement of this motive may be indicative of a much wider syndrome of values and beliefs. Research elsewhere found that gore-watching motivations are related to double standard beliefs about male and female sexuality, illustrated by such views as premarital sexual relations being acceptable for males but not for females.[31]

IMPROVING ON BAD MOODS

Another way in which television functions to influence a viewer's arousal is when it is used to make a person who is in a bad mood feel better. Programme selection in this context will rest not simply on whether or not it is arousing, but in what way. Comedy, drama and game shows, for instance, may all be entertaining in their own way, but invariably the events they contain may not be the most appropriate kinds of material to cheer up someone who is feeling down. Drama and game shows can offer suspense, tension and sad moments, along with a few happy ones. Comedy, in contrast, is aimed at inducing laughter, merriment and euphoria. It may offer a better guarantee of cheering viewers up. Research has shown that to some extent this is all true. Choice of comedy, however, can also vary according to the mood state and type of comedy on offer. Certain forms of humour are hostile and aggressive; this sort of comedy may have a particularly strong appeal to viewers who are in an angry mood (more so than does non-hostile comedy), although this latter pattern is more likely to be found among males than females.[32]

For some researchers in the field, the regulation of moods is a key motivation governing the use of entertainment media.[33] Dolf Zillmann has argued that people tend to view entertainment that enhances or prolongs positive moods or that helps to terminate or diminish unpleasant moods. One of the ways television can help to make children happier is if a well-liked character experiences something good and if disliked characters experience something bad.[34]

Suspense plays an important part in all of this. Increases in suspense and arousal are a function of the viewer's subjective certainty that the hero or heroine will succumb to the dangerous evil forces. Viewers' excitement is all the greater when it seems increasingly likely that the hero will not escape a perilous situation. However, when the drama goes even further and it becomes fully apparent that that he/she will perish, the feeling of suspense diminishes too, and the viewer is then left with only feelings of dread for the on-screen character's inevitable fate.[35]

REASSURANCE AND COMFORT FROM TV

In addition to being entertaining, the information contained in programmes can offer crumbs of comfort. Thus, programmes may be selected and used by viewers not because of expectations regarding the excitement and pleasure they might bring, but because they contain soothing, comforting information. Just when it seems like the world is becoming an increasingly hostile, unpleasant place to live, programmes which depict acts of kindness and generosity may serve to restore faith in human nature. There is evidence that people faced with hostile environments may turn to television and movies not simply to escape but also in search of reassurance. Research with preschool and infant children has shown that, even at a very early age, television programmes may be used in this way. Children who had recently experienced an unpleasant situation, in which an adult had criticised them, opted to spend more time watching a programme in which children were treated nicely than did children who had previously had their appearance praised. Thus, television can provide a means of coping with a harsh, cynical and unfriendly social environment.[36]

Children's reasons for watching television, then, are multiple and varied: they seek to gain information, to be entertained, to pass time, and so on. However, research into the reasons behind their viewing preferences frequently assumes high levels of attention to the screen. But is this necessarily the case? What factors influence *how* children watch TV? It is to this issue that we turn our attention next.

Chapter 3

How do children watch TV?

The previous two chapters have already pointed out that on average children watch television between 2.5–3.5 hours per day according to age, and that the reasons why they watch are multiple and varied. However, the *way* they watch is another important factor to take into account when investigating the nature of children's relationship with the media. Children do not just sit, glued to the screen. The way they watch varies considerably from one day to the next and even from one moment to the next. How do children watch? How much attention do they pay to the screen? Is television viewing a shared activity carried out alongside other activities?

People themselves frequently report that television does not command their exclusive attention. Often, viewing is carried on intermittently, as the individual leaves and re-enters the room where the set is on, or divides attention between looking at the screen and doing other things while in front of the TV. Consequently, time spent viewing is only a superficial indicator of how people use television.[1] Familiarity with having a set in a family household, for instance, is often associated with an increased ability to accomplish other activities in conjunction with TV watching. Thus, children may report doing homework or household chores while watching television. Some surveys have found that a majority of people, children included, report doing something else while watching, for over half of the programmes they watched the previous day. Few programmes are reportedly watched from beginning to end.[2]

Direct observation of how children watch television has further revealed that television holds the child's constant attention a lot less often than we might think. An American study in the 1980s using a time-lapse camera revealed that people may leave their sets on even when they are not actually watching. For a large portion of the total time sets are switched on, they are playing to an empty room. And even when people are present, they may be engaged in a variety of alternative activities at the same time as viewing the television.[3]

Observational data collected via a video camera housed within a special television cabinet placed in six family households in southern England indicated that family members were absent for substantial proportions of the time that the television set was in operation and, even when present, did not pay full attention to the screen for more than a small part of the total time the set was switched on. Viewing patterns varied from family to family. The proportion of observed time the set was playing to an empty room, for example, ranged from 28 per cent to a maximum of 72 per cent. Mothers spent the greatest proportion of observed time fully present (42 per cent), followed by fathers (39 per cent) and then children (34 per cent). While in the room with the set switched on, mothers spent the greatest proportion of time looking at the screen (67 per cent), followed by fathers (66 per cent), then children (49 per cent).[4]

As we shall see, children have been observed to be frequently doing other things such as eating, drinking, dressing, sleeping, playing and fighting. Often they are not actually looking at the screen at all and leave the room for extensive periods while the set is on. As the number of small children in the household increases, however, so too does total set in-use time, but there is also a corresponding increase in the length of time the room is empty while the television set is switched on. How children watch television is also related to their understanding of programmes and to their reactions to different features of programme areas; these are covered in more detail in the next chapter.

THE CHILD'S ATTENTION TO THE SET

As we observed in Chapter 1, children start to pay attention to television from very early on in their lives. A major bone of contention among researchers, however, has been whether children's attention to the screen is mainly an 'active' or a 'passive' phenomenon. In recent years there has been increasing support for the active notion, despite frequent adverse publicity which accuses television of turning children into mentally and physically lethargic 'couch potatoes'.

Adherents to the passive view believe that much of television washes over children and disengages their minds and requires only shallow effort to follow what is happening in programmes. This impression of the way children watch television implies that programmes are more likely to be absorbed passively as a series of disconnected scenes rather than as events which link together to form a coherent whole.[5] Increasingly over recent years, evidence has emerged to indicate that this impression does not reflect the real nature of children's viewing.

Researchers who have observed children watching programmes both in controlled laboratory settings and at home have noticed that children rarely sit quietly and stare at the television the whole of the time viewing takes place. One study of infants watching an episode of *Sesame Street*, for example, found that children frequently looked at and away from the screen, averaging about 150 looks at and away per hour. The child would usually change his or her attention after no more than fifteen seconds of either looking towards or away from the television.[6]

HOW IS THE CHILD'S ATTENTION TO THE SCREEN CONTROLLED?

There are two opposing points of view on this subject. One viewpoint is that children's attention is controlled by the formal features of television; that is, by changing physical stimulation accompanying visual scene changes, background music, sound effects, and so forth. Another view is that children themselves learn to control their attention in relation to things which happen on screen which have meaning for them.[7] But what is the evidence on these ideas about children's viewing? Are youngsters reactive to the events happening in programmes? Or is their attention driven actively by their understanding and interpretation of what is going on?

VIEWING AS REACTIVE

Children's attention to television involves looking and listening – researchers have studied both. Studies of children's visual attention to the screen have tied its onset and offset to specific events or happenings in programmes. This research has provided clear evidence that some attributes of television which children watch are associated with much more looking at the screen than others. When there is a sudden change in the pace of the action, or the occurrence of funny voices, loud noises or appearances by children, young viewers are likely to turn their eyes towards the screen. Such research suggests that these attributes have some control over children's viewing.[8]

If a child's attention is governed by the physical features of a programme, infants and toddlers would be the most tied to such control since they are recognised as being more 'stimulus bound'. One noted researcher, Jerome Singer, has suggested that the 'orienting reaction' is the basis for television viewing.[9] This is a natural response we all make towards something new or different happening in our immediate environment. It stems from a primitive need to know what is going on. Since this response is already established in toddlers by about the age of three months, we might expect to find it happening amongst very young infants while they are watching television. One study has reported that six-month-old infants, when kept near the television at home in a playpen without toys, did pay some visual attention to the screen (49 per cent attention measured over sixteen minutes; 'chance' attention would be about 4 per cent). Under less restrictive viewing circumstances, however, toddlers' attention to television appears to be less frequent.[10]

The length of visual looking at the TV set has been found to increase fourfold in infants aged between 12 and 48 months. This increase is partly connected with increases in the length of looks at the screen, but seem primarily to be due to a dramatic increase, at about 30 months old, in the frequency of looking at the television. Between roughly 2 and 2.5 years old, toddlers exhibit a significant shift in amount of looking at the television.[11]

Up to this age, children appear to show only sporadic attention to the set when it is switched on. Older children begin to develop what seems to be a concept of 'watching television'. This is indicated by the way they position themselves physically towards the set. Thus, although they may still be playing with their toys, the centre of activity is the television, and looks towards it become more frequent. Subsequently, visual attention to television increases throughout the preschool years until the child starts school, after which it tends to level off.[12]

One view is that children's mode of response to television changes systematically as they grow older and pass through progressive stages of intellectual development. As infants up to the age of 5, they are considered to be 'perceptually bound'; that is, very young children are most likely to have their attention drawn to the screen by overt visual or sound effects. As they grow older, those sorts of features, while not irrelevant, become only aspects of a programme's content likely to attract a child's attention. Young children tend to focus on concrete aspects of the programme, most notably changes of pace in physical action and the character types involved. Older children are more sensitive to abstract features of programmes, such as relationships between events and characters, whose meaningfulness derives from youngsters' understanding and following of the storyline as it unfolds.[13]

Proponents of the theory that children react to television, rather than actively seek to pay attention to those things which have meaning for them, also believe that it is sudden, often gimmicky changes in visual action or sound effects in programmes that really control children's viewing behaviour. Thus, television which is rapidly paced with lots of physical changes, visible or heard, will gain and retain a child's attention. However, this style of presentation is not conducive to learning and understanding. If the content is presented too quickly, very little of it will stick. Assuming that this explanation of how television grabs the attention of youngsters is correct, as attention gets greater, understanding should get poorer.[14]

But is this really what happens? The active theory of viewing makes a substantially different assertion. It proposes that the child attends to things he or she can understand. Thus attention is driven by comprehension. On the latest evidence, the active theorists would seem to have it.

VIEWING AS ACTIVE

An alternative impression of the nature of children's television watching has emerged from other evidence. Some scholars have proposed that the degree of attention that children give to the screen is actively and strategically guided by their attempts to understand and follow programmes. They also propose that children begin to learn to do this before the age of 3, and that this process may occur almost automatically, purely as a function of their early experience with television.[15]

As with adults, children rarely need to pay constant attention to the screen to follow what is going on – they are able to detect changes in serials or significant events in programmes even when looking away. Just listening to the soundtrack can provide clues as to when something important is happening and when they should look back at the screen. Even children as young as 3 have this ability to monitor the soundtrack on television whilst looking elsewhere, and have been observed to shift their attention back to the screen when appropriate.

Other studies point to young children's motivation to understand television as a prime driver of their attention. In other words, there is increasing evidence to suggest that children actively direct their attention to television content that has meaning for them. In one study 5-year-olds' level of attention to an episode of *Sesame Street* was observed by placing one group in an empty room and another group in a room that contained potentially distracting toys. Under these conditions, children were found to differ greatly in the amount of time they watched the screen, but there was no difference in the extent to which youngsters followed and understood the programme. However, within the 'toys' group, looking at the screen and understanding were correlated, providing some evidence that attention may be directed by comprehension.

Nevertheless, as had been expected, the presence or absence of toys did make a difference to how much the children looked at the screen. The children who were placed with toys watched on average for 44 per cent of the time, while among the other children, watching averaged 87 per cent. Significantly, the two groups did not differ in how much they could remember overall from the programme. However, there was a connection between the particular aspects of the programme the children could remember and whether they had been paying attention at the moment those parts of the programme were being shown. In other words, if the child's attention was distracted by toys at the precise moment when an important piece of information was being presented, that item was unlikely to be recalled later.[16]

The finding that there were no differences between the two groups is the important one, though. It suggests that even among children whose attention may have been divided between watching the programme and playing with toys, attention to the programme was strategically organised and distributed between the two activities, so that viewing occurred for the most informative bits of the programme. This strategy was so effective that giving the TV more attention did not improve their ability to remember it.

Further evidence that the ability to follow the programme underpins looking at it derives from the fact that when the programme is re-edited and jumbled up, it ceases to hold the attention of very young viewers (aged 3 to 6 years) for very long. Youngsters report thinking most about parts of programmes they can understand and choose not to think about those which have little or no meaning for them.[17]

It is now known that, as they mature, children acquire the intellectual skills necessary to organise specific elements of TV programmes into coherent and meaningful wholes. During their primary-school years, children are more capable of following dramatic plots. They become able to distinguish central from peripheral events in programmes. With such newly acquired comprehension skills, young viewers' attention may be selectively directed towards what they perceive to be the more important story elements in a programme. In other words, children's attention concentrates more decidedly on the main theme or plot, while they become much less concerned about or able subsequently to remember incidental, subplot elements from a programme.[18]

Children, then, learn to monitor the soundtrack of programmes and listen for things which mean something to them. They are already fairly active in this regard by the time they have started school. Anything they hear which is significant and has meaning encourages them to look up at the television, while anything they cannot relate to inhibits attention. Children continue to look at the screen as long as they can follow what is happening. The programme must not simply be meaningful, however, if it is to maintain their attention: there must also be a degree of unpredictability about it.[19]

As children grow older their dependence purely on sound effects decreases. For instance, 11-year-olds exhibit greater depth of understanding television programmes than 5-year-olds, whereas the younger age group follow a programme much better and look at it more often when significant sounds occur. This difference is much less pronounced among the older children. Young children are very responsive to sound effects and other exciting events in the programme. Older children's attention is dependent upon deeper aspects of their understanding of the programme. At this level of viewing, an attention-grabbing event in a programme might consist of a significant development in the storyline, which in itself may not involve exciting changes of pace. The event's significance is only apparent to the child who has followed the storyline and is thus able to place what happens in a context which lends it meaning.[20]

ATTENTIONAL INERTIA

The longer a young viewer continuously maintains a look at television, the more likely it is that he or she will continue to do so. This tendency increases up to a period of about fifteen seconds of looking, after which the probability that the child will continue to look at the screen does not change substantially. Anderson and his colleagues have noted that the inertia pattern characterises *not* looking at the screen as well. In other words, the longer it has been since the viewer last looked at the screen, because of doing something else, the less likely it is that he or she will look back.[21]

To what extent is attentional inertia specific to the types of things being shown in programmes? Do children continue to watch a programme if it is interesting to them or involves them in some way? And to what extent do they fail to return to it if they find it boring? The evidence would suggest that, although attitudes to a programme do depend on what kinds of things it is about, a switch from one item to another is no guarantee that attention will suddenly change. In other words, if one part of a programme is interesting and commands the viewer's attention, there will be a tendency to continue looking, even after a change to a new item or different kind of content which may be less interesting and involving.

Researchers believe that 'attentional inertia' is an important aspect of the way the child watches television. It reflects the fact that even young viewers are actively monitoring television while viewing in order to identify meaningful content. It can drive the child to continue paying attention even when the material being shown is not easy to understand. So for a while, the young viewer tries to make sense of the complex, the new and the difficult. Although in general the child stops paying attention when the going gets really tough, attentional inertia serves to maintain attention further than it might otherwise go. As such, attentional inertia may be part of the means by which the child comes to process a programme that is poorly understood. This may lead the child to explore difficult territory, to work at understanding the unfamiliar and generally to stretch his or her ability to make sense of television.[22]

PROGRAMMES AND THE NATURE OF WATCHING

Children's viewing styles can vary with the type of programme they are watching. We have already seen that children have obvious programme preferences – some programmes are watched more often and liked more than others. Levels of attention vary, too, across different kinds of programmes. In examining the levels of viewing devoted by children to different types of programmes, the role of parental influence cannot be ignored. The amount of television parents themselves watch, together with their reasons for doing so, can shape children's viewing patterns.[23] The extent to which parents and children view television together, however, does vary with programme type. Children will tend to watch programmes designed for a general audience with their parents, while for programmes aimed at the children's audience they will tend to watch much more often on their own. As they grow older, children will watch less and less with their parents, but when the family does watch together, parental choices will tend to dominate. When children watch on their own, however, there appears to be very little carry-over of this parental effect, and this is already true by the age of 7.[24]

American surveys have found that levels of attention to television as reported by families can vary from programme to programme. Claimed attention levels were generally higher than average for peak-time drama series and family shows. Usually, there was greater deliberation and planning to watch these shows. And there was a greater likelihood that family members would report little attention with variety-comedy or variety-music, educational and sports programmes.[25]

Daniel Anderson and Elizabeth Pugzles Lorch have reported a wide variety of viewing styles among children on the evidence of videotapes of families viewing in the home. They speculate that style of viewing is a function of age, viewing environment, relevance of the programme to the viewer, and viewer intention. They cite as an example a 5-year-old girl who looked intently at a favourite programme on Saturday morning but never looked at a hockey game in the evening. In the first case, it seemed likely that the girl wanted to be entertained by television, while in the second instance she was concerned mainly with playing with her father, who was trying to watch the hockey game.[26]

Levels of attention to the set vary with the type of programme. One study, which observed children watching television at home through installed video cameras, indicated that films were the programmes most attended to; on average viewers exhibited visual attention to the TV screen for 76 per cent of the movie's duration. In descending order, children's shows received the next most attention (71 per cent), followed by suspense series (68 per cent), religious programmes (67 per cent), family series (66 per cent), game shows (66 per cent), talk shows (64 per cent), melodramas (59 per cent), sports events (59 per cent), news (55 per cent) and, lastly, advertisements (55 per cent).[27]

The sample was divided into three age groups: children (1–10 years old), adolescents (11–19) and adults (20–75). Overall, the children looked at the screen 52 per cent of the time they were with television, adolescents 69 per cent and adults 65 per cent. Furthermore, interactions were found between the age of the viewer and type of programme being watched in influencing level of viewers' attention to the screen. Children attended most to children's programmes (86 per cent) and least to melodrama and sports (8 per cent). Adolescents paid most attention to suspense (84 per cent) and least to sports

(43 per cent). Adults looked most at films (78 per cent) and least at commercials (52 per cent).

British research involving direct observation of family viewing via a camera hidden in the television set itself has found that the extent to which members of the family were present and paying attention to the screen varied with the type of programme. Full presence, across all family members, occurred principally when children's programmes, thrillers and quiz shows were being broadcast. Children were typically most likely to be present when children's programmes were on, which also commanded the greatest amount of visual attention from children of any programme type.[28]

The ability of children to follow a television programme is affected by the pace at which things happen in it. The view that young children respond to television in a predominantly 'perceptual' fashion suggests that fast pace, short scenes and frequent changes make the best combination to obtain and hold on to children's attention. Despite the fact that many physical features of television have so far emerged, most research shows that rapid pace *per se* has a most significant influence.[29]

The significance of pace on attention can vary with the type of programme. One American study found that children attended to high-paced cartoons more than to low-paced cartoons, but when the content was changed to a magazine format (segments taken from *The Electric Company*), pace had no effect on visual attention. Moreover, children aged 8–9 years had their attention held more strongly by fast-paced cartoons than did preschool children, an age trend opposite to what the researchers expected.[30]

More detailed analysis of what actually is going on during viewing reveals one reason for the complex and inconsistent ways in which children's attention to the screen is affected by the pace of a programme. Pace can actually be composed of several ingredients: changes to a new scene not previously shown in the programme; changes to a familiar scene; and changes in the cast of characters present. These changes are often marked by visual features, such as fades, dissolves, zooms or pans, or by auditory features, such as changes in music, sound effects or speech.[31]

Changes of scenes sometimes elicit attention from a child who is not looking, but for a young viewer who is already watching the screen, scene and character changes can sometimes prompt a temporary interruption of looking. Older children, presumably better able to pursue the flow of a programme, can use scene-change points as the occasion for both starting and stopping a look more so than do younger children. This suggests that, as they get older, children become more aware of formal feature cues marking breaking points in the programme. It appears that for school-age children, scene and character changes are points at which the young viewer decides whether to begin, stop or continue paying attention to a television programme.

Increasingly with age, young television viewers come to attend more consistently and strategically to programmes, and understand more effectively what they view.[32] Other interesting work with young television watchers has further revealed the varying significance of pace with the type of programme being watched. Fast-paced programmes do not consistently receive greater attention than slower-paced programmes. In general, programmes with a continuous storyline receive greater attention than segmented, magazine-format shows. The former also tend to be better remembered than the latter. Pace appears to have a greater impact on the tempo of looking among older children, primarily when they are watching programmes with a continuous story. Increasingly, the pace of magazine shows makes them more difficult for children to follow, and with older children in particular does not cause them to pay the programme more attention.[33]

The implications of this evidence for children's programming are that fast pace does not often enhance attention and may interfere with young viewers' abilities to understand and learn the content of a programme. Children attend more effectively to material presented in story format than in a magazine format.

CONCLUSION

Children's attention to the screen, then, is neither constant nor passive. The amount of attention they are prepared to give to individual programmes is directly related to whether the visual and audio message has meaning specific to them, and whether they are given sufficient time to absorb that meaning. In this regard, the format of programmes is all-important. Therefore, a major controlling factor over how and why they watch particular programmes is to do with how well they are able to follow and understand the information they are offered. But how does their ability to follow and understand television develop? Are there particular factors that hinder or enhance this development? In the next chapter we attempt to answer both these questions.

Chapter 4

How well do children follow and understand TV?

A commonly held belief about television viewing is that it requires little effort. Indeed it is true that for most viewers for most of the time television is watched as a source of relaxation. Yet, in order to get any enjoyment or satisfaction out of television at all, there has to be a degree of understanding. In other words, if programmes cannot be understood, it is unlikely that they will be enjoyed. The ability of viewers to follow a programme and to understand at least part of what's going on is essential to being able to get anything out of television at all – even relaxation. This is just as relevant to children as it is to adults. Since we are not born with an intrinsic understanding of television, it must therefore represent a skill or set of skills which we learn. This learning begins in early childhood from the time we start to watch television.

As we saw in the last chapter, understanding television dictates and even determines attention to the screen. The nature of children's attention to programmes changes with age as their understanding of programmes develops. Among relatively inexperienced young viewers, attention to the television can be affected quite significantly by physical happenings in programmes. Reaction to a change of events is less discriminating among very young children than it is later on in their viewing lives. As children learn about different types of programmes and develop the ability to recognise the particular characters or programmes, they become more selective in the way they respond to visual and sound effects and other sources of physical stimulation which programmes contain. This happens as these physical features themselves acquire meaning. Eventually, it is the meaning that children respond to rather than the physical event.

In this chapter we will take a closer look at different aspects of understanding about television. An implication associated with many commonsensical beliefs about the importance of television is that it 'injects' viewers with new attitudes and examples of how to behave which they take on board without question or resistance. This belief is at best misleading, and at worst wrong. Viewers are not empty vessels – not even young viewers. Nor do they passively accept all that television tells or shows them. There are a number of ways children learn to understand television and make sophisticated judgements about programmes. We shall examine some of these under the following headings:

- children's understanding of the format features of programmes;
- children's abilities to follow television narratives;
- children's discrimination between what is real and what is fantasy on television;
- children's judgements about television characters and their actions.

CHILDREN'S UNDERSTANDING OF THE FORMAT FEATURES OF PROGRAMMES

Researchers have found that young children's attention to television varies with a variety of content and presentation format features. The implication of this work is that children's visual attention to the screen is largely governed by how much they understand what is going on. Two kinds of format attributes have been investigated – visual and sound (or auditory) attributes. The major difference between these is in the way they are able to affect and control attention. Clearly, visual ones can have influence only when they are seen; in other words when the child looks at the screen. Sound attributes, on the other hand, can draw the young child's attention to the television even when he or she is not looking directly at it.[1]

In one study, researchers observed children aged 3 to 5 years continuously while they watched a mixed compilation of programming over a three-hour period. Snacks and toys were available while viewing took place. The children were assessed, principally for the extent to which they looked towards or away from the screen, and according to how much their attention was influenced by visual and sound attributes of the programmes. Which features of the programme made children look back towards the screen when their attention was diverted elsewhere? And which features could maintain the child's attention while he or she was actually watching the screen?

As might be expected, audio or sound effects proved to be the main means of regaining a child's attention, while visual attributes were best at maintaining the child's attention. In other words, some kind of change in the spoken dialogue, background sounds or music could encourage a child to look at the screen, but this look would be prolonged only if what was happening visually proved to be of interest. Both the audio and visual attributes were then examined to assess their potential for either eliciting or inhibiting attention.

In all, seven different types of change in the soundtrack produced visual attention from among inattentive young viewers – change in sound volume, special sound effects, laughter, women's voices, children's voices, peculiar voices and instrumental music. Three sound features inhibited attention – men's voices, individual singing and slow music. Two sound features had mixed effects – the onset of lively music or rhyming elicited attention, but only for a few seconds. Finally, two sound features made no difference to visual attention – group singing and applause. If the child was looking at the television, both visual and sound attributes maintained attention. In all, six visual attributes were found to maintain attention, six terminated attention, and eight were non-significant; three sound attributes maintained attention, three terminated attention, and five were non-significant.[2]

CHILDREN'S ABILITIES TO FOLLOW TELEVISION NARRATIVES

The next question on children's understanding of television concerns how well young viewers are able to follow the narrative or storyline of programmes. Children may pay attention to the screen because of the physical stimulation caused by a programme, for example, because of significant voices they recognise, changes in the tone of the music or other sound effects. But how well do they actually follow what is going on?

Most of the research on children's understanding of television has focused on developmental changes with age. Age trends are not the only important factors, however. It is important to look at the form and content of programmes and how they affect comprehension and growth of understanding. Evaluating the state of knowledge about these matters is not always easy. Comparability of research is often hindered by lack of consistency in the definition and measures of comprehension used by different researchers. Sometimes comprehension has been defined in terms of what children can recall from programmes they have watched. On other occasions, understanding has been indicated by the ability of children to place scenes from a programme in correct sequence. It is unlikely that such different methods measure the same thing. A convenient way to divide up the research is by the age of the children studied. Some researchers have been interested principally in school-age children, while others have focused on infants who have just begun or have yet to start school.

Research with infants and preschool children

Before they start school, children can experience particular difficulties in being able to understand the programmes they watch on television. At the age of 4 or 5, for example, children may be able to recall isolated episodes or scenes from programmes they watch, but are unable to put all the pieces of a story together to form a coherent whole. At this age, children's thinking is concerned totally with life in the present and they have difficulty connecting the beginning, middle and end bits of programmes which occur at different points in time.

At the age when they are about to start school, children usually have trouble following the plots of programmes and do not necessarily recount the events in a story in their proper, original sequence. Even programmes made especially for this age group can cause them difficulties.[3]

Communicating deeper meaning

Even if a programme is carefully produced and succeeds in getting across a good grasp of basic story ingredients to young children, they may still fail to understand the deeper meaning that may underlie it. In one Swedish study, producers tried to communicate an understanding of the situation of immigrant children from Finland. They did so by describing the day-to-day lives of a Swedish and a Finnish girl. The underlying message of the film was 'We are quite alike, after all'. The film did not succeed, even though the children were able to follow the story and relate various details. In order to grasp the message, young viewers had to draw conclusions from the material presented; that is, they had to be capable of inferential reasoning, something they were unable to do since their thought processes were not yet sufficiently developed.[4]

Young children's understanding of television was investigated in a project begun in 1969 at the Swedish Broadcasting Corporation (Sveriges Radio). Rydin and colleagues were investigating preschool children's understanding not only as a means of providing insight into the way they comprehend television, but also as a formative research exercise designed to help produce better programmes.

At the time when interest in preschool programming was growing, in particular following the introduction of *Sesame Street*, Sveriges Radio produced a successful but controversial programme, *Two Ants are More than Four Elephants*. Preschool children and their parents seemed to enjoy the programmes but educators and other critics claimed the 'pace was too fast and the content was packaged knowledge out of context which would not stimulate deeper, activating processes within the young viewers'.

This criticism stimulated further research on a programme called *The Tale of the Seed*. This study assessed children's understanding and retention of information and investigated the effect of accompanying material that was irrelevant to the central theme. Rydin found that repetition of information enhanced learning from the radio version of the programme, but irrelevant details neither increased or decreased children's retention of factual material. In a subsequent study of the televised version, the inclusion of irrelevant details resulted in reduced ability to remember the factual material.

Younger children (of 5 years old) were more distracted by the lack of agreement between audio and visual (e.g. when irrelevant verbal information was not illustrated in the visual display). Rydin suggested that one of the major problems inherent in much of the television programming of the Western world is the fragmentation of the sequence of the programme. This applies both to children and to adults. Thus, the viewer is unable to move with the flow of the programme. This fragmentation, she argues, is the result of the domination of much of the Western world's television by commercial interests. Programmes are fragmented because advertising can be more easily inserted.

School-age children's comprehension of television

Between the ages of 7 and 12, children's thinking is still very different from adult thought processes. At the same time, however, children at this age show some signs of mental maturity. Their command of language, for example, is nearly complete. They also show a growing ability to see other people's point of view. In terms of television, what particularly distinguishes school-age children from younger ones is their ability to draw conclusions from the material presented to them. Their thinking is more flexible and not so closely bound up with the situation in which they find themselves at the moment. When recounting a story, they frequently introduce their own interpretation, which was not part of the original version. Making one's own interpretations and drawing conclusions are part of the mental processing by which we all create structures and contexts for what we perceive in the world around us and help us to remember the things we have experienced.

This development does not happen all at once. Thus, some studies have found that children's understanding of television up to about 8 years of age is poor. In general, up to the age of 8, children retain a relatively small proportion of depicted actions, events and settings in typical programmes; memory for programme content improves significantly between the ages of 8 and 12 years.[5]

Although young viewers attend to aspects of programmes that are obviously salient and have meaning or relevance for them, particularly in programmes produced for children, they apparently lack the abilities necessary for a proper understanding of more complex programmes made for older viewers. While 8-year-olds can follow major, explicitly presented ingredients of a plot, they are significantly less likely than 10- to 12-year-olds to 'go beyond the information given' and make more subtle connections, e.g. relationships between an early and a later scene in a drama. Indeed, younger schoolchildren seem able to perform at little better than chance when tested for their understanding of programmes at this level. Thus, while viewing is active and discerning to some extent, even among young children, the strategic skills necessary for mature viewing of complex programmes develop markedly over the primary-school and early adolescent years.[6]

Drama programmes consist of a series of discrete scenes which are tied together by an underlying theme or storyline. Most peak-time programmes, even though they attract large numbers of young viewers, are not made specifically for children, but for a general audience including adults. Consequently, stories must be somewhat complex and subtle in order to appeal to the adult audience. To understand and follow a plot fully, it is often necessary to make connections between two or more sequences in a programme that are separated by other sequences. Thus, there may be a scene early on in the programme involving a quarrel between two characters, and a later scene towards the end of the programme in which the same two characters are portrayed in altered circumstances in which one attacks the other. The motive for the attack lies in the earlier scene, but viewers must remember that scene and make the connection. Such linkages are essential for understanding plots. Adults who are experienced viewers are usually able to make these connections; young children, however, may often be less able to do so.

Researchers have found, for example, when children are shown a typical hour-long, action-adventure programme and tested afterwards for what they can remember and understand about the story, that those up to the age of 8 are able to remember accurately only about half to two-thirds of what adults have judged as central to the plot. However, by the age of 10 through to 14, 80 to 90 per cent of the central plot is remembered and understood.[7]

Comprehension of TV dramas, however, relies not simply on how much viewers can remember from programmes (although, clearly, accurate memory for events is an important component), but also on the ability to make inferences about what will happen next based on what has just gone before. Storylines often tend to be fairly predictable. Adults learn to predict what may happen next because they have learned how stories typically unfold. Young children, however, have to develop this ability as they mature. Certain studies have attempted to investigate the development of this ability.

One way of examining the relationship between this ability and children's comprehension of TV dramas is to interrupt the programme while children are watching, and ask them at different points in the story what they think will happen next. Studies show that it is not until the age of 10 that children begin to make adult-like inferences. Below the age of 8, usually only a quarter of children are able to make these kinds of inferences, and show that they have followed the story.

As a concrete illustration of this, one American experiment showed groups of children a programme which was interrupted at different points. At one stage, the programme was stopped after a scene in which one of the main characters was asked by an old man, down on his luck, for a dollar. The character, guilt-ridden over his murder of a similar derelict old man earlier in the show, impulsively gives the old man $40. After this scene, children were asked to guess why the younger man reacted as he did.

Children aged 10 and over were able to make the connection between the scene they had just watched and the earlier murder, whilst young children were largely unaware of any such connection.[8]

In the UK, research among children aged between 9 and 16 years found that they were able to follow the storyline of episodes from two British-made police drama series. On story comprehension tests, these children averaged around 70 per cent correct answers, with their performance indicating that they understood both explicitly presented plot material and inferential material implied in the storylines.[9] This study also found marked age differences in levels of programme comprehension. This result was consistent with research findings among American children, where evidence had emerged that accurate retention of TV plots could improve from 66 per cent at 7 or 8 years to over 90 per cent by the age of 13 or 14.[10] The British research found that 15- to 16-year-olds were better than 9- to 14-year-olds, between whom there were few differences. With one of the two police dramas studied, for example, the oldest children in the study scored around 86 per cent correct comprehension, compared with 65 per cent among younger children. With the other police drama studied, differences between age groups were not quite as pronounced, but it was still clear that teenagers understood more than pre-teens. These results were generally supportive of earlier American findings.

Familiarity with programme settings and understanding the story

As children mature, their understanding of their own environment and the world at large improves. When faced with a new experience, they attempt to integrate it into their existing framework of knowledge in order to make sense of it. Does this mean that, when young children are offered a television narrative with settings and character types of which they have some real-life experience, they are better able to follow the plot? In a study designed to investigate this question, Andrew Collins asked if children's recall from programmes would vary with their social background. Children from certain social or ethnic backgrounds were expected to show better understanding of programmes which featured characters and settings similar to those found in their own home environment. The study involved white and black children, from working-class and middle-class backgrounds, and represented three age groups: 7-, 10-, and 12-year-olds. One set of children drawn from each subgroup saw a sitcom featuring white, middle-class characters, while another set viewed a sitcom with a similar plot line, but featuring black, working-class characters. In both stories, the father is offered a better job in another city; his accepting it would mean that members of the family would be separated.

After viewing the programmes, the young viewers were tested for their understanding of the plot, reasons or motives underlying particular actions, their perceptions of how characters felt in different scenes, and their memory of other aspects of the programme not central to the main storyline. Regardless of the programme seen, 7-year-olds' memories of all these things were poorer than 10-year-olds, who in turn were worse than the 12-year-olds. Among children who viewed the middle-class family programme, middle-class 7-year-olds remembered more story content overall than did lower-class 7-year-olds. Among children who viewed the working-class family programme, the reverse was true: compared to middle-class 7-year-olds, lower-class 7-year-olds were better at remembering the main storyline, making judgements about classmates' feelings and recounting other aspects of the programme. There were no ethnicity differences.

Throughout, though, age differences were important, regardless of social background. Older children exhibited a better grasp of the main storyline, were better able to identify causes of events, had better recall of the emotional state of an actor in the scene concerned, and were more likely to remember peripheral content if the main story was understood.[11]

CHILDREN'S DISCRIMINATIONS BETWEEN WHAT IS REAL AND WHAT IS FANTASY ON TELEVISION

Are the events and characters depicted in programmes to be believed or taken for real? How well do children distinguish between reality and fantasy on TV? The reality–fantasy distinction is seen as an important issue because research has shown us that the effects of television on children's subsequent attitudes and behaviour can be significantly modified by their perceptions of how real televised events are. In general, more realistic events have more profound effects. However, most children's viewing is devoted to fictional programmes – there is relatively little attention paid to the news before the age of 10. It is cartoons, fantastic heroes and funny situations which attract most of the young viewer's attention. But even amongst fictional programmes there can be considerable variation in how real different portrayed situations and characters appear to be.

For example, with a programme such as *Tom and Jerry* we all know that the characters are nothing more than animated drawings, and that when they hit each other, nobody really gets hurt. This realisation develops quite early on amongst children, or so it seems. Young viewers are able to enjoy such cartoons in a playful, make-believe way. But what about programmes such as *Coronation Street*, *Minder* or *The Professionals*, where the settings are contemporary, and the characters are human, and may resemble people we know. Under these circumstances, the distinction between what is real and made up is more difficult to make. Indeed, even adults can be confused and taken in by some characters on television.

Anecdotal evidence is available to suggest that TV characters who appear on long-running series may become so familiar to viewers that they are thought to be real people. During the first five years of his appearance in the popular series *Marcus Welby M.D.*, actor Robert Young received over a quarter of a million letters from viewers, mostly asking for medical advice.[12] How did all these people think of Robert Young alias Marcus Welby, however? Did they assume that Robert Young, the actor, must have picked up a certain amount of medical knowledge whilst working on the series? Did they assume that the series probably employed a team of medical consultants who could answer their questions? Or did they actually believe that the character Marcus Welby was a real doctor? Whilst anecdotes of this sort do not constitute empirically acceptable proof of television's influence, they do serve to illustrate an important point. Even the more mature members of the public have many gaps in their knowledge about people, events and institutions in the real world with which they have had little direct experience, but about which something may be learned through watching fictional television.

Most viewers have never been in an operating room, criminal courtroom, a police station or a jail, or a corporate boardroom. Much of what they 'know' about these diverse spheres of activity has been learned from television. Children, of course, have even less experience of life than adults, and consequently may be more easily taken in by the things they see on television.

However, the extent to which people – adults or children – are deceived by television depends to some degree on how specific are the aspects of programmes we are looking at. At a superficial level, the ability to distinguish between types of programmes and their settings is something that develops early on. Even quite young children are able to make crude distinctions between programmes featuring animated and human characters, and quickly come to understand that many of the fantastic heroes they see on television are not real people. Even these relatively easy character discriminations are nevertheless important. One researcher has found, for example, that among 5-year-olds, over half of those he questioned did not understand that TV characters are played by actors. At age 8, over two-thirds knew this, and by age 11 nearly all children appear to have learned this elementary fact.[13]

Considerable changes occur across childhood in the ideas young viewers hold about the reality of television programme content. Up to the age of 7 or 8, the distinction between fantasy and reality is often cloudy. By middle childhood, however, judgements about television's realism become much more refined. News is perceived differently from drama, commercials are distinguished from programmes, and so on. But as cognitive sophistication improves, certain other perceptions develop. The news is categorised as depicting real-life events. But the critical viewer may come to consider ways in which TV news may be inaccurate, biased, misleading and in some ways 'unreal'. By way of contrast, drama programming is recognised as being fictional, but viewers may come to consider ways in which it nevertheless reflects aspects of reality.

Even before they have started school, children can make certain distinctions between which of their favourite programmes are 'real' or 'make-believe'. Children can identify cartoons as make-believe and news as real, but they may be confused about certain other shows.[14]

Distinguishing between different sorts of television characters improves with age; 4-year-olds even find it difficult to explain the differences between animated and puppet characters. At this early age, children are also uncertain about the mechanisms of television and this in turn affects their perception of what is real on television. One example of this confusion is their failure to understand how characters 'get inside TV'. One belief is that TV 'people are made smaller than us', 'they're lowered down by a rope'. Older children, aged 7 to 8 years, may be confused about how certain characters are made. They can, however, usually discriminate between human and animated characters.[15]

Children become more sophisticated about television programmes as they grow older, and this development occurs at more than one level. Deciding about the realism of television may involve comparing television portrayals with real life. Another feature of this area of judgement, however, involves knowing how and why television programmes are put together. This is a subject we shall return to in more detail in Chapter 13, when we discuss how television viewing skills can be taught. For the present, though, we can look briefly at some examples of how children can get confused about the realness of television, and the ages at which they begin to grow out of this confusion.

Accumulating evidence indicates that the knowledge that most fabricated television programmes are made up develops during elementary-school years. One study found that from 5 to 12 the knowledge that television characters were portrayed by actors (and were not real people) gradually improved. Among 5- to 6-year-olds, 58 per cent did not understand this at all. Among 8-year-olds, 45 per cent completely understood that characters were actors; another 26 per cent partially understood it and only 29 per cent did not understand it. Among 11- and 12-year-olds, 65 per cent had complete understanding. Thus, a major jump in knowledge occurred between the beginning and middle of elementary school, but, by the end of elementary school, about one-third of the boys still did not completely understand about actors.[16]

Elsewhere, the age of 8 has been found to be a crucial time, when understanding suddenly improves. Children older than 8 seldom thought of television as offering a 'magic window' on the world. They understood something about the fabricated nature of programming. By the age of 8, children become generally aware that television programmes are made up. How completely they understand this varies, depending on the children studied and on what criteria are established for awareness.[17]

In one study, for example, children were given pairs of programmes and asked to say which of the pair was more real and why. The 10–12s were much more articulate than were those aged 6–8, and gave more criteria as reasons for their judgements. Younger children were more readily able to recognise the reality status of programmes which contained blatant violations of reality, but remained confused about the status of other programmes, such as fantasy drama. But even more difficulty was experienced with realistic programmes (news and sport), live programmes (talk shows and game shows) and comedy shows.[18]

In making reality–fantasy distinctions, younger children tend to focus on physical features of a programme as cues to its lack of reality, including the presence (or absence) of stunts, camera tricks, costumes, props and sets. Distinctions are also dependent on whether a presentation is acted, scripted, rehearsed, live or filmed. The degree to which the show is an acted performance is important here.[19]

Turning next to television versus real-life comparisons, three general strategies seem to be used. These include the category of 'actual', referring to whether or not television content exists in the real world. The second category is of the 'possible', which refers to content which could happen in the real world. And the third category is of the 'impossible', which consists of events which could not happen in the real world. Distinctions made in terms of what is actual are made by children of all ages. Distinctions made in terms of what is possible tend to be used more by younger children, while judgements made with reference to what is impossible have been observed to increase with age.[20]

Reality–fantasy discriminations are made frequently by reference to whether or not the televised content exists in the real world, with little apparent regard for its fictional status. For instance, the child's attention centres repeatedly on specific surface features of programming, such as the means by which programme portrayals violate physical reality. In the absence of such blatant features, the reality of television is often accepted. But eventually, these specific concerns with trickery lead to a more generalised realisation that television is not real life, but rather a representation of it; at the same time, the nature of the television versus real-life comparisons also change. As children mature, they begin to consider more qualities in programmes, and make judgements about degrees of realism.

Children and adolescents can make distinctions between television and real life even though their real-world experiences of certain objects or events may be limited. One study, for example, examined non-delinquent and delinquent adolescents' images of real-life and television police. Teenagers indicated the extent to which they felt each of thirty-six statements accurately described the way television or real-life police are, or operate. Six distinct patterns of perceptions emerged: three of actual police and three of television police. Perceptions of actual police were diverse, ranging from highly favourable to openly hostile, with some mixed feelings in between. Perceptions of television police were relatively homogeneous and positive. Among both delinquent and non-delinquent adolescents there was widespread belief that television police were idealised dramatisations, different from the real thing. Those youngsters who had favourable impressions of actual police tended to see greater similarity between actual and television versions than did those who held unfavourable impressions of actual police. However, delinquents did not on the whole see greater differences between actual and television police than did non-delinquents, despite their greater contact with the police in real life.[21]

Children's perceptions of TV police were investigated further in a British study which focused on two well-known police drama series, *The Bill* produced by ITV and *Juliet Bravo* produced by the BBC. The perceived realism of these two programmes was greater among children aged 8 or 9 than among those aged 15 or 16 years. A similar pattern of age differences emerged in relation to impressions among these young viewers that such programmes can teach valuable social lessons, make viewers think, and evoke empathic feelings. Although such contemporary police dramas were seen by many children as a source of information as well as entertainment, the extent to which children appeared to get involved in these programmes lessens as they enter their teenage years.[22]

Complicating the picture still further, however, is the finding that not all reality perceptions deteriorate as children get older. Although there may be a general weakening of beliefs that fictional dramas are true to life, when children hit their teens, there may remain a residual but firmly established set of beliefs that certain aspects of these programmes are realistic. This happens as children become more attuned and sensitive to different production formats as they grow older.[23] With crime drama programmes which feature violent content, perceived realism has been found to decline significantly with age.[24] With other programme types, children's perceptions of the realism of events, settings and characterisations may exhibit less marked shifts with age.[25] For some programme types, such as family comedies, perceived realism has even been found to increase with age.[26] Such findings reveal how important it is to explore children's reality perceptions with respect to specific aspects of actual programmes. Although broad distinctions across programme genres in terms of their relative realism can provide some indication of how children respond to television, such simplistic measures fail to reveal deeper and more complex perceptual distinctions that children make about programme content.

During the years from about 3 to 12, children gradually acquire an understanding of the distinctions between real and fictional television content.[27] By middle childhood, at least two dimensions appear to be discriminated in children's judgements of reality: factuality and social realism.[28]

Factuality represents a judgement of whether the events portrayed actually happened in the unrehearsed world, and whether the people on screen are being seen in their unscripted life. Factuality is discriminated primarily on the basis of format and form cues. By the age of 7, children recognise cues for live broadcasts of real events (e.g. print on screen, long shots) versus fictional content (e.g. flashbacks, dream sequences) even when content is held constant.[29] They know that certain production conventions indicate certain genres of programming (e.g. laughter track indicates comedy, talking heads indicate news), and they know the basic factuality of each genre of programming.

Social realism, the second dimension of reality perception is similar to the attribute that some writers have called 'plausibility'.[30] It reflects a judgement about whether the televised people and events are like those in the real world. Where the judgement for factuality is 'truth', however unlikely, versus 'make-believe', the judgement for social realism is whether a television representation is true to life, even though it may be known to be fictional.[31]

One significant aspect of these judgements by children is that the perceived reality of television may mediate their emotional responses to the things they see on screen. The nature and strength of children's emotional reactions to a programme may depend upon what perspective they take while watching it. If a programme is perceived as factual, rather than fictional, children may be more likely to imagine themselves in the roles of the people involved. High levels of emotional distress were registered among children shortly after witnessing the explosion of the space shuttle *Challenger*, unlike anything experienced after they had seen comparable fictional depictions.[32] The emotional impact of fictional content can be reduced by reminding children it is not real, but such reassurance is of little help to children younger than about 7 years old.[33]

Under certain circumstances, however, fictional content can produce profound reactions from children just as much as factual programmes. Factors such as the nature of the subject matter and production techniques deployed can override any moderating influences of the broader distinctions which children learn to make between factual and fictional treatments. A study of 9- and 10-year-olds' reactions to, and judgements about, factual and fictional television programmes depicting family conflict found that vicarious emotions were felt in response to both types of programme. The children displayed responsible emotional reactions to the fictional programme, showing understanding of, and empathy with, the depicted family's problems. The documentary version was perceived as more factual than the fictional version, but this did not make any difference to children's emotional responses. One reason for this may be that emotional responses depend more on judged social realism than on perceived reality. Perceptions of factuality depend on both content and the forms or format of the programme. Judgements about social realism, however, depend primarily on content. In this study, the factuality–fictionality distinction was manipulated mainly by variations in production format, while the type of subject matter was similar across the two programmes. The strength of children's emotional reactions was significantly affected by the extent to which they considered the people and events in the programmes as true to life or similar to their own experience.[34]

Findings such as these indicate that children develop a multifaceted idea about the perceived reality of television. Format features are very important because they signal the genre or type of programme a viewer may be watching. When they signal that the genre is documentary, a knowledgeable viewer will generally assume that the content represents people and events in the real world. The viewer may then take the content more seriously and try harder to understand it. The more the viewer identifies with events and people on screen, the more elaborate will be the ideas formed about the subject matter of the programme.

Children's understanding of television and ability to discriminate between different types of television programme can be influenced by those with whom they view. In Chapter 12, we will examine the significant role parents can play in mediating children's viewing behaviour and affecting how children react to the things they see on television. Children do not always watch television with their parents, however. In fact, much of children's viewing is carried out either on their own or with other children, including friends and siblings.[35] Despite the fact that siblings may watch together frequently, the evidence on whether younger siblings can benefit from watching with older ones is mixed. One important factor here seems to be how much older one sibling is than another. When a child watches television with an older brother or sister, their evaluations of programmes remains unaffected unless the older sibling is at least three years older than they are.[36] One reason why sibling coviewing has limited influence on a child's understanding of television is that there tends to be very little conversation about the things being watched between siblings while they are viewing programmes.[37]

In a more recent study, Barbara Wilson and Audrey Weiss found that 4- to 5-year-olds could distinguish effectively between whether a scene from a programme was a dream sequence or represented a normal-time event. Watching with an older sibling, aged 7 to 8 years, did not assist in making this distinction easier. In fact, the presence of an older sibling proved to be a distraction and resulted in poorer dream-sequence identification. However, those young children who watched with an older brother or sister did get less emotionally aroused by what they saw and enjoyed it more than when viewing alone.[38]

CHILDREN'S JUDGEMENTS ABOUT TELEVISION CHARACTERS AND THEIR ACTIONS

We have seen that as children grow older they come to follow the plots in televised dramas more effectively and learn to grasp fundamental distinctions between reality and fantasy content. Another aspect of television comprehension relates to the way viewers evaluate characters in television programmes. Changes in children's perceptions of television characters have been found to occur with age, too. Although there is a tendency for children to ascribe more realism to specific characters with whom they are familiar than to the general category of 'people on TV', this perception tends to decrease with age.

A study of the dimensions used spontaneously by 8- to 12-year-old children to discriminate between pairs of popular television characters found four major dimensions: the humour of the characters; the strength of the characters; the attractiveness of the characters; and the activity level of the characters. 'How much like a real person' characters were perceived to be did not emerge as an important dimension. The significance of the reality dimension seems to depend, however, on the characters that are selected for children's judgement.[39]

Recent evidence shows that a reality factor may in fact colour children's discriminations between television characters. It seems that, as they grow older, children increasingly tend to organise pictures of television characters into discrete groups of human, animated and puppet characters. However, it is not until the age 9 or 10 that children begin to realise that being alive and able to move autonomously are characteristics found only in human characters.[40] Before they are 10 years old, children seem to have an incomplete understanding of the functioning of cartoon and puppet characters. Most children know, for example, that Tony the Tiger is not really alive, but they cannot necessarily explain how the character works. The finding that correct and clear identification of make-believe characters is not always obvious to young children carries important implications for the impact that television may have on these viewers. It cannot be assumed that children under 6, who do not yet have the mental ability to make clear distinctions between what is real and what is fantasy, will respond to television in the same way as more mature viewers.

What kinds of inferences do children make about characters and their actions? Television programmes portray varied persons, behaviours, roles, attitudes, situations and events. These portrayals provide examples of how to behave in different situations which children might on occasion emulate, and are also a source of knowledge about the world. Research has suggested, for example, that children may be influenced in their beliefs about different occupations – such as police work, doctors, lawyers and so on – by the way these things are shown on television. But the extent to which character portrayals do affect children's outlook on the world is determined to a significant extent by the ease or difficulty they have in understanding TV plots.[41]

Another important factor, however, is the way young viewers judge the characters themselves and their actions. If violent fighting or shooting is perpetrated by a character who clearly wishes to harm his victim and who is obviously punished for what he does, the character and his actions would, according to the norms of society, be judged as bad. On the other hand, violence for the purpose of freeing a hostage which earns the perpetrator a medal for bravery would be viewed much more positively.[42] This, then, is mainly true for adults, but to what extent is it true for children?

The motives or reasons for actions and their consequences for victims are potentially important modifiers of children's judgements about an actor's moral character and these depend on young viewers being able to understand a character's reasons for behaving in a certain way.

In one experiment by a leading researcher in this field, Andrew Collins, children were shown edited versions of a TV action-adventure drama. The plot involved a man searching for his former wife to prevent her from testifying against him in a kidnapping case. He finds the house where she is hiding and shoots at her, but his attempt to kill her is thwarted by the arrival of police officers who arrest him and place him in handcuffs before leading him away.

Collins and his colleagues wanted to know how children of different ages would evaluate the moral character of the man. To do this, the programme was interrupted at different points and the children were required to say how good or bad they thought the character to be each time. The interesting finding to emerge was how soon children of different ages recognised the character to be essentially bad. Children aged 10 and over became aware of the character's badness quite early on in the story because of his early intentions to kill his wife. Children younger than 8 began to see the character as bad only when he actually tried to kill her. Even then, many younger children failed to give negative evaluations of the man. For most of the youngest viewers of 7 or 8, it was only at the point when the police handcuffed the man and took him away that they realised that maybe this person was bad – why else would he be arrested by the police? What is even more significant, however, is that even after the programme had finished with the man arrested, some young children still did not see him as bad, having earlier thought of him in fairly positive terms.[43]

These findings show that very young viewers may not make accurate moral judgements about characters at all, or do so only following concrete demonstrations of how good or bad a character is. By the age of 10, however, children become more able to judge whether characters are good or bad on the basis of more subtle information about them.

Children's ability to follow and understand television is mainly dependent on age. As their understanding of the world in general develops, so too does their understanding of television. In the same way as they begin to make moral judgements about peer and adult behaviour in their own environment, similar judgements are also made about the behaviour of television characters. But is it children's 'real-world' knowledge that is shaping these judgements of televised behaviour and beliefs, or is television itself having some kind of influence on their developing perceptions as to what is good and bad in their own environment?

Chapter 5

Does TV improve children's knowledge?

Under the ethos of public service broadcasting, television has been required not only to entertain, but also to educate and inform. Nowadays, from the security of their own homes, people are able to see graphic scenes of wars and disasters or the torments suffered by inhabitants of Third World countries as they struggle to survive. They are invited to journey visually through the human body via miniature cameras, to survey the world beneath the sea or to study close up the insects in their own back gardens magnified thousands of times. Fifty years ago, before television was commonplace, only a few had some real-life experience of any of this, but now the majority of people are exposed to it daily without ever stepping outside their own front doors. Yet how much of this vast range of visual information is actually retained and understood, particularly by children, who may often take for granted television's ability to offer a window on the world?

Television is commonly cited by people as their major source of information about what's happening in the world. In public opinion surveys, samples often claim that they learn a great deal about the world from watching television, and that the news on television is more important in keeping them informed than are any other sources.[1] As we saw in Chapter 2, children often claim that television provides various kinds of learning – in the form of both factual knowledge and how to handle other people and different social situations.

As we shall see, however, research on remembering of broadcast news has consistently indicated that much of what is presented seems to be quickly forgotten, particularly where children are concerned.[2] Yet there is no doubt that children do learn some things from television, both from programmes designed to entertain and from those whose main objective is to inform. This failure to learn consistently from television appears to have something to do with the way it is approached and used in the first place. If children decide to view for amusement or entertainment, much of what they watch will simply wash over them; little will stick. On the other hand, if they are motivated to find out about something through viewing, then learning is more likely to occur.

One body of evidence strongly suggests that how well viewers – young and old – are able to learn and remember from television can depend significantly on how the information is presented. Production practices routinely adopted by television news editors, for example, may result in programmes which present too much information, too quickly, and with built-in (often visual) distractions. Under these conditions, even interested viewers may flounder. Ultimately, though, whether or not children learn from television depends on a mixture of factors which relate to viewers' background knowledge and interests, reasons for watching television, degree of concentration and attention while viewing, and the way that programmes are produced.[3]

One starting point is to review how effectively children learn from television productions specifically designed to impart knowledge to them. Educational television programmes represent one area of television output which has been dedicated to improving children's know-how. Some of these productions are broadcast as part of mainstream television for children, while others have been specially made for schools audiences. An impressive range of schools programmes has been produced over many years in the UK, although these have met with a mixed reception from teachers and children.[4] A considerable body of research has revealed that educational television does have potential to improve children's knowledge about a variety of subjects. Failure to fulfil this potential frequently stems from programme-makers' misunderstanding of audience needs, interests and learning abilities. When audience research is used wisely, however, some very effective, as well as popular, productions have resulted.[5]

A number of innovative and popular educational television programmes were developed in the United States during the late 1960s and early 1970s. The major force behind many of these productions was the Children's Television Workshop (CTW), which combined the talents of educational advisors, professional researchers, and television producers. The programmes made by CTW were carefully crafted pieces of television which were guided by detailed research among members of target audiences. The formula was generally believed to be a success.[6]

The best-known productions of this era were *Sesame Street*, *The Electric Company* and *Feeling Good*. *Sesame Street* was designed to prepare children for school by developing both factual knowledge and thinking skills, specifically those relating to numeracy, vocabulary, the use of language, and understanding the world around them. A basic feature of the making of this programme was that each edition had to have been shown, through research, to have a demonstrable ability to attract and hold the attention of young viewers, and to be something they could follow and understand.

The Electric Company was a programme designed to increase reading skills among primary-school children. It used a magazine format and a variety of attention-grabbing production techniques. Research showed that viewers of the programme outperformed non-viewers on a wide range of reading skills.[7] Children were found generally to respond well to this programme and learned from it the skills it was designed to impart.[8]

Feeling Good was designed to motivate young viewers to take steps to enhance their health in eleven basic areas, such as cancer, alcohol abuse, cardiac disease, nutrition, mental health and prenatal care. The overall aim of the programmes was information accumulation and positive attitude changes. Achievement of desired goals was somewhat fragmentary, but this may have been for other than purely educational or television production reasons.[9]

LEARNING FROM TELEVISED SCIENCE

Children's ability to learn about science from television was studied in relation to an educational programme made in the United States called *3-2-1 Contact*. This series was aimed at children aged 8 to 12 and attempted to get them to enjoy science, to engage in scientific activity and to learn different styles of scientific thinking. The programmes were presented in a magazine format, presenting themes based on opposites, with continuing features such as mystery adventure, animation, live action film, music comedy and special effects. Early assessments of this programme indicated that it had successfully attracted a large following among its intended target audience and that its major educational objectives were being achieved.[10]

Getting science information across to children can sometimes be enhanced by using special features within a programme. With *3-2-1 Contact*, for instance, animal behaviour and the human body were found to have high interest and curiosity value for children. In terms of production treatment, plotted drama was preferred by children over a segmented magazine format. Thus, the challenge to producers may be to investigate new ways of incorporating instructional content into a plotted drama format where a problem is posed and resolved through relations between various recurring characters. The dramatic development of a problem and its resolution can help young viewers to understand better the need for a scientific approach to tackle some of life's mysteries and concerns.[11]

British researchers have examined children's learning from science programmes made both for children and for adults. Some of these programmes dealt with only one theme during a single edition, while others dealt with several distinct items. Science knowledge tests conducted with children before and after they viewed the programmes revealed that young viewers can learn from science broadcasts. These productions could enhance children's ability to recall basic scientific facts and their deeper conceptual knowledge of science. This finding emerged among pre-teens and teenage children.[12]

With single theme programmes, children aged 8–9 years recalled 43 per cent of factual content (compared with 6 per cent by 14- to 15-year-olds) from a science programme made for a general family audience. Comprehension levels were also respectable among 8- to 9-year-olds (55 per cent) and 14 to 15 year olds (74 per cent). With a science programme made especially for children, factual recall was higher among both age groups (66 per cent and 85 per cent respectively), while comprehension was a little lower (51 per cent and 71 per cent respectively).

With programmes that contained more than one theme, recall and comprehension levels again indicated that children can and do learn from such programmes. The children correctly recalled 60 per cent and correctly understood 53 per cent of material tested from these programmes. These global figures, however, conceal significant age differences. Older children generally scored much higher than younger children. Age was also highly correlated with general knowledge. It is possible, therefore, that older children have more background knowledge to call upon and better information-processing skills. Indeed, complex statistical analyses revealed that general knowledge was the key factor underpinning effective recall and comprehension of science programmes.[13]

LEARNING FROM TV QUIZ SHOWS

Children can learn from programmes that are designed specially to entertain. Research among children in Britain has shown that, by watching television quiz shows, children's general knowledge (on those topics covered by questions on the show) can be improved. Thus, even entertainment-oriented shows may provide a source of learning for young viewers.

One important factor here may be the tendency of quiz shows to invoke participation among viewers at home. One of the key reasons given by children for watching quiz shows was 'to compete against the contestants'. This means that, when watching quiz shows, children may be engaged in generating their own answers. This additional mental effort may produce an atmosphere in which they actually learn from these programmes. But effort is not the only factor which may be important here. Generating one's own answer to a question results in better processing of that answer, produces a stronger link between the answer and the question, and this, in turn, results in increased processing of the set of generated answers.

Children aged between 8 and 16 generally performed well in the areas of remembering the general content of each programme (e.g. who won what?), the rules of the game being played (e.g. how contestants achieved passage into the final round), and the answers given to the questions asked in the quiz element of each show. General content recall was best for a programme targeted at adult audiences, but memory for rules of the game and quiz items was best for two programmes aimed at younger audiences.[14]

LEARNING FROM TELEVISION NEWS

Television news brings into children's homes a wealth of information about the world every day. Much of this information will concern people, places and events they have never seen or are unlikely to meet or experience firsthand. As we have already seen, television is not invariably a good or easy medium to learn from. Compared with other forms of communication, its ability to improve awareness and knowledge effectively often pales. It is not always easy to predict when or what children will learn from television.

Television drama is designed principally to entertain, though it can undoubtedly also tell us things about the world. Young audiences and old alike can learn various things about the world, about personal and social relationships, how to behave in different situations, what it might be like to work in a certain kind of job, how people live in faraway places, and so on. Some of this learning reflects truthfully the way the world really is, while some may not. Thus, television drama can influence viewers' beliefs about the world around them, though not always accurately or authentically.

Television news, on the other hand, is defined both by its producers and its audiences as programming designed principally to inform. This is not to say that the news is not also found entertaining. Indeed, it often tries to arouse and entertain. Despite its central aim to inform the public, however, research has shown that audiences often display poor memory for news on television. This happens consistently, even though people subjectively feel that television news provides well for their news needs.

So, just how much does television news improve what children know about the world? Where it fails, can we identify the reasons why? Several different sources of evidence can be distinguished which shed some light on these questions. First, we can look at the role television news plays in the political socialisation of children. Second, we can examine the extent to which frequency of watching the news affects knowledge about recent or current news events. Third, we can test children's abilities to remember stories from individual television news broadcast shortly after they have watched them.

TV news and political learning

Television is widely recognised by the adult public as their major source of news. Much of television news revolves around the affairs of governments and political activity. It is reasonable to assume, therefore, that television could play an important part in the political cultivation of young viewers.

Although the news does not feature among children's stated television favourites, as they grow older and approach teenage years, young viewers gradually tune in to the news more and more. One aspect of this development is children's political socialisation, whereby youngsters acquire knowledge about their political environment and begin to form political opinions. Parents and school are known to have an influence over children's and adolescents' political opinion forming, but there is some indication too that the media can play an important role.[15]

Political awareness has been observed to emerge during elementary-school years with children being able to articulate certain abstract emotional attachments and identification with political figures and institutions. At first these political allegiances are vague and ill-informed. During adolescence, however, they show signs of being founded in specific knowledge about politicians, government and the political process. Political party attachments can often be shaped by the family. Political knowledge, though, has been found to be related to children's and adolescents' use of the mass media and in particular to their interest in news and current affairs.[16]

Watching the news on television may play a part in the political education of young people and is testament to one kind of informational effect that television can have on them. While this effect may not always be powerful, it is there nevertheless. The experts have not always agreed, however, about the significance of the role of television as a source of learning about politics. For some it is a primary influence, while for others its role is secondary to that of other sources.

Only one thing is for sure. Television has a tremendous potential for providing at least some information about government and political affairs. Such topics are covered nightly by news and current affairs programmes which are broadcast at times when millions of young viewers are watching. Those young viewers who take a special interest in watching these programmes might be expected to develop a greater knowledge about government and political leaders than those who do not pay much attention.

One early American study revealed that over half a sample of children said they received most of their information about the President and Vice-President from television: 30 per cent listed television as the most important source of information about Congress, and 21 per cent of information about the Supreme Court. However, newspapers and magazines were mentioned as far more important sources of information about elections, and about candidates and issues, with television running a fairly distant second.[17]

Further insights were provided by a study of 9- to 12-year-olds' reliance on newspapers and television for political information. The children were questioned about their identification with a political party, which party they would vote for, awareness of party interests, laws and the role of government in making laws. Partisan identification and perceptions of party policy among children varied significantly with how much they watched television news or read newspapers. The more children tuned in to either of these news sources, the more they knew. Party voting choice was similarly related to both media. Political interest emerged as an important factor which mediated relationships between knowledge of legal processes and amount of watching television news or reading of newspapers. Increased use of these two news sources made a difference to knowledge of legal processes only among children who were already interested in these matters.[18]

In Britain, one study has yielded weak evidence that television news viewing is related to how much adolescents know about politics. Teenagers of 16 to 18 years were given questionnaires which measured five areas of political knowledge:

- identification of party policies;
- identification of prominent political leaders;
- identification of local political leaders;
- knowledge of parliamentary and local political issues;
- knowledge of who was responsible for various public services.

They were also asked to indicate their interest in politics, economics and current affairs, and their use of television, radio and newspapers. Interest in politics emerged as the best indicator of political knowledge, while sex (boys were better than girls), heavier viewing of television news and talking about politics with others emerged as weaker indicators.[19]

The best way to find out if television is having an influence on the developing political awareness of children is to study viewing and political knowledge growth over time with the same youngsters. One American piece of research studied children aged 5 to 10 years over a one-year period. The researchers administered questionnaires to the children on two occasions one year apart and asked the children whether they discussed news events with parents or friends, whether they had any interest in particular kinds of news topics and whether they ever tried to find out more about a news issue after seeing it reported in the news. The children were also asked whether they viewed evening network television newscasts for adults or the special news slots designed for their own age group and shown on Saturday mornings. (At the time of this study the CBS network in the United States produced a specially designed two-minute sports news broadcast for children every half-hour during children's entertainment programming on Saturday and Sunday mornings.)

News and political knowledge levels, and the tendency to discuss news with others, were greater and more likely to occur among children who watched both more children's news and more adult news among 9- to 10-year-olds. Among younger children, greater news viewing was associated with better knowledge on the second (but not the first) wave of interviews and also with interest in governmental affairs and discussion of the news with others.

The findings showed that more than half the children occasionally or frequently watched television news programming and that reported news viewing contributed to political knowledge, interest and information-seeking. Looking at how these two things changed over time, it became apparent that the influence flowed from watching the news to becoming more politically aware. Young viewers became more knowledgeable about politics over time. There was no indication that children who were initially knowledgeable necessarily sought to watch television news more often.[20]

TV news and knowledge of recent events

Television news provides a daily supply of information about the world. How much does it improve children's knowledge about current and recent events? One way of finding this out is to examine correlations between how often they watch the news and the extent of their knowledge about events in the news.

In a series of studies during the 1980s, psychologist Ed Cairns examined the role of television news broadcasts in providing knowledge about the 'Troubles' in Northern Ireland to younger viewers. This research has been interpreted to show differences in children's knowledge about current social and political problems in the province associated with television news viewing and indicated age-related differences in learning from the news among child audiences.

In embarking on their test study, Cairns and his colleagues hypothesised that even young children living in relatively peaceful areas of Northern Ireland who had not been directly exposed to violence were still aware of the violence going on in other parts of Northern Ireland. They went on to suggest that at least some of this knowledge was probably acquired by children from the news media, particularly from television news. Awareness of what was happening in Northern Ireland was assessed among children from Northern Ireland, who were compared with two sets of children from Scotland; one set of children was exposed to Northern Irish television news broadcasts, while the other set was not.[21]

From this study it was apparent that, while Scottish children who had seen Northern Irish television news broadcasts were more aware of the violence and problems in Northern Ireland than were a control group of Scottish children who had seen none of these broadcasts, the children who revealed the greatest level of awareness were those actually living in Northern Ireland. Two possible explanations were offered for these results. First, although both Northern Irish children and some Scottish children had seen television news from Northern Ireland, the Northern Irish children were probably also exposed to other information sources (e.g. newspapers, family, friends) and hence had greater overall knowledge of events in the province. Second, it could be the case that the Northern Irish children, because of their greater background knowledge about the 'Troubles', were able to absorb more information from television news programmes about this topic and thus increase their superiority. The latter explanation is akin to the knowledge-gap hypothesis whereby the already well-informed benefit more from exposure to the news than do the less well-informed, so that the gap in knowledge between the two groups widens.

Another study investigated the impact of television news viewing on Irish children's knowledge about the problems in Northern Ireland. Nearly 500 11-year-olds living in five different parts of Northern Ireland, some of which were closer to actual violence than others, were asked whether they watched television news either 'never', 'sometimes' or 'frequently', and were also required to complete an eleven-item knowledge test. The latter consisted of

items relating to what were felt to be relatively enduring features of the violence (for example, what the initials RUC and UDR stand for, where the Falls Road and Crossmaglen are, what a control zone and road block are and what the confidential telephone is used for).

It emerged that boys were more knowledgeable than girls, children who lived closer to the violent areas knew more than those who lived further away, and those who claimed frequent news viewing knew more than those who claimed otherwise.[22]

The study falls down on a number of points, however, and solid evidence for a television influence here must be questioned. For instance, we do not know whether boys watched more news than girls or whether children living in violent areas watched more news than those living further away from the trouble spots. Nevertheless, other writers have suggested that at times of trouble people do turn to the news media more often for information about the latest developments.

In a follow-up study, nearly 600 children aged 8 years and 11 years from the North and South of Ireland were selected. Children in the North were from two distinct locations once again: those who had experienced relatively little violence and those who had experienced above average levels of violence. The news viewing and knowledge measures were as before.

Results showed main effects on knowledge for sex and age, but this time not for claimed television news viewing. There was, however, an interaction of television news viewing with age: 11-year-olds who reported greater viewing frequencies knew more. Claimed frequency of news viewing was not related to knowledge levels among the younger children.[23]

There was also no attempt to measure the influences of other important factors. For example, to what extent were differences in knowledge in different areas affected by exposure to other media such as newspapers and radio, or by talking with family and friends? The relationships between reported television news viewing and knowledge about the 'Troubles' may indeed indicate that more knowledgeable children were also more active news seekers. But were they more active seekers of news not only through television, but also through radio, the press and elsewhere? We need to know about all this before we can be sure just what the separate effect of television was upon children's awareness.

Remembering what news programmes said

Some researchers have approached the problem of finding out how much viewers learn from television news by asking people to write down how much they can remember from a news bulletin shortly after watching it. This can be done in two different ways. One method is to contact people at home (usually by telephone or sometimes by sending interviewers to call on them) without prior warning just after the evening's news has been broadcast. They are then asked questions about the stories reported in the programme. The interviewer asks them to recall, without any prompting, all the stories they can remember and may then ask more detailed questions about particular stories. The second method is to bring people along to a central location where they are invited to watch either a live or specially prepared television news programme (usually the latter). Afterwards, they are tested for what they can remember about the programme.

Most of the research carried out with children has taken place either in classroom settings or some other central location. Interest has centred on how much they can remember from individual news programmes or from a series of recently televised programmes, how important their perceptions of the news are to being able to remember it, the kind of news being presented, and the style in which it is produced.

In an American study carried out with children aged 8–13 years, Dan Drew and Byron Reeves were interested to find out more about particular psychological processes which might influence children's learning from a television news story. They wanted to test the assumption that a child's perceptions of a news programme would affect learning.[24]

The children were shown a ten-minute videotape which contained a short news story surrounded either by cartoons or among other news material. Afterwards they were given a ten-item, multiple-choice quiz that asked factual questions about the news item. In addition, they were asked to say whether they thought the function of the item was to inform or entertain, how much they believed the item was accurate and how much they liked the story.

Younger children remembered the item better when it was shown with other news, while older children (11+) did better when it was surrounded by cartoon material. Understanding that the story was designed to inform, liking the story and believing it were all positively related to learning.

Recall of television news varies with the type of story and the way in which it is presented. The presence of film footage in a news item can have a significant effect on how well it is remembered. Dan Drew and Stephen

Reese found that memory and understanding among 10- to 16-year-olds were better for TV news items accompanied by film footage than when presented by a 'talking head' only.

Film had a particularly strong effect on understanding (as measured by in-depth recall accounts) among the oldest children. It was suggested that perhaps film's ability to attract and hold attention enhanced learning. The visuals may have reinforced the verbal content of the news items, although we are not told the extent to which film and narratives were well matched.[25]

Another study has found that children vary in their reactions to, and recall of, violent news on television. In this, male and female teenagers were tested for recall of violent and non-violent news stories presented either audiovisually, in soundtrack only or as written transcripts. Males recalled significantly more than females, and print produced significantly better recall than audiovisual or soundtrack-only presentation.

Recall of violent and non-violent news, however, varied according to both the way in which it was presented and with the sex of the respondents. When presented audiovisually as television news, males were more able to recall violent material than non-violent material; they also scored significantly higher than females on this aspect. On the other hand, females were much better at recalling non-violent material than violent material and scored significantly higher than males. However, when tested via soundtrack-only and written transcripts, there were no significant differences between the sexes and, in both instances, males and females were better at recalling violent content than non-violent.[26]

It would seem that something peculiar to the audiovisual presentation of these news stories caused male and female teenagers to learn from these stories differently. The important feature may have been the nature of the film footage accompanying the stories. It is possible that the females who took part in this study were more distracted by footage of street fighting, shootings and riots than were the males, and that the visuals disrupted females' learning of the story narrative. Males apparently were not affected in the same way by the violent footage and were relatively better able to learn the content of the stories despite it. Indeed, the evidence suggests that the violent items were actually more salient for male teenagers, because they remembered more from them than from the non-violent items. Violence may have been distressing for females, but amusing for males.

Much of the research on children's recall of information from individual television news bulletins has been carried out in artificial viewing conditions. Researchers in the United States, however, have tested children's ability to learn from television news bulletins in the field. This work examined children's learning from *Channel One*, a daily twelve-minute newscast shown in more than 9,800 schools in the USA at the time of the study. The programme was commercially funded and made freely available to schools. Ten minutes of the programme were devoted to news and two minutes to advertising. A study conducted with more than eight hundred 16-year-old high-school students in Michigan found that *Channel One* did benefit the public affairs knowledge of the teenagers who watched it, and that the programme generated increased interest among young viewers in the news topics shown.[27]

IS TELEVISION A GOOD LEARNING MEDIUM?

Some writers have argued that television has severe limitations as an information medium, whereas others have demonstrated that its effectiveness in getting information across to the audience can depend significantly upon the reasons why people choose to watch television in the first place.

Research on children's learning from television, radio and print has indicated a number of factors inherent in the television medium and the way viewers approach television that affect learning from it relative to how well they learn from other media. Television conveys dynamic visual images as a symbol system, in addition to language and sounds or music, which are also conveyed to radio. Print, on the other hand, conveys information simply via the symbol system of language. Television's symbol system, therefore, is able to represent the shape and form of objects and events visually, whereas radio and print can present only verbal descriptions. According to one writer, the crucial difference underlying different patterns of learning the same narrative material, presented via different media, arises from the symbol systems presented by different media rather than from the media themselves. The symbol systems, not the media, vary in their ability to represent certain types of information. Through experience with the symbol systems which characterise different media, children come to acquire the requisite intellectual skills which enable them to learn more effectively from those media. Thus learning from media depends on sufficient development of acts of general skills and skills needed specifically to use particular media.[28]

Research with children has shown that structural differences between the media in the way they represent information can influence which content is conveyed most effectively by television, radio or print. Laurene Meringoff compared children's learning of an unfamiliar story either read to them from an illustrated book or presented as a comparable televised film. She looked at recall of story content and inferences about characters and events.

A subsequent experiment with young children compared story learning from audiovisual (television) and audio-only (radio) presentations of a common narrative soundtrack. Recall of explicit story content was about the same from both media, but there were differences in the kinds of details recalled. Recognition of expressive language was facilitated by audio-only presentation, whereas picture sequencing was augmented by the audiovisual presentation. Once again, the use of general knowledge in forming inferences was more commonplace following audio-only (radio) presentation. The audiovisual (television) version enhanced inferences based on actions. In sum, the radio version promoted the use of verbal content, while in the television version, although verbal content was not totally ignored, more attention was given to visually presented material.[29]

Dutch researchers compared children's ability to remember fictional stories which they either read for themselves or watched on television, and found that print is not necessarily superior to television. Among 12-year-olds, stories watched on television were remembered as well as stories which the children read for themselves, whereas 10-year-olds retained the televised stories better than the printed ones. After three weeks, both age groups remembered the televised stories better than the printed versions.[30]

Other work with youngsters has revealed that it is not only the symbol structures of the media and level of development of appropriate media-specific cognitive skills that mediate learning, but also the amount of mental effort typically invested in learning from different media. Children who saw the televised story remembered more story actions and relied more on visual content as a basis for inferences. Children who were read the story in picture-book form recalled more story vocabulary and based more of their inferences on textual content and background knowledge. It was clear, in other words, that the structural differences in these media influenced which content was conveyed most effectively. The film's provision of more visual information may well have brought this content to the foreground of children's attention, since they apparently relied more on visually provided information in their responses to the programme. The less pronounced visual information offered in the book seemed to permit greater attention to the verbal text. Children who were read the story remembered more figurative language which (having no visual counterpart) relies solely on being heard.[31]

One prominent writer in this field, Jerome Singer, has argued that inherent in the power of television to attract viewers lie its limitations as an information medium. Fundamental to the appeal of television is its constant sensory bombardment in sound and vision. But the fast pace at which television typically presents material is such that it leaves insufficient time for effective cognitive processing. According to Singer,

> The [TV] set trains us merely to watch it. It does not provide us as a rule with a psychological situation that permits us to process the information presented in a manner that will allow us the most efficient use of what we have seen.[32]

Singer refers to television commercials when illustrating how cognitive overload can occur when watching television. The parallel presentation of information in voice-overs, on film and in captions may be simply too much for us to deal with. To some extent, the same principle may apply in the context of learning from the news on television.

News programmes do not have the same objectives as advertisements, nor do they move as quickly in their presentation of information. However, there are certain significant similarities in so far as information may be presented via several channels – narrative, film footage, maps, graphics, captions – simultaneously or in rapid serial progression. The problem fundamental to television (and this includes television news) as an information medium is that it constantly introduces new material before the viewer has been given a chance to grasp properly the visual and auditory material that has just been presented.

An Israeli researcher, Gavriel Salomon, reported a series of studies in which children's preconceptions concerning television and print were investigated in relation to levels of learning the same materials from each medium. In particular, Salomon wanted to know what the effect of knowing one's own ability and amount of effort required to process information from a particular medium would be on actual learning. If someone believes he or she is good at doing something, and that a particular task is very easy, then he or she may invest less effort in performing it and the quality of performance may suffer as a consequence.[33]

In one study, Salomon presented 12-year-old children with a television film or the equivalent story in print. When asked about their ability with each medium, children generally believed themselves to be capable of learning more effectively from television than from print. Salomon also asked the children to explain success or failure in learning from each medium. He found that there were clear differences in the kinds of explanations they gave. Success in comprehending television was attributed by most children to the ease of the medium, whereas success in understanding print was attributed mainly to the readers' smartness. On the other hand, failure to comprehend television was blamed on the viewer's stupidity, while failure to comprehend print was seen to be a function of the medium's difficulty.

The children reported different amounts of effort with television and print. Less effort investment was reported by viewers than by readers. Comparing learning scores for each medium, there was no difference in simple memory, but print produced significantly better inference generation. It was the print group which reported investing more effort in comprehending the story that, on average, generated most inferences.

In a further study, comparisons were made between more and less able children and their learning from television. More than ninety 12-year-olds were questioned about the amount of effort they generally expended in watching television and in reading, and about how worthwhile they thought effort was for each medium. They were then asked to estimate their own abilities to generate inferences and remember from television and from print. Next the children were divided into three groups to watch television or read an easy or difficult passage based on the same film soundtrack.

Afterwards, recall and inference generation, along with effort expenditure, were tested.

Results showed that children reported more effort expenditure in reading the difficult text than in reading the easy text or watching television. Ability correlated higher with information-processing with the difficult text than from the easy text or television film. Ability was associated also with perceptions of how worthwhile it would be investing effort in reading or viewing. More able children thought it more worthwhile investing effort in the difficult text than in the easy text or television film. In terms of learning, high-ability children performed best in the two print groups, and least well in the television group, while low-ability children performed best with television and worst with the difficult text. It would seem that the more able children perceive television to be less demanding than the less intelligent ones, and report less effort investment in viewing than their less able peers. Abler children look down on television. Another interesting result was that children's belief in their ability to remember details correlated negatively with reported investment of mental effort – and in turn with actual learning. The conclusion one is led to draw from these findings is that, since abler children enter the viewing situation with the preconception that television is an undemanding medium, they are inclined not to try very hard to process its contents, and hence don't.[34]

Are these preconceptions sufficient to explain the shallower processing of material from television than from print? Singer, whom we have already referred to above, suggested a range of inherent characteristics of television itself and the way its presents information which may also be significant factors. Television's pace is fast, facts are often crowded together, and its pictorial, mosaic-like qualities impede information uptake. Salomon accepts that television can be processed shallowly and still be enjoyed, unlike print. But this does not mean that television cannot be processed deeply if the preconceptual context of the viewer has been adjusted appropriately. If information from television is not processed effectively because viewers do not believe the medium itself demands or is worth much careful attention or cognitive effort, then perhaps its educational or informational benefits can be enhanced by requiring viewers to invest energy in their viewing.

In a third study reported by Salomon, an attempt was made experimentally to change children's perceptions of the task to be accomplished by watching a television programme. Children from the same age group as the previous studies were divided into groups who either watched a television programme or read the text of the show. These groups were further subdivided into those who were told that the material they were presented with was 'for fun' (low demand) and those who were told to see how much they could learn from it (high demand).

As expected, the high-demand instruction produced reports of greater cognitive effort than the low-demand condition. In addition to this, however, it had certain important effects on learning. In reading, the instruction had little effect; apparently effort is high when reading regardless of pretext. Task demands, however, had especially strong effects on learning from television. High demand produced better learning from television than did low demand. Furthermore, the instruction worked particularly well for more able children. More intelligent children learned considerably more than less intelligent children when told to make more effort.[35]

Children's expectations have been found to influence how much they remember from television news. Dutch researchers invited children, aged 10 to 12, either to watch five television news stories or to read print versions of the same stories. In each condition, half the children expected to be tested on their memory for what the stories were about, whereas the other children did not. Results indicated that children who did not expect to be tested learned more from television than from print versions of the stories. Among children who expected a test, televised and printed news were recalled about equally well. According to the researchers, these findings suggest that children at home, where they watch the news not expecting to be tested for memory of what they have seen, will learn more from televised news than from comparable printed news. It may be that, under relaxed conditions, in a natural viewing context, children can learn more readily from television. Television's advantage over print disappears when a test expectation is created. When children expect to be tested, viewers remember about as much as readers. Television's advantage is undone because readers appear to benefit more from the induced test expectation than viewers do. Under test conditions, readers invest more mental effort in their task, resulting in a significantly higher level of retention as compared to readers who do not expect a test.[36]

Children themselves, then, are aware of television's potential to enhance knowledge and provide information about the world, even though they regard gaining knowledge via television as less intellectually demanding than gaining knowledge through print. However, children also believe that television, particularly through its dramatic representations in characters and situations, offers other kinds of knowledge of particular relevance to them. As can be seen from Greenberg's research, cited in Chapter 3, one of the reasons given by children for watching television is to learn more about themselves and how they should interact both with their peers and adults. But does television have this effect? To what extent is the medium able to teach children about social roles?

Chapter 6

Does TV teach children about social roles?

In the next few chapters we turn our attention to television's influences upon children as they grow up and learn the ways of the world. Children have to learn how to behave in different social situations. Society requires its citizens to follow certain norms or conventions and to adopt appropriate and accepted social roles. In other words, as they grow and develop, children become socialised. During the early years of their lives, children are required to (and do) learn an enormous amount about living in the world with other people. Much of this learning comes from watching and listening to parents, brothers and sisters, peer groups, teachers and other adults. Today, however, television is another prevalent potential source of social learning. Characters on television can provide role models whom children may strive to emulate. Even if they do not directly copy their favourite characters, children may acquire certain values, attitudes or rules from them. A fundamental question about television, therefore, is whether it contributes to children's social development and to their learning of social roles and conventions.

So far we have established that television is a pervasive medium which is readily available to nearly all children. The vast majority of children watch television every day and on average they may spend three to four hours daily in front of a set. Although they may have difficulties early on, children soon learn to understand and follow programmes, become able to articulate refined opinions about what they watch, and make mature judgements about what is real and what is not.

Television is used primarily for entertainment, but it is also a source of information. It can tell us things about the world which we were not previously aware of and it can serve to reinforce what we already believe and know. It imparts information *explicitly* through regular news broadcasts and sets out to teach us things through its educative documentaries and magazines. But television also offers *implicit* messages that are present within all programme areas, be they educational, informative or designed purely as entertainment. For example, if news programmes or documentaries tend to place greater emphasis on one view of a world event or social problem, then this might well have an effect on how viewers perceive the issue, particularly if they are lacking in prior knowledge. Television may also have a more subtle educational or cultivational effect through its drama and entertainment-oriented programming. Events are played out in these programmes which, though fabricated, may nevertheless touch upon circumstances or experiences which are familiar to us. It may thus provide valuable lessons in how to deal with life's problems through its fictional enactments of them.

TELEVISION AND SEX-ROLE PERCEPTIONS

Research has established that children know what sex they are between the ages of 18 months and 3 years.[1] The sex of a person is more than simply a biological gender classification. What sex we are embodies a cluster of conceptions and beliefs about how we are or how we ought to be in the way we display our own character and personality and in the way we behave with other people.

Society holds certain expectations of men and women, and these are not always the same in respect of each sex. Thus, certain characteristics are designated as mainly female and others as mainly male. This is not to say that there can never be any crossover between the sexes of a particular personality trait or pattern of behaviour. Rather, what is referred to here is a classification of convenience, which offers, for the sake of simplicity, a system of socially conditioned stereotypes which are attached to each sex.

Sex stereotypes can limit the roles which males and females are encouraged or even permitted to play in life. Their development in the minds of children is a learning process. It is one aspect of social learning which is geared to produce individuals who as adults conform to social norms. What is the significance of television in the shaping of these ideas about sexuality? This is a subject to which we now turn.

Studies of television's influence on sex stereotyping among children have produced mixed results. To assume that television can impact upon a passively receptive child audience with messages about sex stereotyping, thus moulding innocent young viewers' conceptions of gender, is largely accepted as an oversimplistic picture of what really goes on. Viewers exhibit a degree of activity in selecting what to watch on television, what to pay attention to, and what to remember of the things they see on the screen. Even children respond in a selective fashion to particular characters and events on television, and their perceptions, memories and understanding of what they have seen may often be mediated by dispositions they bring with them to the viewing situation.

What is the evidence? In a small number of surveys, significant links have been reported between personal or parental estimates of children's television viewing and their sex-role perceptions, which have been interpreted as evidence for a television influence.[2] Youngsters who were categorised as heavy viewers were found to hold stronger beliefs than did lighter viewers in what the researchers defined as being a stereotyped direction. Much of this work, however, failed to produce precise measures of what young viewers actually watched.

TELEVISION AND OCCUPATIONAL CHOICE

Some researchers have argued that career or occupational choice are influenced significantly by schools, teachers, careers counsellors, books and catalogues, as well as by parents and peer groups.[3] While these factors may be significant, actual choice of job or career path may also be shaped by the degree of visibility particular occupations attain in the public sphere, particularly through the mass media. The potential role that television might play in this regard is illustrated by the finding that teenagers cite television as a source of occupational information.[4]

One researcher conducted interviews with children of both sexes between the ages of 3 and 6, asking them what they would like to be when they grow up. As well as specific questions about television viewing habits, each child was asked, 'What do you want to be when you grow up?' Then they were required to imagine what they would be if they were a member of the opposite sex. Thus, boys were asked, 'If you were a girl, what would you be when you grow up?' Finally, the children were engaged in a game called 'The OK Picture Game' in which they were shown several pictures, some of which were quite ordinary scenes of situations; others depicted something unusual or out of place, such as a five-legged cat. The interviewer explained to the children that the object of the game was to see whether a picture was 'OK' or not. Among several 'dummy' pictures were three scenes in which traditional sex roles had been reversed – a father feeding the baby, a man pouring coffee for a woman, and a female telephone-line repair person.

Results on career aspirations indicated a strong relationship between sex and envisaged future occupations for both children's own sex and for that of the opposite sex. Boys tended to nominate traditionally 'masculine' professions such as policeman, sports star or cowboy; girls preferred quieter occupations such as nursing. While the actual jobs nominated by girls and boys were different, the tendency to stereotype career aspirations was virtually the same for both sexes. Over 70 per cent of the boys and 73 per cent of the girls chose stereotypical careers for themselves. Even when asked what they would be if they were a member of the opposite sex, in nearly all cases, these youngsters selected what is normally regarded as appropriate for that sex.[5]

Responses to pictures indicate that sex-typing increased as images moved from child-care to husband–wife roles to occupation. The children's beliefs reflected the increasing postwar trend of husbands 'helping' around the house. However, regardless of the growing women's liberation movement, children still showed strong sex-typing with respect to occupational roles. Whilst young children's sex-role perceptions measured here indicated strong stereotyping of ideas about the sexes, to what extent are they affected by television portrayals?

The researcher responsible for this study claims that sex stereotyping of career aspirations was more likely to occur among heavier viewers of television, but she presents no data to back up this assertion. Furthermore, her sample was small and unrepresentative of this age-band and her findings would need to be replicated with other groups of children before they can be confidently accepted.

In a subsequent piece of research, children aged 4 to 12 were interviewed about their viewing, along with their parents, and then given a projective measure of sex stereotyping. The latter was a paper and pencil test which examined children's choice of sex-typed toys. A clear-cut relationship emerged between amount of reported television viewing done by children and the type of toys they selected. The heaviest viewers were found to be the ones who selected toys in the most stereotyped way.[6]

The conclusion of the study was that children learn about traditional sex roles from television. A number of critical questions remain unanswered, however. Why were boys and older children more traditional in their attitudes? Was it their traditional attitudes that made some children heavier television viewers in the first place? What role did parents play, not only in teaching children about sex roles, but also in helping them to interpret what was seen on television? How accurate was parental monitoring of actual viewing among the youngest children? Was the sample of forty boys and forty girls representative of their age groups? Was the projective test a valid measure of children's sex-role development?

Further evidence has emerged of positive relationships between increased viewing of television and more stereotyped beliefs about the sexes. This study examined variations in sex-role prejudice as a function of television viewing, demographic characteristics and family background of children among 155 North American children whose average age was 9.5 years. In general, it was found that these children were not strongly stereotyped in their sex-role perceptions; but, where stereotyping did occur, it was most evident among girls with lower IQs, who had mothers with higher educational attainment and who watched great amounts of television. The same results did not emerge among boys.[7]

LONG-TERM EFFECTS

The studies cited above provide a 'snapshot' of links between reported television viewing and sex stereotypes at one point in time. A different approach was adopted by Michael Morgan who wanted to try and find out if there was a meaningful link between adolescents' sex-role attitudes and television viewing over time. He obtained information from a large sample of teenagers about the extent of their television viewing, acceptance of sex-role stereotypes and educational and occupational aspirations over a period of two years. The results support the view that television cultivates certain sex-role views, although the effects are limited to girls. The heavier TV viewers among the girls became more likely over time to think that women are less ambitious than men and are happiest among children. No such change was noted among boys in relation to the amount of television they said they watched. Among girls, also, the link between TV viewing and sex-role stereotypes was stronger among the middle classes. Both lower-class girls and boys were generally more sexist regardless of viewing levels.

Morgan also reported (again for girls only) a relationship between amount of television viewing in the first year of measurement and subsequent educational aspirations. Interestingly, however, the heavier viewers were the ones who two years later set their sights higher. This result, although predicted by Morgan on the basis of television's over-representation of professional women, runs contrary to the traditional influences reported by most studies.

Although on balance the tone of Morgan's interpretation of his findings points to a sex-role stereotyping effect of regular television watching, in fact careful observation of the details of Morgan's study reveals that his findings are complex and difficult to explain. Correlations between television viewing and sex-role perceptions were made at, and across, two points in time and were compared not only between boys and girls but also between three IQ groups (high, medium and low). Television viewing was significantly related to sexism only among medium-IQ boys and high-IQ girls. No explanation is provided for the result among the boys, whilst the correlations among the girls were interpreted as evidence for television's influence, on the assumption that girls with high IQs are less likely to be sexist in the first place. Unfortunately, the small size of his correlations does not provide strong evidence on which confidently to assume an effect of television.[8]

Further work by Morgan examined the mediating influence of strength of peer group ties upon relationships between young people's television and their beliefs about sex roles. It was hypothesised that teenagers who had fewer friends and peer group contacts would be more susceptible to television's stereotyping effects. The results supported this hypothesis, but also showed that television viewing appeared to exert an independent effect upon adolescent's sex-role perceptions regardless of their own social background or network of social contacts.[9]

Morgan later reported that amount of television viewing was related to adolescents' sex-role attitudes but not their behaviours. However, boys and girls exhibited different patterns of sex-role attitudes and behaviour. For boys who already exhibited strongly stereotyped sex-role behaviour, amount of television viewing made no difference to their sex-role attitudes. In contrast, boys who engaged in less sex-typed behaviour also expressed less sex-typed attitudes, unless they were heavy television viewers. Girls who scored low in terms of sex stereotyped behaviour also exhibited less stereotyped attitudes, regardless of television viewing levels. Girls who showed high levels of sex stereotyped behaviour showed stronger sex-typed attitudes, especially if they also watched a lot of television. Thus, girls who already demonstrate traditional sex-role stereotypes in their own conduct may have these tendencies further reinforced by regular exposure to sex-stereotyped role portrayals on television.[10]

Tannis Macbeth Williams' Canadian study (already outlined in Chapter 1) investigated the effects of the introduction of television on an essentially television-naïve community, and also examined children's sex-role perceptions. Children in the three communities, labelled Notel, Unitel and Multitel, were administered scales to measure their sex-role attitudes both before and two years after television reception was introduced to Notel. A set of Peer Scales asked children to rate how appropriate or frequent certain behaviours are for boys and girls their own age, and a set of Parent Scales asked children to rate how frequently their own mother and father perform certain tasks.

At the outset, children in the television-receiving towns were found to be much more stereotyped on peer ratings than were children from the town with no television reception. At the two-year follow-up point, children living in Notel were found to have become significantly more stereotyped in their attitudes towards the sexes. This change was restricted to the perception of peers, however; no similar change was observed with regard to perception of parents. The researchers concluded that in the longer term television has the potential to shape children's sex-role attitudes and recommended that more women should be presented on television and that special attention should be given to the way they are presented. In Notel also, boys developed stronger stereotyped attitudes than did girls over time after the introduction of television. It would appear then that if television was broadcasting sex-stereotyped messages these were being absorbed more especially by boys.[11]

In Britain, a later survey explored children's perceptions of whether different occupational activities presented on TV were seen to be done principally by males ('boys or men') or by females ('girls or women'). The children were 334 members of a national UK viewing panel, and were aged between 5 and 12. The children were then asked about their own occupational aspirations and an attempt was made by the researchers to link what the children saw on TV with their personal ambitions.[12]

First of all, which of the occupations shown on TV are perceived to be predominantly male or female? From a list of fourteen, some jobs clearly emerged as 'male' and others as 'female'. For instance, 'serving customers in a shop', 'attending to patients in a hospital', 'taking care of baby children' and 'typing in an office' were perceived to be things which were done by girls or women on TV. These were much less often perceived to be done by male TV characters.

On the other hand, 'working a big machine in an office', 'piloting an aeroplane', 'laying bricks to build a house', 'manning a fire engine and putting out a fire' and 'repairing TVs and electric machines' were the occupational domains of male TV characters. There were, in addition, several occupations including 'being in charge of curing a sick animal' and 'driving a police car' which were seen as both male and female occupations. This was especially true in the case of driving a police car, and may imply something about the impact on children of programmes like *Cagney and Lacey*, *CATS Eyes* and *Juliet Bravo*, all of which were popular police/ detective dramas at the time of the study featuring strong female characters..

Girls were more likely to notice female activities, while boys were more attuned to male activities. Thus, girls were much more likely than boys to have noticed female characters in typist jobs and driving a police car. Boys, meanwhile, were more likely than girls to have noticed male characters serving in a shop and working as pilots, builders, firemen and computer operators.

Another interesting finding emerged. Those activities classified as female were commonly seen also to have been performed by male TV characters, among both boys and girls. 'Male' activities, however, were rarely seen as carried out by female characters.

Subsequently, when children were asked which occupations they would like to do, three more from the entertainment industry were added to the list. All three – 'be in a TV serial', 'work the camera in a TV studio' and 'be a singer in a pop group' – were relatively popular choices. Girls were much more likely than boys to want to be soap stars or pop singers, however. Boys were more inclined to want to be camera operators.

Were there any links between the jobs boys or girls perceived their own sex to be shown doing on TV and their own aspirations? The results showed that there were some connections between the two. Thus, the kinds of things females were shown to do on TV corresponded well with the kinds of things girls said they wanted to do in the future. Similarly, the kinds of things males were associated with on TV were largely the things boys wanted to do. Neither boys nor girls were particularly inclined to choose to do the things TV was perceived to associate with the opposite sex.

COUNTERING THE STEREOTYPES THROUGH TELEVISION

There is evidence that children's usual sex stereotypes can be modified if they watch television portrayals which run counter to the typical sex-role depictions. A study in which children were shown episodes from two British TV police drama series found that prior to seeing these episodes children exhibited pronounced stereotyping in their perceptions of male and female police officers. While many of these perceptions remained unchanged even at the end of the study, there were a small number of revised opinions about the characteristics of police officers linked to specific aspects of the programmes seen.

Both series featured women police officers in positions of authority. One episode also showed that the female authority figure kept herself fit by jogging. During the course of the episode, she and a male colleague were shown chasing after a villain. The female officer caught the villain, while her unfit male was left behind in the chase gasping for breath. After viewing the episode, many children shifted their perceptions of the physical fitness and competence of women police officers to a more positive level of evaluation.[13]

The children's opinions about the police exhibited a number of further opinion shifts which were linked logically to specific events that occurred in the programmes. Children's impressions of policewomen improved substantially as a function of observing female fictional police who held superior status positions. There was a reduction in the number of children who felt, for example, that men were better than women at telling people what to do in the police force. These findings illustrate the potential of television drama to effect short-term shifts in children's perceptions where the latter have a specific and direct link to portrayals in the dramatic narrative. The modifications in children's sex-role-related stereotypes reported here resulted from exposure to naturally occurring portrayals in mainstream television programmes. Most of the evidence on television's potential to reduce sex-role stereotyping, however, has derived from studies which have deployed specially produced programme materials.

In a book called *Positive Images*, Jerome Johnston and James Ettema reported on an American project in which television was used to improve children's sex-role attitudes.[14] This project was funded to the extent of $4 million by the National Institute of Education in the US and marked the successful collaboration of researchers, educationalists and TV producers in the production of an entertaining and instructive TV series called *Freestyle*. The main idea of this series was to expand career awareness among children in the 9–12 age range through a number of short stories in which child characters, especially girls, were seen in non-traditional sex roles. Based on attitude questionnaires administered before and after viewing thirteen episodes of the series, *Freestyle* was shown to be successful in making boys more accepting of girls engaging in mechanical activities, football and basketball, whilst girls who saw the series became more interested in these things. Both boys and girls became more approving of men and women who have non-traditional jobs (women as mechanics, lorry drivers or engineers, and men as nurses or secretaries, for example). Their perceptions of appropriate male and female family roles – responsibility for cooking and home repair – also became less stereotyped.

Attempts to study the impact of televised examples of counter-stereotyping on children in Britain have been limited. Kevin Durkin reported two experimental studies, one with primary-school children and the other with secondary-school children. Both attempted to facilitate changes in the sex-role beliefs of young viewers using a single programme in which examples of non-stereotype behaviour were depicted.[15]

The first experiment with fifty-two primary-school children used an edition of a programme called *Rainbow*. This programme had an introductory story and subsequent sketches, cartoons and song and dance sequences amplifying the theme. The story was about a conventional family – father, mother, son and daughter – who suffer an unfortunate event in that the father is made redundant. The mother goes out to work instead and the father is left to take responsibility for household chores and looking after the children.

The children were randomly split up into three groups. One group saw *Rainbow*, one saw a programme about the weather, and a third group saw no programme at all. The youngsters' sex-role beliefs were measured both before and after viewing the programme by sixteen questions concerning stereotypically male occupational roles (e.g. bus driver, doctor, farm worker), stereotypically female occupational roles (e.g. shop assistant, secretary, nurse), stereotypically male domestic roles (e.g. cooking, ironing, shopping). The children were asked to say whether a man, a woman or both could perform these roles. The test was administered for the first time about one week before the programme was viewed, and a second time within a day of viewing.

Both boys and girls in the *Rainbow* group changed their views substantially. The *Rainbow* programme produced a short-term shift of opinion away from stereotyping. The programme seemed particularly effective in modifying children's beliefs about domestic roles. Durkin suggests that this may be because, to some extent, it alerted them to actual as opposed to stereotypical behaviour. Perhaps many of these children already had fathers who helped with the dishes and shopping. After viewing, the children who watched *Rainbow* may have recalled these things more readily. The programme produced less change in beliefs about occupational roles, however. And this may have been because, for these children, such roles were still too far distant from their own experience and concerns for already well-established stereotyping to be changed by just one television programme.

In his second experiment, Durkin attempted to modify adolescents' career beliefs with specially prepared educational films. A total of ninety-nine children aged 12 and 13 years participated in this exercise. They were divided into four groups: one group saw a film introducing traditional career opportunities; a second group saw a non-traditional opportunities film without any explicit attention being given in it to alternative careers for each sex (implicit counter-stereotype); a third group was shown a non-traditional opportunities film in which men and women discussed their occupations more openly (explicit counter-stereotype); and a fourth group saw no film.

The traditional film showed a male doctor, a female nurse, a male plumber and a female secretary. The counter-stereotype films showed the same four occupations, but the actors were interviewed in pairs, one male and one female for each occupation. The difference between the implicit and explicit films was that, in the latter, more emphasis was placed on the reasons why particular actors had chosen a job not normally pursued by their sex.

Children in each group were given a list of twelve occupations consisting of four stereotypically male jobs, four stereotypically female jobs and four 'neutral' jobs. They were asked to indicate in each case whether an occupation was 'just men's work', 'just women's work' or somewhere in between. The general finding was that children tended to rate male jobs as male, female jobs as female, and neutral jobs as neutral. There were very few differences between groups and therefore very little effect of experimental treatment. Even though the films were designed to offer career guidance, they seemed to have very little impact on children's existing stereotyped beliefs about occupations.

TELEVISION AND FAMILY ROLES

Much of children's early learning about social roles takes place in the family. The family is also the place where television viewing patterns become established. In recent years, family life has changed radically in Western societies, most notably with a reduction in the numbers of children, and an increase in divorce rates and single-parent households. With these changes, the concept of the family may be expected to change. Children themselves these days may experience a variety of different forms of the family. What role does television play, however, in shaping children's beliefs about family life? Do typical television families represent those found in everyday life? Are the changes in family life reflected in the way the family has come to be portrayed on television?

Early studies of the representation of the family on the small screen indicated that television emphasised traditional family values and depicted self-contained nuclear families with two parents and two or three children. There was evidence of sex-role bias in family depictions. Family relationships were generally observed as being more central to the lives of women than of men.[16]

Women were shown as more preoccupied with being married, whether they were married, single or divorced. The old-style television portrayals also confined women either to the family context or the work context, but rarely to both. Usually women were shown as mothers and home-makers, with few interests outside the home. The male partner dealt with matters outside the home and was the breadwinner. The female's role was to manage domestic and personal matters.[17]

The lifestyles depicted for men represented a marked contrast to those for women on television. Male characters rarely had much of a family life, and even when they did it generally took second place to their working life. One interesting observation which underlined the emphasis upon the professional as opposed to the personal lives of men on television was that for nearly half of leading male characters, there was no clear indication of their marital status at all.[18]

These representations of the sexes in the family context could give child viewers the impression that, for women, marriage is an all-consuming lifestyle. Women who deviate from this lifestyle put their personal happiness at risk. For men, marriage and the family are depicted, implicitly at least, as largely unimportant or as peripheral to the main purpose of their lives, which is located more centrally in their careers and jobs.[19]

This stereotyping was found to be characteristic of mainstream television drama from the late 1940s until the beginning of the 1980s. This pattern of male and female role portrayals occurred across a variety of different programme genres, including serious action-drama, family dramas, family comedy shows and cartoons. Television family life was also class-biased, with many more prime-time television families being middle-class than working-class. Most heads of households were in professional or managerial jobs, and fewer than one in five families observed had heads of households in blue-collar jobs. Indeed, many of television's families were extremely wealthy and rarely had difficulty making ends meet.[20]

Within working-class families, a distinction could be made between those headed by a rather unintelligent father and those who were upwardly mobile. There was concern raised that these images denigrated the status of working-class families and demonstrated that the only positive thing to do was to strive to move out of a working-class lifestyle. Working-class lifestyle was something to escape from. In contrast, middle-class families were shown much more positively. In these households, both parents were generally capable and competent to deal with most of life's problems.[21]

By the late 1970s, it was reported that American prime-time television depicted about forty to fifty families every week. One in three of these comprised two parents with children or a single parent with children, and one in five were married couples with no children. The remainder were various family groupings – cousins, aunts and uncles, in-laws and so on. Half the marriages were first marriages, but divorce was increasing.[22]

Television's fictional family relationships usually concentrated on immediate family members – wife, mother, daughter, sister and their counterpart male roles. Within the family setting, husbands were usually a companion to their wives and a friend, guide and teacher to their children; they also managed the family finances. Family members were generally positively disposed towards each other, with conflicts unusual and physical attacks rare. Family members were typically depicted as being there to help one another, to provide advice and support. Any conflicts which did occur tended most commonly to be between the husband and wife, or between siblings.[23]

Even during the 1980s, traditional family roles prevailed on television. The father remained the breadwinner and the mother was the nurturant figure looking after the home. Family life on television was not entirely conflict-free, but problems which did arise concerned matters of disobedience and discipline, for which solutions were offered that reinforced traditional values.[24]

Thomas and Callahan looked at family-focused series on peak-time American television during the late 1970s and early 1980s. Television families were classified by their social class and the extent to which family members enjoyed happy and mutually supportive relationships. Working-class television families were found to exhibit more sympathy for the problems of those close to them than did upper-class families, with middle-class families finishing between the two. With greater wealth, family members became less well-intentioned towards each other. Working-class family shows tended to end happily, while this was much less often the case with shows which depicted wealthy families. The implicit message in all of this was that poorer families tended to be happier and more content with their lives than did wealthier families.[25]

The question of whether children learn about family relationships through watching these patterns of family portrayals on television has been addressed by only a limited amount of research. One study which did address this issue surveyed more than 1,000 children, aged 9, 11 and 12 years, in Michigan and California. Family background information was obtained to assign these children to categories of families which were characterised by harmony or conflict. The children were then questioned about how often they watched a number of popular family shows on mainstream television and about their opinions concerning those shows. Children who were regular viewers of family shows held more positive views about the supportive nature of family life than children who were less frequent viewers of these shows, after controlling for differences among the children associated with their own demographic and family circumstances. This relationship between watching family shows and beliefs about family life in the real world became more pronounced the more children believed that the shows themselves contained realistic depictions of family life.[26]

TELEVISION AND RACE-ROLE PERCEPTIONS

Research into the effects of ethnic minority (mainly black) portrayals on television has investigated their impact on white children's perceptions of, and attitudes towards, ethnic groups and on black children's perceptions of themselves. In terms of the methods of research, these divide between

- surveys in which self-report data were collected from children about their viewing habits (in particular their watching of programmes known to contain ethnic minority characters) and their attitudes towards ethnic groups; and
- controlled experiments in which selected groups of children were shown a single episode or edition of a programme or a series of programmes containing relevant character portrayals and tested for reactions or changes in their attitudes contingent upon such viewing.

EFFECTS ON WHITE CHILDREN

Historically, the effects of television on young viewers' perceptions of race can be traced back to studies of motion pictures in the 1930s. This early work gave the first indication that film portrayals could affect children's and teenagers' attitudes towards minority groups. Evidence emerged from the USA that Hollywood-made films could alter white children's attitudes towards Blacks, Germans and Chinese. For example, the major silent production *Birth of a Nation* was found to produce more negative stereotypes about Blacks among those youngsters who had seen the film.[27]

Turning to television, much of the research on the impact of ethnic minority portrayals in programmes dates from 1970 onwards. A division can be made here in terms of the types of programmes whose impact was examined as well as in terms of the research methodology, i.e. survey or controlled experiment. Some studies focused on the impact of educationally oriented programmes produced especially to cultivate and encourage the development of positive racial attitudes. These tended to control the viewing situations and type of material participating children watched. Other studies attempted to find out if commercially made, popular entertainment programmes could affect ethnic or racial minority perceptions.

RESEARCH WITH EDUCATIONAL PROGRAMMING

In the United States, the 1970s saw the production and introduction to television of a number of educational programmes. Some of these included, among their educational objectives, the cultivation of positive, multiethnic attitudes among young children. Prior to these television series, evidence had already begun to emerge that television was an important source of knowledge about nationalities and ethnic groups. White American children, for example, reported obtaining most of their information about other nationalities (e.g. Africans, Chinese, Eurasians and Indians) from their parents and television. With increased age there was greater self-reported reliance on television as the information source about foreigners.[28]

We have already mentioned *Sesame Street* in an earlier chapter; among its educational objectives was included an aim to produce in children a more informed and balanced perception of ethnic minorities. The series was found to have had some impact, though this took time to occur. White children who were regular viewers of *Sesame Street* for two years did exhibit improved positive racial attitudes towards black and Hispanic people. Children who had viewed the series for only one year, however, showed no real shifts in their attitudes. Apparently, sustained viewing for fairly long periods is necessary before television can produce positive attitudes towards ethnic minority groups.[29]

A study with the Canadian version of *Sesame Street* investigated the effects of two types of inserts which depicted ethnic minority children, either Oriental or Indian, in one of two settings. The children were shown either in an ethnic, non-integrated setting or in a racially integrated setting. The other type of insert featured a Canadian boy who was identifiable or not identifiable as French Canadian by whether or not he spoke French. White, English-Canadian preschoolers were shown one presentation of both types of inserts in a nursery-school setting. In each case, after viewing, the youngsters showed a strong preference for playing with minority children as opposed to Whites. This preference, as measured by means of photograph selection, was sharply contrasted with those selections of a control group of white children who did not see the racial integration segments, who preferred a white playmate. Similarly, there was greater preference for the French-Canadian boy over an English Canadian, whether or not his cultural identity was evident. In this study, ethnic or segregated settings and integrated settings were equally effective in inducing positive attitude change towards people of other races. Further, only limited exposure was necessary to produce attitude change.[30]

Research on other educationally oriented television programmes has indicated further positive effects on young children's ethnic minority perceptions and attitudes. One educational series called *Vegetable Soup* was produced for preschool and elementary age children. This series was designed specifically to try to ameliorate some of the negative effects of racial isolation on children. The series featured live and animated characters, which included Euro-Americans, Afro-Americans, Asian Americans, native Americans and Latino-Americans in a variety of settings, roles and activities.[31] An evaluation study indicated that it did alter white children's attitudes towards other racial groups. Boys and girls between 6 and 10 years of age were shown sixteen half-hour programmes over an eight-week period in school. Those who watched the series were more likely than those of similar ages who had not seen it to endorse statements indicating greater acceptance of children of different racial groups, including Blacks, and increased friendliness towards different groups.[32]

A further study produced evidence that educational television can influence white children's attitudes about diverse ethnic and national matters. A television series produced in the United States called *Big Blue Marble* was designed, among other things, to alter children's views about children from other cultures and parts of the world.[33]

Big Blue Marble showed how children in other lands live and grow up. A study with a sample of 9- to 11-year-old white US children found that, after viewing four episodes of the series, white children became more likely to perceive foreign children as healthier, happier and better off, more likely to question whether US conditions were highly superior to those in other countries, and less likely to assume the cognitive superiority of American children.

THE INFLUENCE OF POPULAR ENTERTAINMENT PROGRAMMES

Specially produced educational programmes are designed to influence children's attitudes. In some cases, as we have seen, they do work. In addition to these programmes, however, young audiences are exposed to portrayals of ethnic minorities in popular entertainment programmes, which are not explicitly produced to change racial attitudes. Nevertheless, youngsters who watch these portrayals may learn from them certain things about the characteristics and habits of ethnic minority groups. The extent to which particular programmes contain such portrayals have a specific influence and may be difficult to disentangle from all the others.

It does seem that children are aware of the presence of black actors and actresses on television. Research with 9- and 10-year-old white children in the United States, for instance, has indicated that more than four out of ten could name at least one black television character they would like to be like. Furthermore, at the time that this research was done in the early 1970s, five shows featuring black characters (*Mod Squad, Julia, Flip Wilson, Bill Cosby* and *Mannix*) were mentioned among the white children's ten favourite television programmes. The most frequently mentioned source of information about Blacks was television, and this source was most important for rural Whites who had almost no other source of contact or interaction with Blacks.[34]

Additionally, television exposure to black people seemed to have more impact than personal contacts in the neighbourhood or at school. So those white children with higher levels of exposure to black people through television were more likely to cite black shows among their favourites, and to name black characters as identification figures, than those with lower levels of exposure. However, exposure to black television characters did not seem to influence the racial attitudes of the white children in this study. With the exception of a sharply negative subgroup of urban white youngsters, most Whites in this study felt that Blacks and Whites were about the same on most personality attributes. Neither level of television exposure nor place of residence was related to attitudes towards black people in general or towards black characters on television.

Popular cartoons have been found to have some effect on racial perceptions. One study of cartoons that featured black characters in either the numerical majority or minority, in which racial minority characters were portrayed in either a positive or negative fashion, showed that the racial attitudes of white children between 6 and 8 years of age could be altered after just one such cartoon. Attitude change was measured by the frequency with which children associated positive or negative characteristics with black or white stimuli. Positive portrayals of black characters produced more positive attitudes towards black people and, conversely, negative portrayals produced less favourable attitudes. Further, regardless of characterisation, black people presented in the numerical minority produced more positive attitude change than did black people in the numerical majority. The study suggests that integrated settings were more effective in producing positive attitude change than segregated or predominantly black settings. Similar findings have emerged from studies of other programmes featuring black people depicted either in a favourable or unfavourable light.[35]

The extent to which white children are influenced by TV in their perceptions of races may depend on how much direct contact they have with other races. American research has revealed, for instance, that the greater the contact white children have with black people in real life, the less real they judge TV portrayals of Blacks to be.

LONG-TERM EFFECTS OF TV

Much of the evidence discussed above has derived from research which measured the effects of television on ethnic minority beliefs only in the short term. In the longer term, just how powerful is television's effect on what people believe about other races? In general, the perceived reality of the racial attitudes presented in *All in the Family* and *Sanford and Son* was neutral. However, subjects rated *All in the Family* more realistic in its portrayals of Whites' racial attitudes than they did *Sanford and Son* in expressing Blacks' racial attitudes.[36]

Young viewers' own racial attitudes may affect their perceptions of black characters on television. One study found, for example, that Whites who were antagonistic to Blacks were more likely to report that there were more Blacks appearing on television compared to more favourably disposed Whites. It was highly probable that antagonistic Whites would report that television was more likely to be fair in the presentation of Blacks than would Whites with more favourable attitudes.[37]

EFFECTS OF BLACK PORTRAYALS ON WHITES

A British study focused on adolescents and their parents and divided sources of knowledge about Blacks into two: situational sources involving personal experience, and media sources.[38] It was assumed that either the media may reflect ideas and images which are already commonplace among the viewing public or they may cultivate new ideas and impressions which may not necessarily mirror those which exist in reality. Groups from areas with both high and low immigrant population densities were tested.

To begin with, adolescents were asked what they knew about 'coloured people living in Britain today'. Respondents were free to answer in their own way. Personal experience was the commonest information source mentioned, followed by various mass media. Mentions of personal experience were more common among youngsters living in areas with a high density of immigrants, while media sources were mentioned more frequently by those living in areas with relatively few immigrants. Those youngsters naming media sources most often were also the most heavy users of media, as evidenced by independent measures of media use.

In examining attitudes towards Blacks, no evidence emerged that the mass media made much difference. Ethnic attitudes appeared to be influenced more by personal experience, although the mass media were cited as sources of ideas about the problems caused by coloured people more frequently than as sources of knowledge about good things about the black immigrant.

What about the extent to which viewers felt deprived in their own lives when comparing their own position with that of images of the rich often depicted on television? Would such dissatisfied individuals in turn hold more hostile attitudes towards Blacks? A substantial proportion of those young people who had seen images of wealth portrayed on television felt more deprived in consequence. Among those who said that they did, there was a weak tendency to hold more prejudiced attitudes towards Blacks.

An American study of longer-term effects among young viewers of television portrayals of Blacks on their beliefs about the traits associated with black people was carried out by Charles Atkin and his colleagues.[39] While a basic prediction is that young people who watch programmes featuring Blacks may remember those portrayals or aspects of them, the extent to which their beliefs about black people are *actually* influenced is mediated by a range of important social-psychological variables which include:

- direct contact with Blacks and the extent to which TV portrayals are perceived to be consistent with real-world knowledge;
- motivation to watch television – for relaxation or for information;
- identification with characters on television – strong identification may lead to viewers extracting more information from portrayals and perhaps to stronger influence.

There is evidence that the presumed influence of television, on the basis of what appears on the screen, may not always match its actual influence. Descriptions of content do not always reflect the meanings viewers perceive selectively in that content. In the sphere of ethnic portrayals and racial prejudice, there have been a number of studies of the top-rated US television programme, *All in the Family*. In addition to providing mass entertainment, a secondary objective of this programme was to combat bigotry by poking fun at it and helping viewers gain insight into their own prejudices.

However, the selective perception process seems to prevail with this type of satirical content. Several researchers have reported that authoritarian prejudiced individuals tend to accept the racial slurs of the bigoted character, Archie Bunker. Less prejudiced members of the audience, meanwhile, perceive Archie as a foolish, narrow-minded bigot and interpret his comments as satire.

The Atkin study was carried out with 316 white children aged 9 to 13 years, recruited from two inner-city areas where Whites had varying opportunities for direct contact with black youths and adults. The following measures were obtained:

- extent of watching programmes featuring Blacks;
- motivation to learn about Blacks from television;
- perceived reality of black portrayals on television;
- identification with black characters on television;
- comparisons of black and white television characters;
- beliefs about actual attributes of Blacks;
- beliefs about actual differences between Blacks and Whites;
- beliefs about how many Blacks were in the population;
- beliefs about extent to which knowledge about Blacks was gained from television.

Results showed that effects of televising black portrayals on white viewers appear to be limited and selectively processed. About one in four reported that most of the things they knew about Blacks came from television. The effect of sheer exposure to television programmes with black characters on beliefs about traits of black people was minimal. The only real effect was that greater viewing of these programmes apparently led children to perceive Blacks as funny. Since most black characters appeared in comedy roles, this was not surprising. In the case of beliefs about dissimilarities between real-life Whites and Blacks, there was limited evidence that amount of television viewing had a direct influence. It was young viewers' perceptions of distinctions between TV portrayals of Whites and Blacks that made the most important contribution.

The largest direct impact of television occurred on beliefs about the frequency of Blacks in society and subjective learning. The more Blacks on the television were seen, the higher the estimate about prevalence of Blacks in the real world, and the stronger the feeling that knowledge about Blacks was acquired from television.

The overriding result, that effects on beliefs depend on children's existing perceptions and experiences both of Blacks and television, indicated that television's role may be to reinforce prior dispositions rather than cause dramatic changes. This suggests the important role parents and schools play in shaping the process of learning from television, since these sources directly influence the attitudes the viewer brings to the set.

EFFECTS OF BLACK PORTRAYALS ON BLACK AUDIENCES

Much of the psychological literature on black people's personality development indicates that a large percentage of black adults and children are more likely to reject black models and images than they are to accept or highly value them.[40] This rejection of black stimuli may be so intense that black children will racially misidentify themselves at a rate of between 5 and 54 per cent. Research into how Blacks perceive themselves finds that most Blacks experience a negative or decreased sense of esteem because of their race, although this has improved somewhat in recent times.[41]

What impact do portrayals of Blacks on television have? Will young black viewers identify with possible non-stereotypes that already exist about Blacks? Will exposure to such undesirable role models increase low self-esteem and magnify negative attitudes towards Blacks?

Black children have been found to hold up white TV characters as more attractive role models than black TV characters. Southern black children in the United States, who had yet to start school, were found in one study to imitate white TV models more readily than black ones. Even when the black character was seen to be rewarded for his behaviour, he was barely imitated more than a white character who had been punished.[42]

There is further evidence to suggest that young black viewers regard Whites as more competent than Blacks. In one situation, black children watched a television film of a group of black and white peers choosing toys to play with. After viewing, the black viewers were given the same toys to pick from. All of the black children selected toys chosen by the white children in the film. This imitation of white choices occurred even when the toys selected were smaller or inferior in quality to toys selected by Blacks in the film.[43]

Elsewhere, the imitation of television Blacks by black children has been measured in terms of their willingness to report black shows and characters as favourites. Black children aged 9 to 11 years were found to watch shows featuring Blacks more often than their white counterparts. For example, 61 per cent of Blacks watched nine or more shows featuring Blacks, compared to 21 per cent of Whites. When asked to name three television characters they would most want to be like, 75 per cent of the black children named at least one black character, compared to 43 per cent of white respondents.[44]

Although some of the evidence concerning the influence of television in forming children's perceptions of social roles still seems open to question, the medium's ability to reinforce both positive and negative social attitudes cannot be ignored. If television has the potential to encourage stereotypical views of social groups through its character portrayals, can the actions of these characters have some kind of an effect on the viewer's subsequent action and behaviour? Does television wield some kind of influence on social conduct? It is this question that we turn our attention to next, particularly in terms of antisocial conduct and violence.

Chapter 7

Does TV influence aggressive behaviour?

Over the years, more funding and research effort has been invested in the study of television violence than in any other aspect of television output. Despite all this, there is still considerable disagreement among researchers about the existence of links between violence on the screen and aggressive behaviour among those who watch it.

Nevertheless, evidence that has been published on the possible harmful side effects of viewing television violence, especially where children are concerned, and the widespread public concern accompanying it, have led to calls for stricter controls on the depiction of violence in programmes. In the United States, for example, the setting up and organisation of consumer action groups to lobby against the showing of violence on television has almost become a growth industry in itself.

Exhaustive reviews of the scientific literature on the relationships between television depictions of violence and the aggressive behaviour of viewers have consistently documented how exposure to such content is linked to a likelihood of enhanced aggressiveness among children and adolescents.

Major reports from leading public health agencies in the United States, the 1972 Surgeon General's report and the 1982 National Institute of Mental Heath review, concluded that television played a significant part in the lives of young people and had a general potential to influence their aggressive behaviour. The Surgeon General's report presented findings from a number of original and specially commissioned studies of children and adolescents, which utilised various research methodologies. The overall conclusion of this body of investigation was that regular exposure to television violence is a causal agent underpinning the aggressive dispositions of the young, and may be especially significant among children and teenagers who already exhibit aggressive personalities.[1]

The NIMH report, ten years later, added to the conclusions of the Surgeon General. By now, potential effects of televised violence were being identified for children even before they started school, and for girls as well as boys. Furthermore, television portrayals of violence not only taught aggressive behaviour, but also demonstrated who is most likely to fall victim to violence, thus engendering enhanced fear of violence among certain categories of viewers.[2]

During the 1990s, further reports from the Centres for Disease Control, National Academy of Science and the American Psychological Association have provided further support for the conclusion that the mass media contribute to aggressive attitudes and behaviour.[3] The American Psychological Association established a Commission on Youth and Violence to examine the literature on the causes and prevention of violence. This Commission concluded that American children are exposed to high levels of violence on television, and that heavy viewers of this violence demonstrate increased acceptance of aggressive attitudes and increased aggressive behaviour.

Television violence viewing has consistently been found to correlate with aggressive behaviour over various demographic groups and over time.[4] The correlation has also been observed to occur across a variety of television genres.[5] A comprehensive review of hundreds of experimental and longitudinal studies supported the position that viewing violence on television is related to aggressive behaviour.[6]

The emergent view from the United States in recent years, therefore, is that television is a causal agent in relation to the development of aggressiveness among children, that its influence begins to be felt before the child starts school, and that it continues into adolescence, by which time the damage of cumulative exposure during childhood is done. The case for causality in respect of television violence is therefore proven. The task is not to continue to investigate this media-effects issue, but to monitor what actually appears on screen and control that material which has already been shown to have potentially harmful side effects on young viewers. The cause–effect case is not accepted to the same extent in other countries – for example, in Britain, where it is regarded by broadcasters and many academics as unproven. Nevertheless, there is a concern about the amount of violence on television and the nature and the form it takes.

Is there too much violence on television? It is often claimed that there is. This claim is usually accompanied by the call for tighter controls over the showing of violence on TV. But does this question on its own really mean very much? When talking about TV violence, perhaps we should also be asking 'violence for whom?'.

Calls for the control of violence on the screen necessitate some consideration of what is meant by violence in the first place. How should violent content be classified or defined in order that it may be monitored effectively and, if necessary, limited in the extent and form of its occurrence? It is easy enough publicly to condemn the depiction of violence on TV, but far less easy to arrive at a monitoring system which takes full account of the valued and tastes of the people who matter – the audience. We all have some idea of what we mean by violence. But what one person sees as violent may not be seen in the same way by someone else.

A common method of quantifying TV violence has been to count up incidents in programmes defined by the researchers themselves as violent. But since violence is not the same for everyone, there are problems with this approach. Viewers have their own scales for deciding the seriousness of incidents and their opinions do not always agree with researchers' categories of violence.

We can, nevertheless, begin by looking at estimates of how much violence there is on British television as derived from traditional methods of content analysis, focusing especially on those programmes children are likely to watch. After this we will look at what viewers, young ones especially, mean by violence on TV.

VIOLENCE ON TELEVISION

The basic method used by researchers to quantify the amount of violence on television uses simple counting techniques. Violence is defined objectively by researchers who then code samples of television programmes for any incidents which match their own violence definitions. A number of one-off studies carried out in the United States during the 1950s and 1960s established this perspective with television.[7] These studies fail to provide a coherent analysis of trends across the period, however, mainly because they used different definitions of violence or different indices of the amount of violence in programmes. Most were, nevertheless, interpreted to show that the occurrence of violence in popular entertainment programming broadcast by the majority of US networks was quite commonplace.

One of the most comprehensive analyses of TV violence, and certainly the longest running, was that directed by Professor George Gerbner and his colleagues at the Annenberg School of Communications, University of Pennsylvania. Using a technique founded on a simple, normative definition of violence, this research project monitored samples of network prime-time and weekend daytime programming for all the major American networks for over twenty years from 1967.[8] Violence was defined as 'the overt expression of physical force (with or without a weapon) against self or other, compelling action against one's will on pain of being hurt or killed, or actually hurting or killing'. Further specifications were made that the incidents must be plausible and credible, but that no idle threats should be included. However, violent accidents or natural catastrophes, whose inclusion in dramatic plots was reasoned by Gerbner to be technically non-accidental, were included. This analysis of the violence profile of American network television indicated that violent incidents were prevalent in prime-time, entertainment-oriented drama. More importantly, it provided the model for British research in this field.

Recently, a major three-year research programme was launched in the United States, called the National Television Violence Study. This research has been funded by the National Cable Television Association and administered through a non-profit-making organisation, Mediascope, Inc. The research itself comprised four major components:

- a content analysis of television drama and entertainment programmes carried out at the University of California, Santa Barbara;
- a content analysis of reality (news and factual) programmes carried out at the University of Texas, Austin;
- research into viewers' use of advisories and ratings systems to choose programmes to watch carried out at the University of Wisconsin, Madison; and
- research into the impact of public health measures, including on-air public service announcements and educational programmes containing anti-violence messages and aimed at adolescents in the television audience, carried out by at the University of North Carolina, Chapel Hill.[9]

The content analysis research in this project went beyond traditional methodologies and placed much more focus on the context and form of violence in programmes than previous studies had done. The researchers reasoned that it was important not simply to quantify violence, but also to identify occurrences of those forms of violence which audience research had indicated as most serious in terms of their potential effects upon viewers. The content analysis used a sophisticated random sampling technique to select the programmes to be analysed, covering twenty-three television channels over a twenty-week period. The analysis also distinguished between different units of analysis. Previous content studies emphasised a measure of violent acts per hour. This latest study distinguished between three quantitative measures:

- the PAT level, referring to the Perpetrator–Action–Target sequence;
- the Scene level context, which included an account of immediately adjacent scenes to the violent action itself; and
- the Programme level analysis, which operated at a macro-level and took into account the overall theme of the programme.

The PAT unit most closely resembled the traditional notion of a 'violent act'. The Santa Barbara group's analysis of peak-time drama and entertainment programming found that 57 per cent of 2,693 programmes analysed contained violence. Most of these incidents involved behavioural acts of aggression rather than credible threats of violence or implied violence. The highest percentages of violent programmes were found on cable channels, and most especially on movie channels.[10]

The most common form of violence was that which involved the 'natural capabilities' of a character, which meant various forms of unarmed combat involving the use of different body parts, such as a hand or fist, foot or knee, and so on. One in four incidents of violence (25 per cent) involved handguns. Well over half (57 per cent) of all violent interactions involved repeated acts of aggression, although few acts of violence (3 per cent) were classified as graphic in terms of depicting the violence and its impact from close quarters. In a majority of violence scenes (58 per cent), the violence was neither rewarded nor punished. Violence was almost as likely to be explicitly rewarded (15 per cent of times) as explicitly punished (19 per cent). Nearly half the time (47 per cent) no observable injurious consequences of violence were depicted.

Movies and serious drama were the worst offenders in terms of average frequencies of violent incidents, while comedy series and children's programmes were better than average, though still not completely divorced of all violence. The violence in children's programmes, however, tended to be more stylised, and contained less pain and suffering, less blood and gore, and less realism, but more humour, than most other categories of drama and entertainment programming.

The analysis of 384 reality programmes sampled from the same universe of television output found that 38 per cent contained violence. Nearly one in five additional reality programmes (18 per cent) included talk about violence, though no actual depiction of it. In the average violence-containing reality programme, visual portrayals of violence occupied just over 3 per cent of programme running time. The worst offenders were reality police shows (100 per cent contained violence), 'tabloid' news programmes (85 per cent) and documentaries (73 per cent).[11]

VIOLENCE ON BRITISH TELEVISION

Four major studies of violence on British television have been carried out since 1970. James Halloran and Paul Croll of the Mass Communication Research Centre, Leicester, analysed broadcast material of BBC1 and one ITV region (Midlands) during one week in April 1971. Using the framework developed by Gerbner, they coded violent incidents occurring in fictional drama programmes and news, current affairs and documentaries. At around the same time, the BBC's Audience Research Department undertook a more extensive analysis of TV over a six-month period and analysed content from dramatic fiction, news and current affairs, documentaries and light entertainment programmes. Although broadly the same type of study, the BBC's analysis was not precisely the same as that conducted by the Leicester group.[12]

Each of these British investigations indicated that, although a common feature of programming, violence was not as prevalent on British television as on American television. In fictional drama, the only category of programming in which direct comparisons between American and British findings were possible, Halloran and Croll found that nearly 56 per cent of programmes coded contained violence – compared with a reported 80 per cent of fictional programmes on American television at that time. In nearly 48 per cent of fictional programmes, a major character was involved in violence either as aggressor or victim. The rate of violence on British television drama was nearly three (2.8) incidents per programme (just over four incidents an hour), again substantially less than an average rate of over seven incidents per hour on comparable American television.

In their more extensive analysis of British television content, BBC researchers found a somewhat greater prevalence of violence in fictional drama in terms of the number of programmes containing at least one major violent incident (63 per cent), but somewhat less violence in terms of the rate at which violent incidents per programme – just over two per hour – were recorded.

The prevalence and rate of violent incidents were also found in both studies to vary considerably across different forms of drama programme. Thus, Halloran and Croll noted that the most violent type of programme in the fiction category was the cartoon. All cartoons coded by them contained some violence and the rate of incidents per hour in such shows was nearly thirty-four. None of the cartoon incidents averaged over four per hour. This contrasted with plays, of which 50 per cent were violent, but even then, with an average incident rate of fewer than one per hour, they were unlikely to be very violent programme by programme. After cartoons, the most violent programmes coded by Halloran and Croll were crime, western and action-adventure shows. All programmes in these categories contained violence at an average rate of nearly eight incidents per hour.

Turning to the BBC's analysis of the prevalence of violence for different programme forms or 'themes', once again agreement with Halloran and Croll was not complete. Feature films contained at least one major violent incident in 86 per cent of cases, which compares quite well with Halloran and Croll's 80 per cent figure, whereas the category of programmes labelled as 'TV series' by BBC researchers, which consisted largely of crime-detective, western and action-dramas, contained violence in only 75 per cent of cases, as contrasted with all such programmes monitored by the Leicester researchers. Inconsistencies across the violence measures produced by these two studies for the same areas of television content become even more pronounced when consideration is given to mean rates of violent incidents per programme type. The BBC team coded an average of just over three incidents per hour for feature films, one per hour fewer than Halloran and Croll. But even more significantly, they coded 2.2 incidents per hour for 'TV series', a little over 25 per cent of the average rate of incidents per hour recorded for the crime, western and action-drama categories by the Leicester team. Even when examining particular themes or particular series, BBC violence rate statistics remained lower than those reported by Halloran and Croll. Thus, the BBC reported that westerns contained a higher rate of violent incidents than any other type of TV series; but, at 3.9 incidents per programme, this was still only about half the rate reported by Halloran and Croll for crime–western–action categories.

A later recent study of the portrayal of violence on British television was commissioned by the BBC from the Aston University Communication Research Group, under the direction of Dr Guy Cumberbatch. The research analysed all television programmes (excluding advertisements and Open University programmes) transmitted in four separate weeks on all four channels between May and September 1986. This covered 1,412 hours of television – 930 BBC programmes and 1,148 ITV/Channel 4 programmes.

Once again, 'violence' was defined before counting began. The definition of violence used in this study was 'any action of physical force with or without a weapon against oneself or another person, animal or inanimate object, whether carried through or merely attempted and whether the action caused injury or not'. Both intentional and accidental violence were included. Violent accidents and catastrophes were also covered but acts of nature were included only when violence to victims was shown. Verbal abuse and threats were coded separately. The study reported on the frequency of violence, the pattern of violence and how levels of violence had changed over time. Out of the 2,078 programmes monitored, 30 per cent contained some violence. The overall frequency of violence was 1.14 acts per programme or 1.68 acts per hour. The average violent act took twenty-five seconds, thus violence occupies just over 1 per cent of all television time. However, when boxing and wrestling were excluded, these figures changed to thirteen seconds per act and 0.5 per cent of all television time. If a viewer watched four hours of television a day, he or she would be likely on average to see 6.72 violent acts as defined by the study. Top of the list for violent acts were spy, fantasy, cartoon, war, detective, crime and thriller programmes, and at the bottom of the list came quiz, game and chat shows, along with sport (non-contact). The research found that programmes were more likely to contain violence after 9.00 p.m. than before. During family viewing time prior to 9.00 p.m., when the concentration of children in the audience is greatest, the extent to which violence occurs in programmes on average is much less.

In looking at children's television, the analysis showed that, with the exception of cartoons, violence was rare in children's programmes. Cartoons are another and more difficult matter, especially since there is some argument over whether cartoon violence should actually be regarded as different from, or comparable with, other forms of portrayed violence on television. In terms of a strict mechanical count of acts per hour, cartoons were notably violent, with American cartoons being twice as likely to be violent as British ones. If cartoon violence is to be treated as more than a joke, then cartoons do number amongst the most violent programmes on television. As we shall see in the next section, however, viewers themselves do not take cartoons seriously in this respect.

The latest research in Britain comprised a content analysis study covering four weeks of television broadcast output on eight channels (the four main terrestrial channels and four satellite broadcast channels) which covered more than 2,000 programmes and over 4,700 hours of broadcast material. A complete week of output was taken during each of four waves of off-air recordings running from Monday to Sunday. All broadcast output was recorded around the clock, with analysis focused on programmes and programme previews or trailers, though not covering television advertisements.[13]

Of the programmes analysed, 37 per cent were found to contain violence. A total of 21,170 violent acts were coded over the four weeks' output, of which 71 per cent occurred on the four satellite channels. Each violence-containing programme contained around ten violent acts and five violent sequences (scenes which contained one or perhaps more than one violent act in quick succession). This violence occupied over fifty-one hours or 1.07 per cent of programme running time. On the terrestrial channels (BBC1, BBC2, ITV and Channel 4), just 0.61 per cent of programme output time was occupied by violence, representing a drop on the mid-1980s figure of 1.1 per cent. The general level of violence on television was disproportionately inflated by a small number of programmes which contained exceptionally large quantities of violence. Just 1 per cent of programmes across the eight channels were found to contain 19 per cent of all violent acts coded. Further, just 2 per cent of the programmes monitored were found to contain 46 per cent of all the programme running time occupied by violence.

Most violent acts (70 per cent) occurred in drama programmes, with cinema films being the biggest single drama genre contributor (containing 53 per cent of all violent acts). The most commonly occurring form of violence involved the use of a body part (42 per cent) or a hand-held weapon (31 per cent). More than a third of violent acts (36 per cent) depicted no injuries to victims, but few acts were found to be extremely graphic in terms of their portrayal of pain, blood and horrific suffering.

PERCEPTIONS OF TV VIOLENCE

Research into programme content indicates that violence is commonplace on television. But how salient is it for viewers? Viewers can be highly discriminating when it comes to portrayals of violence. They do not invariably read into television content the same meanings as do researchers.

Merely knowing how often certain pre-defined incidents occur in programmes does not tell us how significant these features are for viewers. Thus, viewers' perceptions of how violent television is may not accord with objective counts of programme incidents.

One BBC study showed that when viewers were asked to fill out a questionnaire about specific programmes shortly after they had been broadcast, in which reactions to violence and other aspects of the programmes were probed, whether or not a particular programme was perceived as violent did not depend on how many 'violent' incidents it contained. Nor was there any strong relationship between perceiving a programme as violent and verbally reported emotional arousal. Assessment of violence as unjustified, however, was associated with negative evaluations of the programme.[14]

Realism was an important element in viewers' perceptions of televised violence. Real-life violent incidents reported in the news or shown in documentaries were generally rated as more violent than violence presented in fictional settings. These exploratory findings were subsequently corroborated in a later study, in which viewers' perception of violence as portrayed in a range of fictional programmes was investigated. From this research, it emerged that familiarity of surroundings is one of the most powerful factors influencing viewers' perception of television violence. The closer to everyday life the violence is portrayed as being, in terms of time and place, the more serious it is judged to be.

CHILDREN'S PERCEPTIONS OF TV VIOLENCE

Are children's perceptions of TV violence similar to those of adults or are they more in line with the researchers', who have based their analyses strictly on number of incidents irrespective of context? Van der Voort conducted a study of children's perception of TV violence at three schools in Holland.[15] In all, 314 children were shown full-length realistic crime drama (*Starsky and Hutch* and *Charlie's Angels*), two adventure series (*Dick Turpin* and *The Incredible Hulk*) and fantasy cartoons (*Scooby Doo, Tom and Jerry, Popeye* and *The Pink Panther*). Immediately after showing each programme a post-exposure questionnaire was filled in measuring ten perception variables:

- readiness to see violence;
- approval of violent actions seen in the programme;
- enjoyment of the violence seen;
- evaluation of the programme;
- emotional responsiveness;
- absorption in the programme;
- detachment while watching;
- identification with the programme's chief characters;

- perceived reality of the programme;
- comprehension and retention of programme content.

Van der Voort investigated whether programmes perceived to be realistic were also more absorbing for children who would thereby respond to them with more emotion and less detachment than they showed towards programmes perceived to be more fantastic. Thus, *Starsky and Hutch* and *Charlie's Angels* were perceived to be realistic, while *The Incredible Hulk*, *Dick Turpin* and cartoons were seen as fantastic. Realistic programmes were watched with more involvement, more emotion and less detachment. The two crime drama series mentioned above were regarded as containing the most violence of any of the programmes the children were shown.

Van der Voort found, in fact, that 9- to 12-year-olds' judgements of the amount of violence programmes contain differ little from those of adults. He makes the important point, however, that children's violence ratings do differ from those of content analysts who analyse the amount of violence a programme contains by means of the systematic observation of programmes recorded on videotape. Programmes that are extremely violent according to 'objective' content analysis can be seen by children as 'hardly containing any violence'. Thus, although content analyses have identified cartoons as being among the most violent of television programmes in terms of numbers of objectively identified incidents per hour or per show, such programmes tend to be seen by children as containing hardly any violence at all.

On the basis of the above findings, both with adults and children, it is clear that viewers classify programme content differently from the descriptive counts of objectively defined programme violence, where narrow definitions of violence are usually employed. In reflecting the attitudes and perceptions of the audience, research into the amount of violence on television ought, therefore, to include at least some subjective input from viewers. This would provide an indication of which types of programmes or portrayals viewers themselves regard as violent and with what degree of seriousness.

THE EFFECTS OF TV VIOLENCE

Does TV violence cause social violence? There are two things we need to consider here. First, what kinds of effects are we talking about? Second, how are the effects measured and to what extent can we believe the evidence?

Mechanisms of effect

We will consider four kinds of effects here. In each case they refer to a psychological mechanism or process through which TV violence is hypothesised to produce changes in the attitudes or behaviour of viewers.

A fifth mechanism, known as catharsis, is discussed in the next chapter, which deals with the pro-social effects of television on children's behaviour:

- Arousal
- Disinhibition
- Imitation
- Desensitisation

Arousal

The arousal hypothesis suggests that watching violent television programmes can arouse viewers and make them more excited. This kind of effect is not restricted to violent content; sexual or humorous content can have the same effect. The emotional arousal itself is conceived as being a non-specific physiological response; it is defined by the individual in terms of the type of material he or she happens to be watching.[16] Thus, according to the hypothesis, if viewers are watching a highly amusing comedy they are likely to interpret their arousal as amusement. But if they are watching a programme containing violence they may interpret their arousal as anger.

Disinhibition

According to this hypothesis, watching violence on television may legitimise the use of violence by the viewer in real life by undermining social sanctions against behaving violently, which normally work to inhibit such behaviour. Research carried out under contrived laboratory conditions has supported this hypothesis and shown that viewers may behave in a more aggressive manner after watching film violence and especially if they are already in a bad mood before they watch it.[17] As we shall see later, however, there are problems with laboratory research of this kind, which throw question marks over the validity of this evidence.

Recent years have seen a new theoretical development on the original idea of how aggression in viewers might be stimulated by screen violence, which proposes that when people witness a violent media event, it activates thoughts or ideas about violence which stay with them for a period of time. When such an idea is activated, it may evoke other related thoughts, through a process known as 'priming'. Once these thoughts have come to mind they may influence a person to behave aggressively in a number of ways.[18]

Research has indicated that aggressive ideas can be activated through exposure to media violence which may in turn 'prime' other aggressive thoughts which can have important consequences for how people are likely to behave in different social situations.[19]

Imitation

This is the type of effect which has, over the years, probably attracted more publicity and attention than most. This hypothesis assumes that viewers, most especially very young ones, are inclined to learn from behaviours they see performed by TV characters, and copy such actions themselves. It is hypothesised, for example, that children may learn that violence is a useful and appropriate way of overcoming one's problems. Alternatively, young viewers may copy their heroes' behaviours to become more like them.[20]

In specific laboratory settings, research findings have indicated that children can be encouraged to behave in more aggressive ways following exposure to violent behaviour on film or TV. This effect has usually been attributed to 'observational learning', in which children imitate the behaviours of the models they observe.[21] The actual importance of imitation effects cannot be determined by laboratory experiments alone, however. It is essential to find out and establish that there are actual linkages between normal everyday viewing experiences and enhanced propensities to behave in a violent way.

The modelling and disinhibition perspectives propose that instances of violence depicted in the mass media may be emulated by members of the audience. Although more than one psychological mechanism has been implicated in this type of media influence, the fundamental feature throughout is that media influence operates in one direction. The media act upon audiences and bring about changes in their character. There is little consideration given to the expectations of audiences when they approach the media or of how audiences may discriminate between different kinds of media content and different kinds of violent portrayal. One-off exposure to media violence may have little effect. Is there a tendency, however, for certain viewers to seek out violent material and to enjoy repeated exposure to it? Does this phenomenon, if it occurs, serve to reinforce pre-existing aggressive tendencies in the individual? Alternatively, do certain individuals turn to the media as a source of ideas about how to behave in problematic situations, and utilise television as a source of guidelines or 'scripts' about how to react in various situations?

According to some media researchers, the relationship between viewing violence on television and the level of aggressiveness in young viewers builds over time, with some children and teenagers appearing to be more susceptible to develop a television dependency. Poorer academic achievers, those with less developed social skills and social networks, and those who fantasise about violence a lot all tend to display greater aggressiveness. Such children also tend to spend more time watching television. In addition, children who identify more strongly with aggressive television characters and perceive television violence as being more realistic also tend to display more pronounced aggressive tendencies. Thus, according to this social development model, a mixture of developmental factors seem to combine with television to promote aggressiveness.[22]

An investigation of children's reactions to the popular series *Mighty Morphin Power Rangers* produced evidence which suggested that children became more aggressive in their styles of play after watching an episode from this programme. The Power Rangers are a racially diverse group of friendly adolescents who are ordered by their elderly white leader, Zordon, to transform or 'morph' into superhero-type characters in order to battle monsters sent to Earth by the evil Rita Repulsa, a shrill Asian woman intent on taking control of the planet. The programme features scenes of stylised violence involving the Power Rangers and a host of evil counterparts, many of whom have a toy-like quality.

In a classic experimental design, fifty-two elementary-school girls and boys, aged between 5 and 11 years were randomly assigned either to watch an episode of Power Rangers or to a control group which did not see the episode. All the children were observed both before and after the programme while playing in their classroom. The researchers reported that children who had watched the *Power Rangers* episode exhibited a greater number of aggressive acts the next day at play than did children who had not been shown the episode. Indeed, children who had watched the episode committed seven times as many actions classed as aggressive as did the other children. This pattern of behaviour was much more pronounced among boys than girls, and was manifest in the boys' emulation of the Power Rangers' martial arts-type movements.[23]

Desensitisation

According to this hypothesis, repeated viewing of violence on TV leads to a reduction in emotional response to violence on the screen and to an increased acceptance of violence in real life. The argument runs that young viewers become increasingly used to violence in programmes if they watch a lot of this sort of television. As a consequence, demand grows for more and more extreme forms of fictional violence as that which viewers become accustomed to seeing loses its 'kick' and hence its appeal.

Researchers have expressed concern that exposure to large amounts of film violence may desensitise children to real-life violence. Although the mechanism through which desensitisation might occur is unclear, it is possible that watching violence may increase the child's tolerance for real-life violence either by implying that such behaviour is normal or by making real-life violence seem trivial by comparison. Furthermore, desensitisation might occur through reduced emotional response to violence after viewing film violence.

Just a few attempts have been made to provide practical demonstrations of televised violence's desensitising effect on children. These have investigated either the effect of TV violence on young viewers' own disposition to act responsibly (by trying to stop what they believe to be a real fight) or the degree to which they show an emotional response to violence.

Two studies, for example, looked at whether watching televised violence would make any difference to the response of 8-year-old children who witnessed a real fight between two other children in the playroom. Would they be any more or less likely than children who had watched a non-violent programme excerpt to warn an adult about what was happening? In the event, the youngsters who viewed violence were less likely to behave responsibly and seek the help of an adult.[24]

Further research has shown that children who are relatively heavy viewers (over twenty-five hours of viewing on average per week) were much less responsive to TV violence, in terms of physical measures of emotional arousal, than were relatively light viewers (fewer than four hours per week).[25]

Further desensitisation effects have been demonstrated with more graphic forms of violence, although this research has generally been confined to young men in their late teens and early twenties. Repeated exposure to films portraying violence, often within a sexual context where women are the victims, was found to shift the attitudes of college-age men such that they became less sympathetic about rape victims and more lenient in their judgements about alleged rapists.[26]

Repeated exposure to graphic depictions of film violence may lead viewers to adjust their emotional reactions to it. The violent material may be regarded as less disturbing, less offensive, and even as less degrading to the depicted victims. This cognitive shift in the way a film is judged may lead viewers to re-evaluate other aspects of the film as well, so that it becomes less anxiety-provoking and even more enjoyable. These altered perceptual judgements and emotional reactions may then be carried over into judgements made about victims of violence in other more realistic settings.

RESEARCH METHODS

We now turn to consider how the effects of TV violence have been measured. A common argument levelled against the broadcasters is that advertisers would not spend vast sums of money on commercials if they did not believe that television can affect consumer behaviour. Yet broadcasters still claim that television violence has no effect on the social behaviour of viewers. Is there not an inconsistency in this argument? But is there really a conflict here? Television advertisements are different from programmes; they are messages designed to get across to the audience information about a particular product. The effect on buying behaviour is not invariably direct and does not act equally on all viewers. The main aim of television advertisements, as with advertising through any medium, is to rouse awareness of an item's existence, especially among that segment of the population that is most likely to be in the market to buy. There is an element of persuasion contained within most adverts, of course, but the main aim is to say to those people who may already be interested in buying from a particular product or service range, 'Here is one example of the thing you want to buy which you might wish to try first.'

Television programmes, on the other hand, are not designed to persuade or to sell objects or ideas. This is not to say that ideas are not learned from them, because research tells us that indeed they are. But any 'effects' of programmes are incidental and, by their very nature, therefore, are much less likely to occur. Furthermore, it has been established that whether viewers are affected by programmes, together with the shape any influence takes, depends on how they approach television in the first place. By and large, viewers learn from television when they want to; otherwise, they do not.

There have been many studies of TV violence, but these can be condensed down to a handful of basic research methods, each of which has crucial design limitations often sufficient to cast doubt on the validity of the findings. Most of the work done so far can be broken down into four categories:

- laboratory experiments
- field experiments
- correlational surveys
- longitudinal panel studies

Laboratory experiments

These are designed to demonstrate a casual relationship between watching a violent event on TV and increased viewer aggressiveness. Typically, however, these studies test only small unrepresentative groups of people under highly contrived unnatural viewing conditions. Their measures of TV viewing and aggression tend to be so far removed from normal everyday behaviour that whether laboratory findings have any meaning in the outside world is something which can be debated quite strongly.

It is worth outlining the nature of some of this research. Through laboratory experiments, researchers have tried to demonstrate empirically that television violence can have a variety of different kinds of effects. These include encouraging children to imitate examples of violence they see in programmes, reducing socially learned inhibitions which normally act to discourage children from behaving aggressively in everyday life, and increased desensitisation to violence in real life consequent upon continued and regular exposure to violence on television.

A series of experiments by Albert Bandura and his associates in the 1960s addressed the imitation issue. Bandura believed that children could learn antisocial behaviour through observation. In other words, by watching favourite television characters behave violently on screen, young viewers could identify with these actors and their actions, and might under appropriate circumstances be inclined to mimic them. A demonstration of this effect was provided through an experimental design in which children were shown a character on film behaving in an aggressive manner towards a large plastic 'Bobo' doll before being placed in a playroom with lots of toys, including the doll. Other children were put in the playroom having either seen the same actor not behaving violently, or having seen no film at all. While observing the children playing, Bandura and his colleagues noted higher levels of imitative aggressive behaviours (towards the 'Bobo' doll) among children who had seen the violent example than among other children. In a variation of the original experiment, Bandura found that if the film character was seen to be rewarded for his behaviour, he was more likely to be copied than if he had been punished or if nothing had happened to him.[27]

Research subsequently showed that social sanctions and prior experience in the play situation were among a number of factors which could affect the nature and extent of mimicry. If an adult, watching with a child, praised the film actor's behaviour, the child was more likely to imitate it than if the actor was criticised for behaving the way he did. Criticism could reduce imitation. If the child had been given an opportunity to play in the room full of toys before watching the film, thus establishing their own forms of play, the actor had less influence on their behaviour than if they had been given no chance to play with the toys beforehand.[28]

In addition to imitation, there is some concern that television violence may have adverse effects on children's social behaviour by weakening socially learned inhibitions against behaving aggressively. The leading protagonist to have carried out laboratory experiments designed to prove the existence of this type of effect is Leonard Berkowitz. Although nearly all Berkowitz's studies were carried out with college students, the principles addressed are believed to apply also to younger viewers.[29]

The nature of this research was usually to take male American college students and to place them in a contrived situation in the laboratory, where they are first of all either intimidated and thus angered by an accomplice of the experimenter, or treated in an innocuous fashion. Then they are given the opportunity to watch either a violent or non-violent clip, or no clip at all. Finally, each participant is given a chance to get even with their antagonist. The technique here was to enable participants to deliver electric shocks to the other person every time they made a mistake on a bogus learning task. The findings usually revealed that angered individuals who watched a violent film clip expressed more aggression than did either non-angered participants or those who had been angered but watched a non-violent clip.

Evidence of desensitisation effects has emerged from experiments in which children are shown either a violent or non-violent clip from a television programme and are subsequently put in a situation where they have to monitor other children younger than themselves and warn the experimenter if those children start to misbehave themselves at all. Children shown a violent programme sequence tend to take longer to give a warning about the violence or misbehaviour of other children compared with similar children who have not watched any television violence. These results are interpreted as showing that watching television violence may produce a greater tolerance of real-life violence among those who watch it.[30]

The main problem with these experimental studies is their artificiality. They are unrepresentative of reality in their settings, their samples and in their measures of behavioural aggression. The validity of the electric shock procedure, for example, as an indicator of aggression in real life, must be seriously doubted. Further, the norms governing what is acceptable or unacceptable behaviour in the laboratory differ from those in the outside world. The participant is invited to deliver an electric shock to another person and complies because he feels that this is what the experimenter expects of him. The distressful consequences that the participant's action may have for the victim are perceptually reduced through a process of devolved responsibility for what happens on to the experimenter, and there is no threat of punishment or retaliation contingent upon the participant's 'antisocial' behaviour. Indeed, the question of whether the participant actually perceives his behaviour as deviant or antisocial is not investigated, and yet for most people (children included) this is an important factor affecting whether or not they behave violently in real life.[31]

Experimental studies have been interpreted to provide a clear demonstration of a link between viewing film violence and aggressive behaviour among children. Furthermore, because the children are randomly assigned to film-viewing conditions, and because the experimenter can hold constant all factors except which film was seen, causal conclusions can be drawn. These studies do not simply show an associative link between viewing violence and aggressive behaviour, but from them we can also conclude that viewing the violent films may have caused the increase in aggressive behaviour in that particular situation. The ability to draw causal connections is an important advantage of laboratory studies. In more naturalistic studies, it is often impossible to distinguish whether the connection between viewing violence and aggressive behaviour means that children who watch TV violence become more aggressive or that aggressive children choose to watch violent shows, or some combination of both. However, the advantages the experimental study gains in terms of control are lost when applied to the real world. For instance, a number of factors differ in the experimental study from the everyday life of children:

- The films are very short, about three minutes long instead of the half-hour or hour-long shows children usually watch on television.
- Aggressive behaviour is measured immediately after viewing; thus only the immediate, rather than long-term, effects are studied.
- The situation in which aggression occurs is very permissive, and any realistic consequences of behaving aggressively (such as peer retaliation or adult sanctions) are absent.
- The aggressive behaviour measured is often unrealistic, consisting of aggression against inanimate objects or pressing a lever to hurt someone. Thus, although we can be quite certain about what occurs in the laboratory, we are left with a great deal of uncertainty concerning how much the process demonstrated in the laboratory accurately reflects what happens in children's lives.

Field experiments

To avoid some of the problems associated with the laboratory study, while retaining some of its advantages, social scientists have conducted field experiments. In these studies, children are randomly assigned to view violent or non-violent television programming for a period of a few days to a few weeks. Measures of aggressive behaviour, fantasy or attitudes are taken before, during and after the period of controlled viewing. In order to ensure control over actual viewing, children in group or institutional settings have been studied. The two most common of these settings have been nursery schools, and residential schools or institutions for adolescent boys. With one exception, all of these studies have confirmed the results of the laboratory studies; in general, children who view violent TV are more aggressive than children who view non-violent TV.

Two particular studies have indicated this kind of link among preschool children. In one study, the researchers found that the children who watched a ten-minute aggressive cartoon for eleven days were more aggressive during a free-play situation than were children who had watched non-aggressive cartoons. In another study, preschool children were shown either violent or neutral or pro-social television for ten to twenty minutes a day for four weeks. The researchers found increased levels of aggressiveness during play only among those children who were initially more aggressive anyway and who were then shown a diet of violent cartoons.[32]

The field experiments involving adolescent boys have either taken place in residential boarding schools or in institutions for delinquent teenage boys. Using several measures of physical and verbal aggression, these studies have found an increase in some measures of aggression in boys watching violent films, and an increase in other measures of aggression only among those boys initially high in aggression who viewed violent shows.[33]

The field experiment has some of the advantages of the laboratory study, in particular the random assignment of viewers to viewing conditions. It also avoids some of the disadvantages of laboratory studies in that real TV shows are used, they are viewed in a natural setting, and aggression occurs in a situation where naturally occurring consequences are present.

There are, however, limitations to most field studies. The situation cannot be as well controlled as in a laboratory and thus the researcher is not as certain that the only difference between groups is the kind of TV viewed. One limitation is that often subjects cannot always be assigned to viewing conditions completely at random. If the residential setting involves natural group-living conditions such as cottages or dormitories, the researcher must sometimes assign groups rather than individuals to viewing conditions. To the extent that boys are not assigned randomly to these existing groups, they then are not assigned randomly to viewing conditions.

The individuals studied are often not representative of children in general. This is particularly true of the studies of adolescent boys in residential living settings. These boys may be different in important ways from adolescent boys living at home (for example, the delinquent boys are probably more aggressive). Furthermore, we know nothing from these studies of the effect on adolescent girls. Equally, the field-study environments, when the viewing and the aggression occur, are not representative of the living situation of most adolescent boys. While problems of sampling and environmental validity are less serious with the preschool studies, there is the problem of lack of control over the total viewing situation, since the children's home viewing is not controlled during the study.

Even with these limitations, however, the results of the field studies confirm the findings of the laboratory studies, replicating the basic finding that an increase in violent viewing is related to an increase in aggressive behaviour in a more naturalistic setting.

Correlational surveys

These improve on experimental studies in terms of the representativeness of samples, but often fall down in the accuracy of their measures of exposure to TV violence. The basic approach in correlational research is to obtain a measure of viewing violent TV and to relate this to a measure or group of measures of aggressiveness. The ultimate goal is to demonstrate a causal relation; the first step is to find that some relation exists. Viewers often have to identify or recall from lists of programme titles which ones they like best or watch most often. Occasionally, more effective diary measures are used, but even then assumptions are made about the probably violent content of programmes viewers say they have seen, which are not backed up by any better evidence. If some doubt exists about amounts of violence watched on television, there must also be doubts about the evidence offered on the supposed effects of this conduct. In any case, correlation surveys are unable to demonstrate causal relations. They can simply show where degrees of statistical association exist between certain correlations of attitudes or behaviours and patterns of TV watching. And even then, the small size of most of the correlations indicates some very weak associations indeed.

In contrast to the experimental designs, the correlational survey does not assign people to groups at random, but rather uses already existing groups of people who differ in their exposure to television or to violent content. Thus, what the naturalistic study loses in terms of control and thereby the ability to make causal conclusions, it makes up through its usefulness as a means of assessing effects in real life.

Consequently, the results of naturalistic studies are more mixed than those of field experiments or laboratory studies. Two early studies did not find a relationship between presence or absence of TV in the home and teacher reports of aggressive behaviour or scores on an aggression scale – although, in the latter case, there was a modest link with aggressiveness among 15-year-old boys who watched a lot of TV and read less.

Among researchers who have looked at the relationship between self-reports of favourite shows and self-reports or peer ratings of aggression, some have found that children who prefer violent programmes were themselves rated as more aggressive, in other cases as less aggressive, or that no relationship as such emerged at all. The most consistent results from naturalistic studies have been those in which overall amount of viewing violent TV was related to certain measures of aggression. Two studies in particular have reported a positive association between amount of violent TV viewing and self-reports of aggressive behaviour.[34]

Longitudinal panel studies

These represent perhaps the best kind of studies of TV effects. They can test causal hypotheses and they usually employ sound sampling methods. The aim of this type of investigation is to discover relationships which may exist or develop over time between TV viewing and social attitudes and behaviour. In this respect, such research addresses the notions of the cumulative influence of television violence. This view posits that the link between watching television and personal levels of aggressiveness should increase with age and repeated exposure to televised violence.

So far, however, the evidence from these studies has been equivocal. Some researchers have claimed to have found a strong link between watching of TV-violence-containing programmes in early childhood and the subsequent development of aggressive tendencies among children and adolescents in later years.[35] Other researchers, using similar procedures, have concluded differently.[36]

In the United Kingdom, a major investigation of the impact of television violence on the behaviour of adolescent boys was carried out by William

Belson.[37] This study used a simulated panel survey. In other words, the respondents were not actually studied across separate points in time, but were questioned retrospectively at a single point about their habits over previous years. Detailed and lengthy interviews with these teenage boys revealed a relationship between certain aspects of their claimed viewing behaviour and self-reported attitudes and dispositions towards the use of violence in their lives. In particular, the more the boys claimed to watch particular types of dramatic television content – classified by Belson as containing violence – the more likely they were to report having used aggression themselves under different circumstances. Belson's results have not been universally accepted and critics have questioned the validity of the biographical information obtained from his young respondents about not only their current viewing habits and behaviour, but also those they tried to recall from ten years earlier. The study does indicate usefully that certain types of programming may have a more significant impact than other types on antisocial behaviour among young viewers, and that it is not sufficient to examine only the overall amount of viewing that is done.

In an attempt to make causal inferences from naturalistic studies, one study which used panels of youngsters interviewed on more than one occasion found that, for boys, the amount of TV viewing at the age of 8 tended to be more strongly correlated with peer ratings of aggression two years later than with peer ratings at age 8. Furthermore, there was no relationship between early aggression and later TV viewing. The authors infer from this pattern of conditions that the earlier TV viewing caused the later aggression.

Another major panel survey with children was sponsored by the National Broadcasting Company in the United States. Some 3,200 elementary-school children and teenagers participated in this research. The primary-age children were surveyed on six occasions and the teenagers on five occasions over a three-year period (May 1970 to December 1973).[38]

The aim of the research was to find out if there were links, either at any one point in time or over time, between the character of television viewing and the propensity of aggressive tendencies among the children and teenagers under study. Among the primary-school children, evidence about verbal and physical acts of aggression was obtained from school friends, while the teenagers reported on themselves. Television viewing was measured by giving respondents check-lists of programmes available on the major networks which had been pre-classified for their violent content. Thus, not only did the researchers obtain some indication about general viewing patterns but also more specific information about levels of exposure among these young viewers to violent programmes.

During the analysis phase, the researchers assessed linkages between aggressive behaviour and levels of claimed viewing of different types of programming among different subgroups of children as well as among children as a whole. Only small statistical associations were found in any of these cases. Further analyses showed that, compared with the influence of family background, social environment and school performance, the significance of television viewing as an indicator of aggressiveness was very weak. This led the authors to conclude that television viewing was not a factor in the development of aggressive behaviours among the children and teenagers in their sample.

Another major study of the long-term effects of television violence spanned more than twenty years. Initial contacts were made with 875 children in the United States when they were aged 8–9 years. Nearly half of these children were contacted again ten years later. Correlational relationships were computed not only at these two points in time, but also across time, between measures of their exposure to television violence and of their personal aggressiveness. The researchers reported that viewing of television violence was significantly correlated with aggressiveness at age 8 and again at age 18. Furthermore, earlier viewing of television violence was linked to later aggressiveness.[39]

The correlation over time, however, was weak and only found among boys. A more significant problem is the rather simplistic measure of exposure to television violence which was based on nominations of the respondent's three or four favourite programmes. While at age 18, respondents made their own nominations, at age 8, these programmes were selected by parents. The measure of aggressiveness was also problematic and relied at age 18 on peer recall of how respondents had allegedly behaved a year earlier. These flaws seriously undermine the validity of these results.[40]

The same respondents were later followed up at age 30. Nearly all those who had been reinterviewed at 18 were located again. The study reported that those who had been more aggressive as children and teenagers continued to be among the more aggressive of the sample as adults. Although seeking to find evidence to support their earlier conclusions about the role of television in the development of personal aggressiveness, this later analysis revealed that there were other factors which underpin an individual's aggressiveness quite independently of how much television he or she watches. Some suggestion emerges that a significant genetic component operates in this context.[41] If this is so, certain individuals may be pre-programmed to develop more aggressive personalities and to exhibit a preference for violent media content. This view is supported by research conducted in the United Kingdom among pairs of siblings who shared genetic material and a common home environment. There was no evidence here that intra-pair differences in aggressiveness were significantly linked to differences in levels of watching television in general or of programmes which were classified as violent. However, more aggressive siblings tended to enjoy watching violence on television more.[42]

The American twenty-year study was extended internationally, with further surveys being launched in Finland, Poland, The Netherlands, Israel and Austria. Little data emerged from either Australia or children studied in Israel, who lived in a rural location, to support a link between television viewing and aggression. Weak links were suggested by the studies among children who lived in an urban location in Israel and among children in Poland.[43] The Finnish work corroborated the American findings. The Dutch study moved off in a different direction when its researchers decided to develop their own measures of television viewing and aggression rather than adopt what were seen as inferior measures from the original American study. The Dutch results failed to support the view that television violence is a likely long-term factor of any significance in the development of personal aggressiveness.[44]

In Canadian research by Tannis Macbeth Williams, which we discussed in Chapter 1, unobtrusive observations of children's behaviour were used, in addition to teacher and peer ratings of aggression, in a community where television had recently been introduced for the first time. We may recall that in this study the impact of television on the local population of young people was examined in three towns which at the outset either had no television reception (Notel), only one channel (Unitel) or several channels (Multitel) available.[45]

The major finding of the study was that the aggressive behaviour in the playground of grade-school children (aged 6 to 11) increased in Notel over the two-year period, while playground aggression in Unitel and Multitel showed no increase. This pattern of increased aggression was true for

- both physical and verbal aggression;
- girls and boys;
- longitudinal (children aged 6 to 7 prior to TV reception, and 8 to 9 two years later) and cross-sectional (children of same age at each testing) samples;
- children initially high or low in aggression;
- children who were either heavy or light viewers.

The evidence in support of the hypothesis that viewing violence leads to an increase in aggressive behaviour is very strong.

CONCLUSION

Television violence continues to feature prominently in public debates about the regulation and impact of the world's most prevalent mass medium. Much of the focus of concern has been on the reactions of children to violent depictions in programmes. We do not argue with the sincerity and significance of this public anxiety. Children's minds and social consciousness are malleable and immature in many ways. Young viewers may be susceptible to subtle influences (often intended) of television, to which most adults are immune. Whatever might be considered as appropriate viewing fare for grown-ups may, therefore, not be suitable for children, who may take what is shown the wrong way.

What is questionable, then, is not the significance of the issue, but the validity and reliability of the research evidence about television violence. Television is accused of showing too much violence. When measuring violence on television, however, researchers often begin by setting up an 'objective' definition of violence which does not necessarily reflect the public's perception. Physical incidents or body counts provide a measure of something, but not necessarily what ordinary viewers would themselves consider to be violence.

For viewers, and this applies to children as well, context is important. Viewers can and do discriminate between types of programmes and the way in which different programmes depict events. These perceptual discriminations are significant mediators of how viewers respond to television. They affect programme preferences, evaluations of how tasteful or offensive programmes are thought to be, and behavioural reactions to programmes.

We have seen that, in the end, anxieties about television violence rest on the supposed harmful effects it may have on viewers, particularly on the young and impressionable. There have been many studies of the influence of television violence (although the actual number is often grossly overstated), but these can be condensed to a handful of basic research methods – laboratory experiments, field experiments, correlational surveys and longitudinal panel studies. In each case, the methods have shortcomings, which are sufficient to cast some doubt on the validity of their findings. This is not to say that all the research is useless; rather the point is made as a note of caution to be borne in mind when interpreting what research results really show.

Over the years, a substantial body of research literature has built up on the subjects of television and the effects it might have on audiences. The conclusions reached from this research effort have been mixed. One major review of evidence, twenty years ago, concluded that the cause–effect relationship between television violence and audience behaviour had not been clearly demonstrated. It was noted, at that time, that support had been forthcoming for the imitation hypothesis, but that the results could not be accepted unequivocally. One of the central problems rested on the fact that different researchers had advanced different measures of aggression and of the incidence of violence on the screen. This made it difficult to derive any coherent body of assumptions about television's effects upon its viewers.[46]

This open verdict was repeated many years later following a further review of available evidence. The conclusion here was not to dismiss the possibility that television violence could have harmful effects on children, but to state that so far the research evidence had failed unambiguously to demonstrate such a link. Key problems identified by this review were the inadequacy of the raw data and the analytical methods used, and the viability of the way the results were often interpreted.[47] Not all reviewers of the evidence have reached this conclusion, however.

Using an analytical technique known as 'meta-analysis', some researchers have attempted to pull all the prevailing evidence together to assess which direction of causality, if any, the overall body of evidence points towards.[48] In the first of these exercises, Scott Andison examined sixty-seven studies published over a twenty-year period and found evidence overall pointing to a weak positive correlation between viewing television violence and viewer aggression. Ten years on, Susan Hearold examined 230 studies produced over a period spanning around fifty years to 1977 and reached a similar conclusion.[48]

The latest such analysis by Haejung Paik and George Comstock analysed the findings of 217 studies from 1957 to 1990 and implemented a sophisticated mode of analysis which carefully separated out the evidence deriving from different categories of methodology.[49]

Once again, the conclusion reached was that the body of research evidence indicated an effect of viewing television violence upon subsequent aggressiveness among viewers. These sorts of analyses provide a useful synthesis of the empirical research evidence, but focus on the statistical results, tending to treat the results from all studies as having equivalent status, regardless of methodological weaknesses which might undermine the validity of the measures upon which statistical analyses were computed.[50]

The debate about television violence will continue both in the public and academic spheres. Whether or not there is too much violence in programmes is a subjective question as much as it is a scientific one: the answer lies, to a large extent, in prevailing public taste and opinion. Values change constantly and are reflected in what is deemed to be acceptable viewing fare. On the question of whether or not television violence has any direct effects on viewers, the answer is neither simple nor straightforward. Much depends on the type of effect to which reference is being made and on the method used to measure television's impact. From the range of research completed so far, it has become apparent that the measurement of television's effects, and of factors that mediate those effects, is highly complex. Often, researchers have relied upon methodologies that inadequately represent real-world television-viewing experiences and upon conceptual frameworks that omit important contributory variables. Although some progress has been made in eliminating the nature of certain types of television influence, we are still a long way from knowing fully the extent and character of television's influence on children's aggressive behaviour.

Chapter 8

Does TV encourage good behaviour?

Concern about possible antisocial influences of television far outweighs the consideration given to any other area of children's involvement with television. How far is the perception of the box in the corner as a 'one-eyed monster' justified? The possibilities that television's examples of bad behaviour provide models to be copied by susceptible young viewers cannot be treated lightly. But the assumption, which commonly seems to prevail, that television has been demonstrably proved to have a bad influence, oversimplifies both what 'the box' brings into the home and how children get involved with it.

Television programmes contain many examples of good behaviour, of people acting kindly and with generosity. It is equally logical to assume that these portrayals provide models for children to copy, too. In this chapter, therefore, we turn to the question of whether television encourages good behaviour among children. Although not as extensive as the work on television violence, an important body of research exists which indicates a variety of ways in which television can or might, under certain circumstances, have soundly beneficial and desirable effects on children.

THE NOTION OF CATHARSIS

One pro-social possibility, which runs counter to much established thinking on the subject, is that watching violence on television serves to provide an outlet for pent-up aggressive drives. According to the catharsis hypothesis, originally proposed by Aristotle, accumulated aggressive urges are supposedly drained after watching violence, with the result that the individual behaves less aggressively. In its strongest form, the hypothesis holds that anyone can purge their aggressive impulses through vicarious cathartic experiences. This form of the catharsis hypothesis is currently in general disfavour, after passing through successive periods of uncritical acceptance and controversy. As we shall see, however, a weaker form of the hypothesis has been proposed and some evidence has emerged which suggests that for some people catharsis may be possible as a response to TV violence.[1]

Rather than thinking of catharsis as a process which can occur in anybody, increasingly researchers have suggested that if such a discharge of hostile feeling can occur at all, it is probably restricted to certain types of personality. It has come to be theoretically conceived as a dimension of human skill or competence involving the ability to fantasise, daydream or use one's imagination.[2] These mental faculties are not equally well developed in all people. There is some evidence, though, which we look at later in this chapter, that children with lively imaginations are better at shifting their mood from one of anger to one of more positive emotional feeling, thus reducing the likelihood of overt expression of aggression. Furthermore, such children are better equipped to get rid of their hostilities through films or television programmes with which they become emotionally carried away.[3]

Much of the evidence for catharsis as linked with the way people respond to televised portrayals of violence has derived from the work of Seymour Feshbach. In the 1950s and 1960s his work provided several early demonstrations that individuals can harmlessly discharge their aggressive impulses either through fantasising about violence or through watching fictional portrayals of violence under controlled laboratory conditions.[4] Later, at the beginning of the 1970s, Feshbach and his colleague Jerome Singer reported a reduction of aggressive tendencies among teenage boys under more natural conditions after they had been encouraged to watch mainly violent television programmes.[5]

Over 600 teenage boys, from three private residential schools for middle-class boys and four residential treatment homes for boys lacking in proper home care, had their viewing diets manipulated over a six-week spell. During this period, some boys were shown a minimum of six hours per week of primarily violent programming, while other boys were shown primarily non-violent programmes. Additional hours of viewing were allowed so long as they involved the assigned programme types. A behaviour rating scale was completed daily by a member of the staff familiar with the boys' activities throughout the experiment.

The teenagers who watched mainly non-violent programmes exhibited higher levels of physical aggression against their peers than did those who watched mainly violent programmes. Thus, the boys who saw mainly non-violent programmes had twice as many fights as the other boys and were more likely to provoke fights.

The study has not been received without criticism and an attempt by another researcher to replicate its findings under similar conditions failed.[6] Problems with it stem from the unknown amount of violence there may have been in non-violent programmes, something that was not checked. Programmes which other researchers have labelled as violent, such as cartoons, found their way into the non-violent diet. It is not known either how attentively the children in each condition actually watched television. Finally, there were complaints among some teenage boys in the non-violent diet condition because they were not permitted to watch some of their favourite programmes. The frustration caused by being deprived of programmes they liked and would normally be able to watch may have contributed towards these boys' increased aggressiveness.

While there may be problems with the interpretation of Feshbach's results and a question mark hangs over the validity of the strong form of the catharsis hypothesis, there has recently been some discussion of a more idiosyncratic way in which catharsis might work. It could be that catharsis is more likely to occur among certain types of people than others.[7]

In place of the simplistic catharsis framework based on the 'hydraulic' model of aggression as a reservoir of psychic energy which can be purged via fantasy – a non-specific vicarious activity available to all individuals – there is an alternative conception that views fantasy as a dimension of human skill or competence. This imaginative capacity may be manifested among children as skills in creativity, daydreaming or fantasy play behaviour. Thus, the practised young daydreamer can turn to fantasy activity in dealing with frustrating problems or situations, whereas the less experienced daydreamer may be unable to do this and is limited to the direct expression of anger through aggression. It is known that youngsters who are adept at fantasising can reduce their aggressive feelings not only through vicarious involvement in fantasy portrayals of aggression, but also by daydreaming about non-violent, imaginative themes such as being successful at school, going out on dates and so on.

A series of interesting experiments by Grant Noble in the 1970s showed that children's reaction to televised or film violence was not invariably to become more aggressive in their subsequent play or interactions with other children; sometimes violent portrayals encouraged them to play more imaginatively and less destructively.[8] The type of violence made a difference. Highly stylised, fictional portrayals of violence subsequently encouraged children to be friendlier and less hostile towards each other, while more realistic portrayals of violence, especially where the victim was seen, resulted in increased aggressive tendencies.

Realistic violence, such as that contained in a televised wrestling match, made both aggressive and non-aggressive boys more aggressive afterwards when they played with other children. Stylised violence as shown in a western, however, produced more imaginative play among boys already known to be prone to aggression. At the same time it also made relatively well-behaved boys more boisterous with other children, though less so than did watching wrestling.

Individual differences in imaginative play behaviour and in the ability to fantasise or daydream may underlie differences among children in their responses to TV violence. Youngsters who are particularly skilled as daydreamers may be able to reinterpret their aggressive feelings and use their fantasies to shift their mood from one of anger to a more positive, pleasant emotion, thus reducing the likelihood that they will show any overt expression of aggression.

One researcher has tested this idea by comparing the reactions of children who were either skilled or not adept at fantasising in their reactions to violent and non-violent film material.[9] In a manipulation of how children felt, two accomplices of the researcher were employed to annoy the children by interrupting them while they were building a toy. Next, the children saw either a film containing violence, or a non-violent film or no film at all. Finally, the children were placed in a room of toys, some of which they could have played with in an aggressive fashion. Their behaviour at play was observed, unknown to them, for a further ten minutes, during which they were scored for any aggressiveness they displayed.

Children who were skilled daydreamers exhibited significantly less aggressiveness at play after being given an opportunity to watch either violent or non-violent film material than when they had watched nothing. Among youngsters who were not adept at daydreaming, none of the film material, regardless of whether it was violent or non-violent, made any difference to their behaviour.

Children who were high fantasisers seemed to be able to reduce any anger they had while generally improving the way they felt while watching violent and non-violent film sequences. For some children at least, fictional violence can have positive effects. This research throws some doubt on the popular view that violence on television and in motion pictures is harmful to all children, even if they view a great deal. It seems that in the case of some youngsters, particularly those who have highly developed imaginations, the effects of these materials might even be beneficial. Violent as well as non-violent television programmes may provide a means through which some children can reduce their angry feelings. It should be noted that so far such beneficial effects of viewing media violence seem to apply only to those children who are active and regular fantasisers. Children with low levels of fantasy activity are unable to deal with their aggressive feelings in this way and may actually become more prone to react aggressively following exposure to film violence. Thus, the same television programme could have beneficial or harmful results depending upon youngsters' abilities to use it in active and positive ways to improve how they feel.

What is required at this stage are developments in several new directions, and perhaps the following ideas may provide some useful indicators:

- experimental research showing the extent to which individuals differ in fantasising capabilities;
- closer examination of relationships between fantasising or imaginativeness and reactions to various kinds of TV content;

- collection of data to show what proportion of youngsters have sufficient fantasising abilities to use television dramatisations in a constructive way to control their negative emotional and behavioural tendencies.

CAN TELEVISION TEACH GOOD BEHAVIOUR?

A growing body of evidence indicates that televised examples of good behaviour can encourage children to behave better. Research has shown that young viewers can learn how to behave in a more socially acceptable or desirable fashion through watching not only specially produced educational programmes, but also examples of good behaviour contained in more popular establishment programmes produced for the mass audience.[10] The evidence for pro-social effects of television can be grouped into four types:

- laboratory studies with prepared television or film materials;
- laboratory studies with broadcast materials specially produced for social-skills-teaching purposes;
- laboratory studies with programme materials from popular TV series;
- field studies relating amount of viewing of pro-social television content to strength of pro-social behaviour tendencies.

Using these various techniques, researchers have investigated the potential of television to affect children's levels of displayed generosity and unselfishness, their friendliness and deferred gratification in contrast to wanting immediate rewards for anything they do.

RESEARCH WITH PREPARED MATERIALS

Specially prepared film and television materials have been found to influence several different types of children's self-control behaviour, including courage, delay of gratification and adherence to rules. Controlled study has also been made of television's ability to affect charitable behaviour among young viewers.[11] Several researchers have demonstrated the therapeutic potential of television material, particularly with regard to helping children overcome fears. Showing preschool children, who were initially afraid of dogs, a series of films that depicted other children approaching and playing with a dog resulted in substantial decrease in their fear of dogs. The same effect failed to occur following exposure to films of Disneyland. Similarly, successful film examples have been reported to help cure children's fear of the dentist.[12]

Further important work has shown that specially prepared television material can help lonely, self-conscious children to make friends more readily. Thus, youngsters who have difficulty getting on with other children can be encouraged to take a step back while watching fictional scenarios in which examples are portrayed of how to mix with others in various social situations.[13]

Brief television portrayals have been used to influence children's self-control regarding delay of gratification and the impact of symbolic models on viewers' adherence to rules. For instance, children have been found to be more willing to wait for a valued reward after watching a videotaped sequence of an adult modelling delay of gratification in the same way and explaining why he or she has done so.[14] In another study, children were shown, on television, a child of their own age conforming to an explicitly stated rule while playing a game. These children were less likely themselves to deviate from this rule than were other children who had not seen the television example.[15]

Another example of self-control has been examined in studies which were carried out to see if television programming could influence children's 'resistance to temptation'.[16] The typical situation involved observations of 7- and 8-year-old boys playing with toys in a games room. While left on their own in this room they were forbidden to touch or to play with one particularly attractive toy. On average, around six minutes and forty seconds would go by before a boy in this situation would touch the toy. However, if the boy had watched a TV programme showing another boy of around the same age playing with similar toys, though not going near the forbidden toy, the average boy would wait nearly eight minutes before transgressing. If, on the other hand, the boy in the programme was seen to play with the toy, young viewers were apt to touch it subsequently within three minutes of being left in the games room. These effects were found still to be present one month later.

The way in which television's portrayal of good behaviour or bad behaviour can influence children to behave similarly may depend on whether youngsters watch on their own or with someone else of their own age. One American study examined 5-year-old boys' reactions to a short film depicting a male character behaving in an aggressive manner towards a person costumed as a clown and compared this with their reactions following a film in which the same character acted in a friendly, helpful manner towards the clown. Each child saw only one of these films. However, in some cases, these young boys watched on their own, while in others they watched with a companion.[17]

Afterwards, when the film had finished, the boys were taken to a playroom which was located in the experimenter's 'own trailer'. Here, they were introduced to the clown figure in person and left to talk and play with him for a short period, during which the experimenter went away. The children were at this time monitored unobtrusively by hidden observers.

These observations revealed that children who had watched the aggressive film depiction were significantly more likely than those who had seen the other version to play with the clown more 'aggressively', that is, they made more hostile comments, played shooting games, hit the clown with a mallet and, when in pairs, were more aggressive towards each other. These effects were more pronounced among boys who had watched the film in pairs. In contrast, boys who watched the friendly version were in turn more likely to behave in a constructive, friendly way towards the clown. Viewing in pairs with a companion made no substantial difference to the friendly film's effects.

Children's charitable behaviour may be influenced by televised examples of people making donations. One demonstration of this type of effect emerged from a series of controlled experimental studies with 6- to 9-year-old children. These youngsters were shown a specially constructed videotape film showing a character playing a bowling game and winning gift certificates.

In a different version of the film the bowler could either give some of his certificates to a charity or keep them all for himself. In addition, sometimes he also preached the merits of giving to charity. After watching this film, children were placed in a similar situation and were observed to see how much they would give their winnings to charity. The results were that children who saw the videotape in which the character gave to charity were more likely to make donations themselves than were those who saw the character behave selfishly. The bowler's actions spoke louder than his words, since preaching about giving to charity made little difference to how the children behaved.[18] Children's charitable behaviours may be short-lived, however. Although televised examples of generosity can encourage children to be more giving, this effect may have worn off within a week or two.[19]

Television may influence children's friendliness and affectionate behaviour. Demonstrations of this effect have been made in laboratory settings and under more natural viewing conditions. In a controlled viewing environment with specially prepared television material, nursery-school children have been observed to express greater affection towards a toy clown after watching an adult TV character do likewise on screen. However this copycat behaviour was more likely to occur among boys only if the affectionate character was male; a female character showing affection had no effect. The study suggests that at this early age children already select to follow appropriate models for them, and perceived similarity of TV characters (in this case being of the same sex) can be important.[20]

RESEARCH WITH BROADCAST MATERIALS

A number of special television productions have emerged from major television companies – especially in the United States, but also in the United Kingdom and Sweden – which have been designed to enhance the social maturity and responsibility of young viewers. One of the most notable examples of this type of production is *Sesame Street*. This series was primarily aimed at teaching disadvantaged children living in urban ghettos a variety of social and mental skills which they would need in school. Its appeal, however, has been extensive and it has attracted a far wider and more heterogeneous audience than that for which it was originally intended. While it is undoubtedly a very successful programme in terms of popularity with audiences around the world, what evidence is there that *Sesame Street* and similar types of programmes have pro-social effects upon young viewers?

There is some evidence that children as young as 4, and certainly those aged 7 years, are able to identify and remember the cooperative and helping behaviours emphasised by certain segments of the show. Another programme, *Mister Rogers' Neighbourhood*, which has also been made to improve children's social awareness and social skills, has been found to have similar effects.[21] For instance, children aged 4, who were shown four episodes of the series depicting characters attempting to understand and help a stranger, were better able to behave in more helpful and cooperative ways than were children who saw different programmes.[22]

Some educational programmes appear to be better than others at encouraging children to behave in a more friendly manner towards their peers. Among children aged between 3 and 5, for example, American researchers found that watching *Mister Rogers' Neighbourhood* produced much friendlier dispositions both among children and between the children and adults over a period of several days. Watching *Sesame Street* had the same impact, but only among those children who tended to be poorly behind in the first place.[23]

The success of pro-social messages in broadcast programming in getting through to children and influencing their values and behaviours can depend upon the supplementary application of support training. Examples of pro-social behaviour on screen may not only enhance the likelihood that children who see these portrayals will adopt this behaviour themselves when in a similar situation, but may also generalise to new and different situations.[24] Such generalisation effects have not always been successfully achieved, however.[25] It has been argued elsewhere that these negative results occurred because the programme extracts used in these studies failed to observe the production integrity of broadcast educational material. Production quality was poorer and the extracts used in these experiments seldom allowed an opportunity for rehearsal of the key behaviour portrayals.[26]

The impact of pro-social messages may be further enhanced when the programme in which they occur is free of antisocial conduct.[27] What also seems to be important to the effectiveness of pro-social television is the opportunity subsequently to discuss, rehearse or in other ways examine the pro-social messages themselves.[28]

Pro-social behaviours depicted in educational programming produced for broadcast television have been shown to enhance the extent to which preschool children will exhibit similar behaviours in free play, when sufficient opportunities are provided for such behaviours to occur. In an

American study with children from a day-care centre, aged 3–5 years, boys and girls watched either pro-social or neutral educational programming. The material shown to the children comprised videotaped segments from *Sesame Street*. After viewing, the children were guided through activities designed to elicit rehearsal of the pro-social behaviours depicted in the programme.[29]

Results showed that such televised examples can be used effectively within day-care settings and, if designed to, can enrich the social education of preschool children. The children who watched the *Sesame Street* segments containing exclusively pro-social content showed clear signs of increased cooperative, helping, sharing, giving, comforting and affectionate behaviours compared with similar children who had watched programming with no overt pro-social content. The effectiveness of the programme was believed to reside in the way it depicted pro-social behaviours with stories that unfolded in real time which contained examples of pro-social conduct that were integrated with the storyline. After viewing had taken place, there were plenty of opportunities for the children to practise what they had seen. The children were given the freedom to try these behaviours out for themselves through a regime which deliberately toned down the role of teaching staff in determining how the children would play.

RESEARCH WITH POPULAR DRAMA MATERIALS

There is growing evidence, then, that appropriate, specially manufactured television programmes or film clips can influence children's altruistic tendencies, in the short term and under contrived conditions. However, these studies have used a comparatively narrow range of television and film materials. Even those experiments which used actual broadcast material from network television generally featured only carefully selected clips from educationally oriented programmes. Their results may not, therefore, be generalisable to the portrayals found in existing, action-oriented television dramas, which usually attract the largest audiences among children as well as adults and are often of the type found at the centre of the television violence controversy. Although fast-moving sequences typical of many action-adventure shows on television may contain examples of aggressive behaviour which could conceivably be imitated, does the occurrence of pro-social behaviours in this type of fictional context also provide salient imitation cues? The answer, at least for contrived viewing conditions in research, appears to be 'yes'.

Television dramas depicting pro-social behaviours can encourage children to behave unselfishly. One study with 5- and 6-year-olds had the children divided up to watch one of three unedited programmes – an episode of *Lassie* in which a small boy risked his life to save an endangered puppy; an episode of *Lassie* that featured dogs in a positive light but portrayed no example of a human helping a dog; and an episode of *The Brady Bunch*, a family situation comedy. After viewing, children were first introduced to a situation engineered so that they were faced with a choice between persisting at a button game, or breaking off from the game to push another button that would bring assistance to (fictional) puppies in distress, thereby reducing the number of points they could win. The illusion of a troubled puppy was created by asking the children to monitor a kennel by earphones and to press the button if they heard barking over the earphones, thus signalling to the attendant that the dogs might be in distress. Children who saw the dramatic example of a boy helping a dog in the *Lassie* episode chose to help puppies in distress more quickly and for a considerably longer period of time than children in either of the other two conditions.[30]

From a practical point of view these results imply that it is possible to produce television shows featuring action and adventure which have appeal for child and family audiences which at the same time have socially desirable, as opposed to antisocial, influences upon viewer behaviour. However, it should perhaps be carefully noted that throughout these experiments the helping behaviour portrayed in the television episode and the behaviour required of the child in the post-viewing situation were very similar in nature. Can pro-social content occurring in popular television series have more general effects upon dissimilar as well as related viewer behaviours?

Several pieces of research from the United States and Australia have explored this question. These have shown that popular television programmes can provide examples of sociable effects which may generalise to good behaviour other than those shown in the programmes.

One study with Australian preschool children examined the effects of a specially controlled diet of television on the youngsters' social behaviour. The experiment used a selection of episodes from television series, including *Lassie, I Love Lucy, The Brady Bunch* and *Father Knows Best*.[31] First of all, these programmes were content-analysed and classified in terms of the amount of 'pro-social' behaviour they depicted. On this basis they were divided into two sorts: 'pro-social' and 'neutral'.

The children were assigned to watch either 'pro-social' or 'neutral' programmes for half an hour each day, five days a week for four weeks. They were tested one week before and again one week after conclusion of the special viewing diet on measures of sociability. Regular watching of pro-social programmes was found to be associated with an increase in helpfulness among boys and in cooperative behaviour among boys and girls. The precise behaviours measured were quite different from anything depicted in any of the programmes. This indicated that when young children watch standard television programmes in which the main characters display concern and consideration for others their own consideration may increase.

Another study showed children either an episode of *The Waltons* or a television film in which people were not very helpful towards each other. Children who saw *The Waltons* were more likely to help an experimenter who dropped an armful of books than were those who watched the other film. This effect did not generalise across other situations, however. Thus, the results provide only some evidence that ordinary broadcast material can enhance the goodness in people.[32]

FIELD STUDIES OF PRO-SOCIAL TV EFFECTS

What happens outside the laboratory, though? Do programmes such as *The Waltons* have an effect on how children behave towards each other in their everyday lives? One way of finding this out has been to monitor children's viewing habits and social activity and conduct over time in natural surroundings. One survey where this was done obtained information from children about the programmes they watched and classified their viewing diets in terms of the number of programmes they watched that contained either antisocial or pro-social behaviour examples. Thus, each programme watched was coded in terms of how much antisocial or pro-social content it usually carried. Children's own behaviours were rated through self-reports and teacher reports. Findings revealed that the less TV they watched in total, and if they watched a lot of programmes with high levels of pro-social content, the more likely they were to behave in a pro-social manner.[33]

In a comparison of the relative influence of pro-social versus violence viewing, correlations obtained between viewing habits and pro-social behaviour were lower than those obtained between viewing habits and aggressive behaviour. However, there are several reasons for this which point to limitations in the current state of research in this field and offer a number of potential lines of enquiry for future research.

First of all, children learn quite early that they should help or share, and thus television's pro-social content only reiterates what they already know. Aggressive behaviour, on the other hand, is generally punished in a child's home and school environment, and seeing it performed with frequent success on television contrasts with its treatment in reality. It may be useful for future studies to find out the extent to which children of various ages clearly differentiate pro-social and antisocial behaviours and their outcomes in reality and in television's fictional drama, and for these studies to obtain measures of the relative salience and attractiveness of these behaviours for the child.

A second point also concerns the manner in which pro-social and antisocial or aggressive behaviours are presented on television. Pro-social behaviours are very often subtle and verbally mediated, whereas aggressive behaviours are blatant and physical. Because young children learn better from simple direct and active presentation, they may be more likely to learn from violent, rather than from pro-social, portrayals customarily shown on television. At present, no evidence is available to show that these differential portrayal characteristics produce differences in perception and learning of pro-social versus violent content.

Finally, content analysis has shown that televised pro-social behaviours are predominantly performed by female and non-white characters rather than by male white characters in television drama. Thus, the relative influence of pro-social and violent behaviours may be compounded with the types of characters that normally portray them. It is important for future research to assess the relative amounts of pro-social and violent behaviours performed by specific leading characters. If it is to be assumed that their preferential production treatment makes their presence more noticeable, then their actions may provide sources of learning and behavioural influence for young viewers.

By the late 1980s, some indication had begun to emerge that the pattern may be changing somewhat in a positive way. Barbara Lee, formerly of the CBS television network in the United States, has reported findings from an analysis of pro-social portrayals on American prime-time network television entertainment programming. Over 1,000 pro-social incidents were recorded from 235 entertainment programmes.[34] The portrayal of helpful and altruistic, affectionate and cooperative behaviours was prevalent, though more frequently occurring in some types of programmes (e.g. action-adventure). Pro-social behaviours were usually depicted as successful in working out whatever conflicts existed and easing people's problems. In over half (56 per cent) of the incidents, the pro-social behaviour was intended to resolve an immediate problem or conflict. In eight out of ten of these cases, it was rated as being wholly or partially successful in problem-resolution. Most of the good behaviours observed occurred among those who were relatives or friends. This accounted for three out of four pro-social content incidents.

TELEVISION AND MORAL JUDGEMENT

Much of the research on the potentially good effects of television has focused on different kinds of social behaviours relevant to character. Little research has studied whether television has any direct influence upon moral reasoning and judgement. Early critics were particularly concerned about the ethical and moral views taught by television, which were seen as exerting a corrupting influence. One view is that television often shows that illegal or immoral actions often work. Even law enforcers on television are depicted bending the rules, ignoring moral codes and indulging in questionable conduct. The implicit message in this content is that being bad often works better than being good.

In contrast, defenders of the medium have argued that television impact upon the moral reasoning of its youngest viewers is primarily a positive one. Television programmes regularly raise a host of moral issues in an interesting fashion which attracts and retains the audience's attention. People are confronted with an array of moral issues and dilemmas which are discussed or acted out in its drama and entertainment programming, as well as in its factual and educational productions. Serialised dramas depict characters wrestling with moral problems often at great length in a context which invites audiences to identify with events and situations. Television talk shows feature ordinary members of the public baring their souls in front of millions, often focusing on the most intimate aspects of their private lives. Through these kinds of experiences, television can function as a kind of moral teacher or counsellor, encouraging viewers, young and old, to reflect on important moral issues.[35] So far, though, there has been little research either to confirm or disconfirm any effect of television on the moral reasoning and values of children.[36]

Research into the development of moral judgement has been dominated by the work of Kohlberg.[37] Under this framework, the child's moral reasoning is thought to develop through a series of stages, with each successive stage representing a more enhanced level of understanding of the moral order of the social world. At each step along the way, the child learns a sequence of critical features in relation to differentiating between right and wrong. Under this system, one rudimentary conclusion is that if an act is not punished, then it must by definition be deemed ethically acceptable and therefore morally right. A key question is whether television contributes to this mode of reasoning.

One attempt to find an answer to this question involved a study of boys and girls aged 4–5 years, 7–8 years, and 10–11 years. These children were interviewed initially to find out more about their moral reasoning capabilities. In addition, the mother of each child assisted by keeping a television diary for two weeks for her child and provided extensive background information about the family's viewing habits. The researchers then used statistical techniques to examine relationships between reported family and child television viewing and the child's moral attitudes and values.[38]

Among the younger children, heavier television viewing was moderately associated with less advanced moral reasoning on each of a series of moral judgement measures taken. This relationship did not emerge among the two older age groups, however. Among the 4- to 5-year-olds, it was total amount of television viewing rather than preferences for particular kinds of programmes which was linked to nature of moral values. There was no indication, therefore, that the tendency to watch certain kinds of programming is especially likely to impair young children's moral development. Among children aged 7 to 8, however, stronger preferences for watching situation comedies featuring families were associated with a better developed understanding of the importance to help people in need. This was an interesting finding, in that it reflected the themes of many of these shows. Less encouraging was the reported finding that this kind of understanding was relatively weak among the oldest children surveyed; those who had a special liking for adult-oriented action-adventure shows. The dearth of research on television and moral reasoning means that our understanding of the nature and significance of any role it plays in teaching children the difference between right and wrong remains patchy.

CONCLUSION

In this chapter we have discussed the pro-social potential of television. Despite widespread criticism of television for promoting antisocial behaviour and undermining the moral fabric of society, there is evidence that it may provide a channel through which hostile impulses can be harmlessly dispersed. Furthermore, televised examples of good behaviour can encourage children to behave in friendlier and more thoughtful ways towards others.

We began the chapter where the previous one had left off – with the subject of TV violence. The catharsis hypothesis proposes that, through watching televised violence, youngsters may discharge their aggressive urges harmlessly and be less likely to behave aggressively with others. We dismissed a major US field study of boys in public institutions, which examined and claimed to produce evidence in support of the catharsis hypothesis. Close scrutiny of this study by others resulted in doubts being cast on its major conclusions. An attempted replication failed to yield consistent findings. However, interest in catharsis encouraged further research and a modified hypothesis.

In a weaker form of the original idea, it has been proposed that catharsis can occur but that it is dependent on the ability to fantasise or daydream. Children who daydream vividly seem to be better able to discharge their aggressive urges through media portrayals of violence. The *type* of violence is important, too. Obvious fictional portrayals seem to offer better possibilities for the harmless reduction of aggressive feelings amongst young daydreamers than do realistic portrayals of violence. Imaginative fantasising is a cognitive skill and, although it is more evident in some children than others, it can be improved through appropriate training. This would seem to offer a route through which young viewers can be equipped with the ability to use their experience with televised violence in a socially beneficial and constructive way.

In addition to taking advantage of vicarious involvement with television violence to provide a means of improving the child's mood, another way television can have a beneficial impact on children is through the portrayal of kindness, generosity, being helpful and socially responsible. These portrayals have been shown to exert both short-term and longer-term influences on similar behaviours among children. Television can have such socially desirable effects not simply through its educational programmes, but also when pro-social portrayals feature in its entertainment and drama productions made for non-popular consumption.

Although research on the pro-social effects of television still has a long way to go, the early signs are that this area of television content has important social-behavioural influences which need to be examined in greater depth. Through both specially designed campaigns and educational fare, as well as through its fictional entertainment output, television can play a positive role in helping to build cultivated and socially responsible young people. It is possible that pro-social content may counteract antisocial content to some extent, and finding out which pro-social television material is most effective in this respect may provide valuable alternative programme-content control guidelines to simply cutting violence.

Chapter 9

Does TV advertising affect children?

ADVERTISING: WHY THE CONCERN?

On many television networks around the world a not insubstantial proportion of TV airtime is filled by advertisements. Controls over advertising on television are more rigid in some countries than others. For example, rules governing the amount of advertising content in each broadcast hour, and the frequency with which advertising breaks can occur during a single programme, place more restrictions on television advertising in Britain than is found in the United States. Even so, the number of advertising breaks during the course of each day's programming on British television, especially during peak time, is sufficient to merit empirical consideration and exploration relating to the impact this material has on the audience.

In the United States, anxieties over the influence of television advertising, especially on children, have resulted in parental movements on a national scale which have voiced their concern at the highest levels.[1] On an intuitive level, at least, this concern of parents for the mental and behavioural welfare of their youngsters, who may be exposed to thousands of commercials during their young lives, should not be regarded as trivial or unwarranted. Very often, the standards of production of television advertisements are equal to or even better than those in programmes and consequently their impact on the attention of the television audience should not be underrated or ignored. Furthermore, the faces and voices prevalent on television advertisements are often the same as those seen and heard in other contexts on popular television shows. One ought not to be too surprised, therefore, if young children confuse programmes and advertisements.

Given these similarities between programming and advertising, how difficult is it for children to distinguish between the two and how susceptible are they, therefore, to commercial appeals broadcast on television? The answer to this question is not certain because research in this field lags behind that on effects of other types of television content such as violence or sex – at least in the academic sphere. There is, of course, ample research conducted by advertising agencies and others involved in the advertising industry. This proprietary research rarely surfaces outside the agencies responsible for conducting it and seldom enters into discussion about the efficacy of television advertising. Although increasing numbers of academic studies have emerged during the 1970s and 1980s, our knowledge of the ways children are affected cognitively, emotionally and behaviourally by commercial messages on television is still limited.

Many parents and critics fear that children are particularly susceptible to commercial appeals because young viewers lack the necessary cognitive skills to defend themselves against what are often highly attractive and skilfully worded persuasive messages.[2] Other undesirable consequences of television commercials listed by their critics are that they lead youngsters to pressure parents into purchasing products unnecessarily and thereby often create conflict within the family, and that the number and nature of televised commercials to which children are exposed before they leave school are such that they are likely to be socialised into over-materialistic ways.

The first published work in the area of advertising was an American study carried out with 400 children aged 6 to 12 years, who were asked to list as many products advertised on television as they could remember. They were given fifteen minutes to do this. Even the youngest could recall some products, with children generally producing an average of twenty. The three most recalled products were detergents, beer and cigarettes, which were not directly advertised to children.[3]

A few years later, a book called *The Hidden Persuaders* emerged which painted a picture of people – the innocents – being manipulated by advertisers who used sophisticated selling techniques to persuade people to buy things they do not really need anyway. This was a highly rhetorical statement about the impact of advertising, but not effectively backed up with hard evidence. Nevertheless it set the scene for future thinking about advertising.[4]

CHILDREN'S REACTIONS TO ADVERTISING

Many early instances of advertising adopted a very simplistic understanding of the way advertising works. Where children are concerned, for instance, there is assumed to be a straightforward cause-and-effect relationship between the advertised message and the behaviour it recommends. In other words, on watching an advertisement on television children may be directly encouraged to go out and buy the advertised or attempt to persuade someone else – a parent perhaps – to buy it for them. This view of the influence of advertising fails to take into account the full complexities of the process, however. It ignores children's ability to process and evaluate advertisements, just as they do with programmes, prior to deciding whether or not to believe the commercial appeal or to act upon it.

Growing concern about children's susceptibility to more subtle messages in advertisements has, on occasions, prompted broadcast regulators to act against specific commercials, as witnessed when the Independent Broadcasting Authority, which regulated advertising on television in the UK in the 1980s, judged a commercial for Levi's 501 jeans as too sexy to be shown during children's programmes or on Saturday afternoons. One writer warned that such steps reflected a reaction to a trend in the pursuit of selling whereby the barriers are being shifted to a point many will find unacceptable.[5]

The first advertisement in the Levi's campaign, Nick Kamen's launderette commercial, was marked with a touch more humour than sex. The next, however, used a 14-year-old girl, shown after parting from her boyfriend, lying on her back dressed in T-shirt and knickers, suggestively pulling on the Levi's he had left her. A third commercial in the series had a muscular stranger coming downstairs in an American Midwestern boarding house, dressed only in shirt and underpants. He smoulders at the owner's daughter as the father looks on with suspicion; he sighs as he pulls on his Levi's taken from the fridge and then rides off into the desert, leaving an obviously aroused woman behind him.

The advertisement was extremely well made – but to what end? It is not just increasingly explicit sex that advertisers are using; it is a whole range of immoral practices, from attempted murder to squeezing a man out of his job. Two more examples illustrate this point.

In a commercial for Pirelli, again a beautifully crafted little piece of drama, the male protagonist set out in his car – but the woman in his life had tampered with the brakes. Thanks to Pirelli tyres, he survives.

Then, there was the bought woman in a Volkswagen commercial. This time the mistress walked out; symbolically she threw away a succession of expensive gifts including the expensive fur. But she kept the keys to the Volkswagen Golf.

The concern among some writers is that, while using 'immorality' to sell goods, the advertisers are also selling the immorality itself. Another worry is that audiences will grow accustomed to this style of advertising and be less aware of its gradual influence upon them. To what extent is this alarmist viewpoint substantiated by what is known about the effect of advertising on children – and with what children themselves know and understand and have to say about advertisements?

Increasingly, research has revealed that children exhibit a growing sophistication about advertising during their formative years. Although early on in life they may have no proper understanding of the dishonest character of advertisements and their purposes compared with programmes, this soon changes. Research has shown that advertising does not directly influence its audience. It may, nonetheless, play an important role in children's consumer socialisation, teaching them consumer values and ways of expressing them.[6] The potential impact of the message can be determined by a whole range of other factors. In this chapter we shall examine the nature and extent of television advertising's influence on children. We can begin by examining some of the substantiated facts about children's experience with television advertising and then explore what children themselves think about television commercials.

MAKING SENSE OF ADVERTISING

Although advertising is designed ultimately to manipulate consumer behaviour, this influence is mediated by what people think about advertising *per se* as well as about specific advertisements. Before a commercial can change people's minds about what to buy or encourage them to favour one brand over another, its message must be taken in and examined. Viewers must pay attention to their TV sets for this to happen. They must pay sufficient attention that they are able to remember the commercial or the elements of it that the advertiser hopes will make their product more appealing. However, the influence process also depends on what viewers know about the aims of advertising and on how much they believe what advertisements tell them.

Thus, in the context of the impact of television advertising upon children, several important questions need to be considered.

- Are children aware of advertisements as distinct from programmes?
- Do children understand what advertisements are about?
- Do children remember and believe what advertisements tell them?
- Are children likely to respond to advertising by wanting the things advertised for themselves?

CHILDREN'S DISTINCTIVE AWARENESS OF TV ADVERTISING

Before advertising can affect young viewers, it must impinge upon their consciousness in some way. Although there has in the past been concern about the effects of subliminal advertising, solid support for the efficacy of this sort of advertising from research has failed to materialise. In any case, the use of subliminal images or messages in TV advertising in the UK is outlawed.

Even though presented in a normal, perceptible way, children may not necessarily notice advertisements. If they look away from the screen for a minute or two, the message may easily be missed. Another problem, especially with very young viewers, is that they simply may fail to make the distinction between programmes and advertisements. The two may run together as an indistinguishable montage of images and voices.

Children's attention to TV advertising can be measured in a variety of ways. Children can be asked directly whether they watch and remember advertisements, or parents can be questioned about their children's reactions to TV ads. A more objective method used by some researchers has been to make their own direct observations of children's attention to the screen during ad breaks. The latter have the advantage that they monitor children continuously while watching television and that running logs are kept by independent observers of levels of attention during actual viewing. Evidence derived from the reports of children or their parents may lack the same degree of measuring because it relies heavily on the often fallible memories and dubious vigilance of respondents when required to monitor their own or others' viewing behaviours.

Parents, for example, have been found to provide higher estimates of children's attention to TV adverts than independent, continuous observations typically viewed. Both types of evidence, however, have indicated an increase in attention to screen during ad breaks with age. Thus, when, in one American study, sixty-five mothers were invited to report on the home viewing of their children (aged 5 to 12 years), they indicated lower levels of attention among younger children than among older ones.[7]

Younger children also tended to pay less attention throughout the advertisements as compared with older children. Children aged 5–8 years were at full attention 67 per cent of advertisement viewing time, and 9- to 12-year-olds averaged full attention 75 per cent of the viewing time. Older children's attention when a series of advertisements was presented in a block tended to drop towards the end. Older children tended to make more critical comments about adverts they saw than did younger children.

In an observational study in which researchers placed video cameras in family homes, somewhat lower levels of attention to television advertisements were found. They found that children up to 10 years old whom they observed watched adverts only 40 per cent of the time they were on air, while 11- to 19-year-olds watched them 55 per cent of the time they were on.[8]

Even direct observations of children's television viewing by trained monitors do not always produce the same impressions of young viewers' attention to the screen. Much depends on the setting in which viewing takes place. For example, observations made of children's viewing in schools have found higher levels of attention to advertisements than ones made in home viewing contexts.

Another indication of children's awareness of advertising is their ability to recognise or recall it. As with their level of attention to ad breaks, children's memory for advertisements changes with age. As they get older, children become better at remembering adverts and are able to recall more about different TV ads.

It would appear that there is a major change in the type of information retained from advertisements between the ages of 5–6 and 8–9 years.

Younger children tend to recall single elements from the commercials whereas older children tend to recall more product and commercial plot-line information. Recognition (measured by selection from a range of alternatives) seems to be uniformly poor, ranging from a level slightly above chance for 5- to 6-year-olds to an average level of 70 per cent for 8- to 9-year-olds (based on a chance recognition score of 33 per cent). There can be a high degree of variability across children, however.[9]

Despite generally low recognition and recall scores, young children seem to find certain features of advertisements more salient than others. In particular, commercial slogans, jingles or unusual, humorous elements may stand out far more than brand names.[10]

CHILDREN'S UNDERSTANDING OF TV ADVERTISING

There are two principal issues concerning children's understanding of TV advertising. The first concerns their understanding of what TV advertising is about. What is the purpose of advertising? How does it differ from programming in its aims? A second important feature of children's understanding relates to how much they are able to follow and interpret the appeals made by adverts for the commodities being advertised.

For children to understand the purpose of TV advertising, however, they must be capable of making a series of important discriminations. They must be able to:

- distinguish advertisements as separate from programmes;
- recognise a sponsor as the source of the commercial message;
- perceive the idea of an intended audience for the message;
- understand the 'symbolic' nature of products, character and contextual representation in commercials;
- to discriminate by example between product as advertised and products as experienced.

When interviewed or questioned in general terms about TV advertising, children's ability to describe the differences between advertisements and programmes has been found to improve considerably with age. Usually, very young children below 8 years old express a certain amount of confusion when asked to define the nature of television commercials. Older children, on the other hand, are able to distinguish between programme and commercial material on the basis of an overall understanding of each message's meaning.[11]

To measure children's awareness of TV advertisements as distinct entities from programmes without relying purely on youngsters' personal accounts, some researchers have monitored changes in children's levels of visual attention whilst they are actually watching television. One consistent finding is a tendency often for children to exhibit a drop in visual attention to the screen during an advertising break compared with their amount of looking at the screen while watching prior programming. In addition, children's looking at the screen may continue to decline across the ad break and over the course of subsequent breaks in a programme. Age differences are, once again, very apparent.[12]

The smallest decreases in attention tend to occur among the youngest viewers (5- to 7-year-olds) who displayed higher and more stable levels of visual attention to both advertisements and programmes than do older children. Young and immature children may exhibit a higher degree of stability in their visual attention to programmes and advertisements, whereas older children show a higher degree of differentiation in when they look attentively at the screen.[13]

In one illustration of children's patterns of looking at television across different kinds of material, one group of researchers showed groups of 6-, 8- and 10-year-old children a fifteen-minute television programme in which was embedded a commercial break consisting of two advertisements. While viewing this material the children themselves were videotaped and their attention to the programme and the advertisements was assessed. Attention dropped during the time the first advertisement appeared, and decreased even further during the course of the second advertisement. This effect occurred whether the advertisements were presented in the context of a live-action or an animated programme and was observed over eight different types of advertisements, indicating that it was unlikely that the drop in attention was specific to particular kinds of advertising or programme content.[14]

Studies which use children's visual attention to the television screen as a measure of their ability to discriminate between programmes and advertisements can be difficult to interpret. Attention to an advertisement or a programme may shift because of differences in certain physical features, such as the kinds of images being shown, the background music and so on. This does not necessarily mean that children are making a conceptual distinction between an 'advertisement' and a 'programme' and thus choose mentally to switch off when the ad break occurs.[15] The children's attention may shift according to how interesting or boring they find what they are watching and not just because they know what is coming next (i.e. an ad break) and therefore do not need to watch.

Although shifts in amount of looking do occur among children when watching programmes and advertisements, these may signify little more than superficial perceptual responses to these two types of material and may not confidently be interpreted to represent a deeper, conceptual differentiation between advertising and programming.[16] A more precise measure of children's understanding of television advertising is needed which explores what they actually assimilate from individual commercials.

The level of attention children pay to television advertising can be influenced by a variety of production features residing within the commercial itself. Visual scene changes and changes in the nature or amplitude of the soundtrack can affect audiences' attention.[17] Advertisements which contain a large number of visual changes in scene, action and characters, and which have fast-paced production features – such as rapid cutting between camera shots, zooming in and out of close-ups and fading the picture up or down to a brighter or darker level of lighting – can hold the child's visual attention. On an auditory level, lively music, sound effects, unusual voices, children's and women's voices and laughter are all effective for maintaining attention.[18]

Children often monitor television advertisements via the soundtrack even when they are looking away from the screen. When their interest is triggered, they will turn to look at the screen again and maintain eye contact with it for as long as the commercial engages their interest.[19]

Music plays an important role in this process since it may both attract and hold the young viewer's attention, and increase the likelihood of repeat viewing and listening whenever the advertisement appears, enhancing its potential impact.[20]

Most studies, however, reveal that music is by no means an isolated element of a commercial, and only functions in relationship with other features of an advertisement, such as dialogue, type of voice, and visual elements. As a result of this, the salience and impact of music will vary from advertisement to advertisement, and it is not realistic to expect that the relationship between music and consumer response will be consistent.[21] For young people it is, of course, probably the type of music played during the advertisement that is of great significance.

WHAT DO CHILDREN REMEMBER FROM TV ADVERTS?

From the perspective of the advertiser, a successful advertising campaign is a memorable one because the opportunity to buy a product following its appearance on a television advertisement is usually delayed. Therefore, it is the information which the viewer has stored, and is subsequently able to retrieve from memory about the advertised brand, that will influence the decision whether or not to choose that brand rather than others from the same product category. However, measures of children's memory for advertising content may also provide an indication of how children come to understand the nature and purpose of advertisements as distinct from programmes.

It seems that, although there is generally no intent among young viewers to seek information from television commercials to use in a purchase decision (except perhaps at Christmas time when they may be looking for gift ideas), children may nevertheless use information which they have already learned from commercials when asking parents for specific products at a later date.[22] Advertising may also influence a child to buy a particular attractive or highly valued attribute rather than other brands of the same type. Children may remember certain aspects of TV adverts better than others. Furthermore, it seems that the better children are able to retain and understand factual and emotional appeals made about products by advertisements, the more they distinguish adverts from surrounding programmes.[23]

Researchers can sometimes underestimate children's understanding of television, however, especially when they use techniques which are insensitive to the subtleties of what children pick up from what they watch. One illustration of this is the way children are tested for what they can remember about adverts. Recall measures may not always be sufficient to tap memory (and therefore perhaps comprehension) performance of children on television commercials. When asked to recall freely, younger children may not always understand what is required of them and inevitably lack the skill to articulate their thoughts as clearly as older children. Instead, recognition scores may be a more sensitive means of measuring memory, especially among very young viewers. Fortunately, using recall, one study found that 8-year-olds showed considerably better overall memory for the product appeals contained in commercials than 3- to 4-year-olds. But, when recognition measures were used, this difference was substantially reduced as the percentage of younger viewers remembering the commercial products elements increased substantially.[24] Another study provided children aged between 4 and 10 years with photographs of animated presenter characters from either programmes or food commercials and asked them to identify the characters. On the basis of recognition scores, it was found that even children as young as 4 years could distinguish between animated characters as they appeared in programmes or commercials, and could also link those characters from food commercials to their respective products.[25]

Memory for advertising may be a significant factor at the point of purchase. Research suggests that when children have to choose a brand out of a wide range of largely similar products, one of the factors that will influence their choice will be the most salient advertisement for an available brand retrieved from memory, rather than the most recent television advertisement seen or heard.[26] The child's memory for advertisements, however, is a very complex issue. Brands do not simply exist in isolation in children's minds; they are clustered in groups of products having similar characteristics. Consequently, a commercial for one brand may increase the salience of related brands from the same product category.[27]

DISTINGUISHING ADVERTISEMENTS FROM PROGRAMMES

One significant aspect of children's understanding of television advertising is their ability to tell the difference between commercials and programmes. The suggestion made by some researchers – that with growing maturity and viewing experience children develop their own 'cognitive defences' against the influences of advertising – rests on an assumption that they can recognise a commercial in the first place.

Early signs that advertisements are distinguished from programmes emerged with the observation that children's level of visual attention would often shift when a programme broke for a commercial.[28]

Children's ability to make this distinction develops with age. It emerges, however, very early. A number of researchers have noted that by 5 years of age, most children can consistently distinguish advertisements from programmes.[29] One study found that 3- to 5-year-olds applied the terms 'programme' or 'commercial' correctly about two-thirds of the time when a videotape with programming and advertising was stopped at random points.[30] Research that does not rely on children's verbal abilities has found that children as young as 3 know the difference between television programmes and advertisements.[31]

The symbolic meaning of products grows stronger between the ages of 9 and 11. Children of this age have been found to possess the ability to describe the kind of child likely to own familiar products when photographs of these products are shown to them. Product symbolism tends to be stronger in girls than boys, and is better developed in middle-class children than working-class children. After the age of 9, children show steady improvement in understanding the ambiguous wording, humour and imagery found in advertisements.[32]

Children's ability to distinguish between programmes and advertisements on television can also be influenced by advertising-related factors. Sometimes these factors can make it easier for children to distinguish advertisements; on other occasions, such factors make it more difficult. The use of popular television characters or animated cartoon heroes in commercials may lead children to become more confused about what they are watching.[33] There is no universal agreement on this issue. At least one author has observed, however, that the use of licensed characters (such as Walt Disney characters or the Smurfs) within an advertisement removes some of the formal distinctive features of advertisements and may therefore lead to confusion among younger children as to whether they appear in an advertisement or a programme.[34]

Another phenomenon which has been considered within the current context is the existence of a wide variety of advertiser-initiated, product-related shows and programme sponsorship. Although these commercial and promotional schemes go beyond the usual form of spot advertising, they nevertheless represent a form of marketing designed to raise brand awareness among young consumers. Furthermore, for some observers, this form of commercialism represents an insidious kind of advertising in which the real purpose of ostensibly entertainment-oriented programming is little more than an extended advertisement for a product.[35]

The selling purpose of TV advertising

Another important aspect of children's understanding of TV advertising is the ability to recognise the selling motive of adverts. A key component of the selling motive is the persuasive intent of advertising. If children are unaware of the persuasive purpose of advertising, they could be more vulnerable to its influences.[36] Most researchers agree that the awareness of the purpose of television advertising is a very important step in the child's acquisition of the necessary skills to become advertising-literate.

There is consistent evidence that younger children who do not understand the persuasive intent of commercials are more likely to perceive them as truthful messages, whereas older children who can discern persuasive intent tend to express sceptical attitudes towards commercials. Results of various survey studies indicate that, below the age of 6, the vast majority of children cannot readily explain the selling purpose of advertising. Between the ages of about 5 and 9 years, the majority of children come to be able to recognise and explain the selling intent of advertising.[37]

In a British survey, when children were asked, 'What is the main reason they have advertisements on TV?', eight out of ten (80 per cent) replied that it is because the advertisers want to sell you something, while around one in eight (12 per cent) thought it is because they want you to know something. Fewer than one in ten (8 per cent) did not know. These responses did not differ by age or by social class, but they did differ by sex. The girls in the study were even more likely (84 per cent) than the boys (75 per cent) to indicate that the main purpose of advertisements was to sell something; the boys were more likely to indicate that they did not know the main purpose.[38]

Children's verbal replies to questions about what television advertisements are and why they are shown have thus revealed significant improvements in understanding. In all such studies, however, the apparent growth in understanding has to be weighed against the relative abilities of younger and older children to articulate the differences between programmes and advertisements, regardless of whether or not they actually make the distinction in their own minds.

Research in which understanding of the purpose of television advertisements has not relied on the children's verbal abilities, but in which children merely have to point at pictures in order to indicate what the character in a commercial wanted them to do, has revealed that, although the grasp of concepts improves with age, children as young as 3 years of age have exhibited some understanding of selling intent.[39]

Children's trust in TV advertising

Whilst understanding of the nature of TV advertisements appears to improve as children get older, belief in the truthfulness of advertising appeals tends to decline. Before they begin school, there is widespread belief among young viewers that TV adverts tell the truth all the time. While few believe this at age 8, hardly any still do at age 12.[40] The advertising industry can therefore begin to suffer from a credibility gap among quite young children.[41]

At the same time, children's attempts to influence parents to buy advertised products seen on television show a marked decline. In general, it seems that as children grow older they understand more completely the selling motive underlying television advertising and become less responsive to commercial appeals. Older children make more numerous and more refined judgements about television commercials and develop a cognitive mechanism against persuasion.

A survey of British children's views about TV advertising asked a national sample of 4- to 13-year-olds (over 500 children) if they thought that advertisements on television tell the truth. Only a few (6 per cent) thought that advertisements 'always' tell the truth, while rather more (15 per cent) thought that they 'quite often' are truthful. Most (60 per cent) felt that advertisements tell the truth 'sometimes'. Nearly one in five (18 per cent) thought that it is not common for advertisements to tell the truth, while a small number (2 per cent) felt that advertisements were never truthful. Perceived truth in advertising was not found to differ according to the sex or social class of the children, but age did make a difference. The youngest children were most likely to believe that advertisements told the truth, while older children became more sceptical.

Attention to advertisements would seem to vary across children. Around one in three (31 per cent) said that when advertisements come on they watch them all, while even more (37 per cent) said they watch most. Relatively fewer claim to be less attentive; fewer than one in five in each case said they watch around half the advertisements in a break (15 per cent) or watch just a few (18 per cent). None of the children said that they did not watch any. Responses to this question did not differ by age or social class, but there was a significant, although not large, difference between boys and girls. The girls reported greater attention to advertising than did the boys, a phenomenon which other research indicates carries over to adulthood.

Furthermore, amount of exposure to advertising was positively related to the perceived truthfulness of advertising; those who said they paid more attention to advertisements were also more likely to say they believed more of the advertisements. And those who said they were more attentive were also more likely either to give positive or negative opinions about advertising.[42]

Despite their scepticism, young consumers often have favourable attitudes towards specific advertisements.[43] A study carried out among children aged 9 and 10 in Belfast, Northern Ireland, found that two-thirds believed that advertisers tell the truth only some of the time. Despite this negative global opinion towards advertising, most of the children said they enjoyed particular advertisements, especially the ones featuring humour.[44]

DO CHILDREN WANT WHAT THEY SEE ADVERTISED ON TV?

Television advertising is designed to influence consumer behaviour either by encouraging consumers principally to switch from one brand to another or to remain loyal to the one they currently buy. To some extent, advertising may also be concerned with creating markets for new brands. When looking at possible influences of TV advertising on children, it is important to make certain crucial distinctions between them and adult consumers. Children do not always have the means to buy many advertised items. Although children today have more personal disposable income than at any time hitherto, they are often reliant on parents to buy things for them. This situation commonly changes with age. As they get into their teens, young consumers have money of their own to spend – either from part-time jobs or pocket money. They also have more freedom and independence to go out on their own than during earlier years. Thus new opportunities to spend open up to them. To some extent, therefore, advertisements may probably direct themselves at youngsters who have their own money to spend. Alternatively, advertising may operate through encouraging children to approach their parents with requests to purchase items.

Research in a number of different countries, including the United States, Britain and Japan, has indicated that children's requests for advertised products can result in conflicts within the family.[45]

A study by Adler and his colleagues asked more than 700 American children aged 4 to 10 years whether they urged their mothers to buy toys they had seen advertised on television. Children who were heavy viewers of television were more likely to ask for advertised products (40 per cent) than infrequent viewers (16 per cent).[46]

The amount of parental pestering that occurs can be reduced if children are more usually involved in family purchase decisions and if parents discuss television and advertising with them.[47]

The extent to which children ask their parents to buy them things they have seen advertised on TV can vary across items. Most researchers agree that children are more likely to make requests for products which are frequently consumed by them, such as breakfast cereals, snacks or sweets, or for products that are of particular interest to them, such as toys or those with special offers.[48]

Products which are usually requested also vary importantly according to the child's age, with requests for toys, breakfast cereals and sweets being more frequent with younger children (aged 5–7 years) and requests for clothing or records more frequent among children aged 11–12.[49] There is no firm evidence, however, that children necessarily become generally less demanding as they get older. It has been observed that requests for some toys advertised in the pre-Christmas period became less frequent, but this may simply reflect a declining interest in toys anyway as children grow older.[50] Requests for TV-advertised products which are relevant to children of all ages, such as snack foods and soft drinks, tend not to decline with age.

In Britain, one survey (referred to earlier), found, on asking a national sample of children whether they had asked their parents to buy them something they had seen in an advertisement on television, that 85 per cent said that they had, while just 15 per cent claimed not to have done. Asking for something they had seen advertised on television was done equally by boys and girls. However, there were differences by age and social class. For the age groups, there was a drop-off in such requests among older children: 97 per cent of 4- to 5-year-olds, 94 per cent of 6- to 7-year-olds, 86 per cent of 8- to 9-year-olds and 71 per cent of 10- to 13-year-olds claimed to have made such requests of their parents. For the social classes, there was a substantial lessening of such requests reported among the higher social classes. Requests were reported by 81 per cent of children from ABC1 households, by 84 per cent of C2 households and by 92 per cent of DE households. Some 66 per cent claimed that their parents had bought them something advertised on television after they had requested it. The rate of buying did not differ by sex, age or social class.

Those children who did report that their parents had bought something were asked what it was, and then their responses were grouped into several major product categories, constructed on the basis of the responses received. The distribution, by category, of items purchased was food/cereal (15 per cent), toys/dolls (44 per cent), toys/others (28 per cent) and all others (13 per cent). What was bought for the children did not differ by sex (note: Transformers were considered as male dolls) or by social class, but did differ by age. By age, the results are linear; that is, they increase or decrease consistently across the four age groups, with the following results: the oldest were more likely to have received a cereal purchase (21 per cent) by comparison with the youngest (7 per cent). The youngest were more likely to have received a toy/doll purchase (51 per cent vs 11 per cent) and a toy/other purchase (31 per cent vs 21 per cent). The oldest were more likely to have received some other purchase (15 per cent vs 6 per cent).[51]

To what extent do parents acquiesce to children's requests? From the same survey, most of the children reported that they had asked their parents to buy them something they had seen advertised on television; a sizeable majority of those making the request were granted it. The children were asked to identify one such product. In all, the children identified 161 different products that had been purchased at their request. Three different products dominated these purchases: My Little Pony was cited by forty-eight youngsters (9 per cent of all the youngsters in the survey);

Transformers were cited by forty-four (8 per cent); and Barbie products by thirty (6 per cent).

No other single product was cited by as many as twenty of the youngsters. However, twenty-six of them responded to the question with the generic term 'toys'. Eighty-nine children each cited one specific product, and thirty-two products each were cited by two children. The dominance of toys as the item requested from parents is apparent already; it is further emphasised by the fact that the next four most-mentioned products of parental-induced purchase were also toys – Care Bears (15), Star Wars (13), Sindy (12) and He-Man (12). A majority of the children specifically attributed a toy purchase requested by them of their parents to a television advertisement.

IS THERE A BEHAVIOURAL EFFECT OF TV ADVERTISING?

Research into the way children respond to television advertising is ultimately concerned with the impact advertising has upon children's behaviour. Does television advertising affect children's purchasing of goods? Two types of methodology have been applied to this problem: experimental research and survey research. The former attempts to manipulate children's exposure to television advertising in order to measure its direct effects upon their subsequent behaviour. The latter examines relationships between levels of advertising exposure over time and purchase behaviour patterns. Studies which have adopted an 'experimental' methodology have generally supported the view that the impact of television advertising on children is considerable, whereas survey research studies have more usually indicated that advertising effects operate at a fairly low level.

In experimental studies, children are allocated to various viewing conditions. Some of the children will generally be shown advertisements, usually for various kinds of toys or snacks. After being exposed to advertising materials under controlled viewing conditions, the children will be given an opportunity to select a snack or toy out of a range of items. The key findings rest on the product choices that are made. If there is a tendency to select those items for which commercials have just been seen, rather than items not featured in the commercials, such a result is taken as evidence of an effect for advertising.

There are a number of drawbacks to this kind of research. First, it does not actually examine children's *purchase* behaviour, but only deals with the child's choice out of a number of prizes which are offered as a free gift. Second, the effects that are measured are short-term effects, since the 'choosing phase' usually takes place immediately after exposure to the advertising. Third, it does not explore any of the processes that mediate between watching advertising and eventual product purchase. Fourth, it does not stimulate the natural activities of television viewing and consumer behaviour. Thus, experimental research suffers from having limited external validity.[52]

In contrast to experimental research, many researchers have used survey research to study the effects of advertising on children's purchase behaviour.[53] Most research studies that follow this approach emphasise that television advertising is only one of a large number of simultaneously interacting influences on children's purchase behaviour. Consequently, they tend to conclude that television commercials have only a minor role in influencing children's purchase behaviour.

Survey research tends to examine naturally occurring behaviour, not that under laboratory conditions. The weakness of survey research, however, lies in the difficulty of attributing causality, because assessing the direction of cause–effects relationships on the basis of correlational data is problematic.

Survey research studies also face other methodological problems. Rather than measuring actual behaviour, researchers using this approach tend to rely on respondents' self-reports about their behaviour. The accuracy of such reports depends on how sharp respondents' memories are.

Reports by children that they ask parents to buy them items advertised on TV, or from parents that their children make such requests, provide subjective evidence of an impact of TV advertising in young people's consumer behaviour. It is difficult to check the reliability of this evidence, however, since it is dependent on the ability of respondents to provide accurate accounts from memory that such advertising-related behaviours occur.

A more objective way of assessing the effects of TV advertising on consumerism is to examine links between research exposure to this advertising and the level or nature of consumption for particular commodities. In relation to young people, one area that has come in for close scrutiny in recent years is the role of advertising in alcoholic drinks consumption. Increased concerns about excessive drinking amongst young people, and particularly about under-age drinking, have led to calls for more stringent controls over alcohol advertising.

There is evidence that alcoholic drinks adverts are among the most popular advertisements on TV. This has led some critics to argue that advertising plays a significant part in encouraging children and teenagers to experiment with drink. A number of published studies, which include large-scale surveys and controlled experiments, have attempted to produce evidence to clarify whether or not this influence occurs.

One American survey of teenagers aged 13 to 17 used questionnaires which respondents had to complete themselves and which asked them about their use of various mass media, their personality profiles, family background, alcohol consumption patterns and attitudes towards drinking. Virtually no effects of exposure to televised alcohol advertising on level of consumption emerged for the sample as a whole. However, certain orientations or predispositions to advertising were shown to make a difference to advertising influences.

Teenagers who were highly motivated to attend to advertising, because they thought they could learn something from it about how to behave in social situations, were found to be influenced by exposure to alcoholic drinks advertisements. Likewise, among teenagers who attended to advertisements as a means of vicariously participating in desired activities and lifestyles, there was a statistically significant effect of advertising on consumption.[54]

There are some important caveats to consider, however. First, even under those conditions in which a significant advertising effect was found, the magnitude of the effect was largely trivial. In no case was more than 1.5 per cent of the net variance in consumption associated with advertising exposure. Second, the fact that particular orientations or attitudes to advertising facilitate even the minimal advertising effects found in this research points to the role of parents in socialising children towards media use and consumption behaviour. Developing 'resistance' to commercial persuasions in adopting particular orientations towards advertising is part of the process by which children learn rational consumption attitudes and behaviours from their parents.

Survey research generally identifies the causes of consumer choices as deriving from a variety of factors, including consumers' own personality characteristics, abilities to weigh up different sources of information about products and brands, family background (with all the examples of consumer behaviour experienced in that context), current fashions and peer pressures to conform to these trends, as well as disposable income (which covers the bottom line of being able to purchase).[55] They stress that, quite often, effects from television advertisements on children's product and brand preferences, and eventual purchase behaviour, will be mediated by the way parents and children talk to one another, by styles of parental discipline, and by how members of the family in general interact with one another.[56]

The role of parents and society is illustrated by the fact that a product which is unacceptable to the parent will actually be vetoed, and that there are many examples of products (e.g. new sweets) which failed to establish a market among children despite being heavily advertised.[57] Even if advertising can persuade children to try out a new product on one occasion, the product itself will have to provide the necessary reasons for the child to buy it again. If the product fails to meet the child's expectations, it will not be bought a second time, regardless of the total amount of advertising devoted to it.[58]

Chapter 10

Does TV affect children's health orientation?

A knowledge base is being cultivated concerning modern diseases and disabilities which places emphasis upon prevention and self-care more than professional medical treatment and costly cures. If patients can learn to take care of themselves, they will stay healthier, avoid illness and the soaring medical costs that accompany medical treatments.

In the world of fast-developing communications technologies, families will have access to greater amounts of information that will help them to manage their own health. Television may be one vital source of such information. To some extent, though, it may already represent a source of influence through its factual programmes about health-care, medicine and medical developments and drama programmes centred on the work of fictional doctors and hospitals. In the pre-electronic media era, medicine was generally family-centred. Family folklore and recipes for medicinal compounds and remedies embodied preventative and curative practices.[1] In one sense, we are witnessing a return to the family-centredness in medicine and health-related matters through the family's use of information and advice sources provided by the mass media.

Television has been acknowledged as an important source of information about health and medical matters for many years.[2] In Britain, documentary and magazine programmes about health and medicine have been prominent in mainstream television schedules for the past twenty years.

While television has been used as a channel through which to provide direct communication to people about specific health topics, it also serves as a wider source of health information which viewers may acquire incidentally as a consequence of watching programmes that contain portrayals with health-related implications. Portrayals of illness, the medical profession, and patient behaviour in television drama (both serious and comedy) can leave their mark. Indirect messages about health may also derive from portrayals of lifestyle behaviours such as eating patterns, smoking, alcohol consumption, dangerous driving or use of seatbelts, illicit drug use, and sexual promiscuity.

Although many infectious diseases have been conquered as a result of advances in medical science, many chronic illnesses such as heart disease, stroke, high blood pressure and hypertension, in which lifestyle can play a major part, account for substantial numbers of deaths every year. Nutrition and dietary patterns, smoking and alcohol consumption are included among the major risk factors for lifestyle disease. The growth of concern about the spread of sexually transmitted diseases such as AIDS have drawn increased attention to sexual behaviour as a lifestyle 'risk' factor.

Medicine and health are common themes in television's fictional drama programming. It was observed quite a few years ago that, in American soap operas, up to half of all characters may be involved in health-related events of some kind.[3] Problems depicted most often include psychiatric disorders, heart disease, pregnancies, car accidents and infectious diseases. Medical drama series have a long history and have proved to be among the best-liked television shows.[4]

There has been concern in particular about television's portrayal of certain kinds of behaviour which, although often socially acceptable, nevertheless are known to cause physical harm when indulged in to excess – as is often shown on television. The depiction of smoking, drinking alcohol and the use of other drugs has given rise to concern because of the potential social learning which might occur among young viewers.[5]

Another aspect of health and medicine shown commonly on television is the health profession and the treatment of ill-health or physical injury. American research has indicated that in general there tend to be many more health or medical professionals in American television serials than in real life.[6] Television doctors tend to be portrayed as highly competent and nearly always make correct diagnoses, even though their patients often withhold vital diagnostic information from them.[7] Medical dramas have been very popular with audiences. American series such as *Dr Kildare*, *Ben Casey*, *Marcus Welby M.D.*, *St. Elsewhere*, *ER*, and *Chicago Hope* have attracted large audiences on both sides of the Atlantic. UK productions such as *Peak Practice*, *Casualty* and *Medics* have been major ratings successes in Britain. Anecdotal evidence has indicated that viewers often take these fictional series seriously and may write in to the leading characters, the actors playing those roles, or to the producers, requesting medical advice.[8] Thus medical dramas would appear to have the potential to exert widespread influence in relation to public knowledge and beliefs about illness, medical treatment and health care.

The potential role of television in shaping young people's health beliefs, attitudes and related behaviours is considered by some researchers to derive from stereotyped patterns of health-related portrayals on television and the observation that many viewers watch television non-selectively.[9]

In establishing the effects that television might have upon young viewers' health-related knowledge and habits, therefore, it is important, first of all, to look at how health and medical matters are displayed on television and then to find out if there are any links between what viewers see on screen and the beliefs, attitudes and behavioural intentions they hold.

GENERAL HEALTH PORTRAYALS

A variety of health and related issues occur on television. Coverage of health issues can occur in specially produced factual programmes as well as featuring as central or peripheral aspects of television fiction. Television can provide information about illnesses and the causes of ill-health. It can portray health-promoting and health-damaging behaviours. It can also show how the medical profession works. Thus, viewers can, potentially, apprehend a wide range of health and related messages from television.

Television has been used as a communication channel by health campaigns, and these messages often take the form of public service announcements. Health campaigns may also be promoted through special television factual productions, advertisements and fictional dramatisations. These vehicles have been used to convey messages about heart disease, sexually transmitted diseases, smoking addiction and alcohol abuse, family planning and personal safety. Television has provided information about many types of disease such as cancer, stroke, hepatitis, venereal disease, AIDS and child-associated illnesses. Some diseases have clearly attracted more attention than others among broadcasters, and health campaigns have, more often than not, achieved mixed success in getting their messages across.[10]

The high profile attained by certain diseases such as AIDS has drawn greater attention to health-related topics in more recent years. Brief televised public service messages on heart disease, smoking and crisis centres have been more helpful. Despite these efforts, information about most major health issues such as cancer, stroke, hepatitis, venereal disease, child-care, lead poisoning and family planning has not been very comprehensive.

Studies of peak-time and weekend daytime programming on major American television networks, for example, found that dramatic pro-grammes were dominated by themes involving action, power and danger. In many action-adventure series, leading characters could often be seen behaving in ways which put their health and safety at risk. Even so, few accidental fatalities were seen to occur as a result of high-speed car chases, use of firearms and other dangerous pursuits.[11]

EARLY OBSERVATIONS

Health has featured as a theme on television for many years. Early on, however, it was observed that few television characters appeared to suffer ill-health. One study of American television in the 1950s found that, out of a sample of 1,700 fictional characters catalogued during one week's programming, only one suffered from a physical illness and just twelve had a serious mental illness. Only five of these characters died natural deaths, with most being killed in violent incidents.[12]

Other American researchers noted that substantial numbers of fictional programmes on US network television have either focused, or at least touched upon, health and related issues, where such issues have included depictions of physical or mental illness, medical treatment, doctors, smoking or health in general.[13] Television fiction does tend to dramatise health and illness, however. One study found that patients portrayed on television were usually those suffering from complaints requiring intensive medical care and treatment. Fictional medical practitioners tended to care for their patients' emotional well-being as much as their physical condition, often getting more involved in their private lives than doctors in real life would normally be expected to do. Comic elements in situation comedies and emotional relationships in soap operas were found to obscure the small amounts of specific health information such programmes would actually contain.[14]

In the National Institute of Mental Health (NIMH) report, *Television and Behaviour*, George Gerbner and his colleagues urged health-care professionals to examine the health messages contained within television entertainment programming in order to understand the images portrayed on television regarding health.[15] They argued that, in utilising television in the service of successful health campaigns, it is important to be aware of the full range of health-related messages already presented in programmes and advertisements. Not all of these (often implicit) health messages could be expected to reinforce positive health campaigns.

In examining general health messages on television, these researchers noted that prime-time television characters were rarely shown to have any type of physical impairment; in fact, almost none even wore glasses. Only 2 per cent of major characters were physically handicapped. They tended to be older, less positively presented, more likely to be victimised, and were almost never shown on children's programmes. Characters suffering from mental disorders, however, did appear on prime-time programmes with some frequency – about 17 per cent of prime-time programmes involved a depiction or theme of mental illness.

Moreover, about 3 per cent of major characters were identified as mentally ill and, in late evening programmes, this percentage doubled. The mentally ill were also disproportionately depicted both as perpetrators and victims of violence. Mental illness was also found to be closely connected with aggressive tendencies amongst major drama characters. These profiles were observed to reinforce early studies of mass media depictions of mental ill-health which were interpreted as cultivating a stereotype that the mentally ill are dangerous.[16]

In an analysis of the most watched fictional scenes on American prime-time television during the 1979–1980 season, researchers found that medical and health-related content appeared with considerable frequency. Health-related scenes averaged 3.3 per episode and 5.5 times per hour on prime-time programming. These incidents usually involved older adults, young children and women. One particularly interesting observation was the apparent lack of concern among patients or medical professionals about the cost of medical treatment.[17]

Elsewhere, researchers have observed that television portrayals connected with health and medical matters bore little resemblance to the significant issues which characterised real life; principally, lack of attention to chronic illnesses, rising medical costs, and competition for patients privately able to pay for treatment. One-third of illness-related coverage was found to occur in television advertisements for pharmaceutical products, especially cold and pain remedies. Peak-time programmes accounted for another third of coverage, daytime serials made up almost one-fifth, news magazines more than one-tenth, and evening news broadcasts less than one-twentieth of the coverage. Whenever illness was featured, however, it tended to take centre stage.[18]

DIET AND NUTRITION

Eating and drinking are commonly shown on television entertainment programmes. In popular soap operas and drama serials, dialogue often takes place around the dinner table or over breakfast. Food products are also among the most frequently advertised items on television. Both types of content have been acknowledged as having potential effects upon young people's dietary habits, with certain health-related consequences. Media researchers have tried to establish the nature of the messages about diet and nutrition that are conveyed explicitly or implicitly by programmes and advertisements, and the impact such messages might have upon nutrition-related attitudes and dietary behaviours.

The role of advertisements

The source of concern relating to the possible effects of advertising upon children's and teenagers' diets stems in the first instance from the observation that young viewers may be exposed to thousands of commercials on television every year. Even twenty years ago, when there were far fewer television channels than today, it was noted that an American child might see 22,000 television advertisements each year, 5,000 of them for food products, over half of which were high-calorie, high-sugar, low-nutrition items.[19] At least half of the advertising in children's programmes was found to be for sugared cereals and sweets, usually present as snacks to eat between meals.[20] Indeed, sugar-laden products promoted by most food advertisements on children's television were of precisely those kinds that the

US Senate Select Committee on Nutrition and Human Needs urged should be reduced in children's diets.[21] Other observers reported that less than one in ten television advertisements on US network television generally presented healthy foods such as fruits and bread; most were devoted to mass-produced, packaged and marketed foodstuffs of fairly low nutritional value.[22]

Even with legislative restrictions on the amount and types of advertising permitted in children's programmes, the number of advertisements on television continued to increase. Thus, children, by the late 1980s, could be exposed to many more advertisements on television than previously.[23]

The kinds of products advertised in commercials in children's programmes continued to be dominated by toys, cereals, sweets and snack foods, and fast-food restaurants.[24] While toy commercials may dominate in the two months leading up to Christmas, food commercials tend to dominate for the rest of the year. Very often, these advertised foods are highly sugared products such as pre-sweetened cereals, cakes, sweets, soda and biscuits, rather than healthy food such as fruit or vegetables.[25]

The evidence about television advertising indicates that it presents a variety of food product choices to children, but hardly promotes a healthy diet. The food products which are predominantly advertised on television tend to be high in sugar and fat content and low in nutritional value. The question arises, therefore, as to what this kind of advertising teaches children about food and eating. Television advertising may affect children's knowledge, attitudes or behaviour. In the first instance, what impact does this advertising have upon children's nutrition-related knowledge?

One view is that if children repeatedly see advertisements for snack foods or foods with high sugar content from an early age, they may develop limited ideas about what represents a balanced nutritional diet. The research evidence on this point is by no means conclusive, however. Indeed, some research suggests that children may develop clear ideas about what the relative nutritional benefits of different foods are (including sweets and snacks), which may be unrelated to levels of exposure to television advertising for these foods.[26] Sweet, snack foods were associated with obesity, dental caries and being sick. Although many children clearly eat and enjoy such foods, they realise that they should not exist on a diet which comprises nothing else.

Evidence from another study indicated that children aged 8 to 11 years showed poorer nutritional knowledge the more they were reportedly exposed to television advertising. One interpretation of this finding was that the kinds of nutritional phrases used in advertisements such as 'part of a good breakfast' or 'fortified with essential vitamins' failed to get through to children of this age, or simply confused them.[27]

Nutritional messages within television commercials are assimilated by children, who evaluate food products accordingly. One study experimentally manipulated the way a particular food product was extolled within a television commercial. In one version, the product was described as being 'chocolatey, rich and sweet', while in another version it was said to be 'healthful, vitaminy and nutritious'. Afterwards, children aged 5–9 years who had seen the nutritional version were more likely to describe the product as having high nutritional value compared with same-age children who watched the other version.[28]

Children's abilities to identify the health risks associated with certain food products varies with age. Younger children are less capable than older children, for example, of identifying that sugared food consumption is related to tooth decay. Thus, advertisements for sugared foods are less likely to be critically appraised by younger children on the basis that such foods may cause dental health problems.[29]

Further evidence has indicated that different kinds of advertising messages have different effects upon children's food preferences and consumption patterns. Regular exposure to advertising for sugared food products was linked to greater consumption of these products by children. Exposure to advertising for healthy foods (or non-sugared foods) tended to dampen enthusiasm for sugared foods to some extent. Educational programmes which promoted nutritional food consumption were also found to reduce the impact of advertising for sugared foods. Many of these observed effects, however, were only measured in the short term and did not establish whether such educational material exerted longer-term effects upon children's nutritional knowledge and food preferences.[30]

The role of programmes

Food consumption is emphasised not only in advertisements but also in programmes. The general impression, however, is that nutritional patterns depicted in mainstream programming depict anything but a balanced and relaxed style of eating. On American prime-time drama, for example, three-quarters of all characters were found to be depicted eating or drinking or talking about doing so.[31] These behaviours occurred, on average, nine times an hour. Much eating involved snacks consumed in a hurry rather than relaxed eating at a table. The diet was seldom nutritionally balanced and frequently consisted of fast food. Snacking behaviour was found to be particularly frequent in children's programmes, where regular meals were seldom depicted and snacks most often comprised high-calorie, high-fat food.

Overeating and obesity is a health problem for many people in modern Western societies. It represents a problem whose seeds may be sown in childhood, when eating patterns and food preferences are initially socialised. On television, however, being overweight seldom seems to be a problem. Despite the fact that not many fictional characters on television eat a balanced, nutritional diet, relatively few suffer from weight problems.[32] Children and young people were rarely overweight, despite television's emphasis upon high-sugar, high-fat-content foods for young people.

Television programmes may contain many subtle, indirect messages about health that derive from the lifestyles often depicted. Health portrayals embedded within the content of dramatic and entertainment programmes may provide a source of example to young people, and may play a part in shaping their early eating and drinking habits.

The impact of general entertainment programming may be incidental and subtle compared with the effects of advertising, which directly promotes certain forms of food products. However, programmes can also be utilised in a more deliberate fashion to promote healthy eating. One American study presented children with a full-length television programme called *Fat Albert* that carried the message that junk food is bad and fruit and vegetables are good. This programme used animation and comedy to get its message across. Even when the programme was embedded with commercials for sugared foods, it was effective at reducing the number of sugared foods the children chose from a range of options.[33]

DRINKING

The social learning argument has been applied to depictions of alcohol consumption on television. Portrayals of heavy consumption of alcohol in association with successful personal or professional outcomes for characters on television may promote the impression that heavy drinking is a socially desirable behaviour. The evidence of the real world is that, while moderate alcohol consumption (principally wine consumption) may have health-promoting effects, excessive drinking may result in damaged relationships and physical damage to self or others.

The damage associated with the use (or abuse) of alcoholic drinks is one of the most pressing public health issues of the day. Although the use of alcohol is well integrated into the social fabric and is a regular part of daily living for a large number of people, the consequences of drinking to excess can be far-reaching and severe. Over the past ten years, there has been a steadily growing concern about the role that television might play in socialising drinking habits, especially among young people. Once again, there has been concern about the particular roles played in this context by both advertising and programming.

Emphasis has been placed especially upon the potential influence of television advertising for alcoholic beverages. Although television commercials for these products are aimed at adult markets, a number of survey studies have revealed the popularity of advertisements, in particular for various brands of beer and lager, among children and teenagers.[34]

In addition to the alcoholic drinks advertising on television, the depiction of drinking behaviour in programmes is also a source of concern. On television, although as many as one-third of characters drink alcohol, few are depicted with drink problems.[35] Alcohol consumption is most often linked with leading male characters and is often done at home. There is a view that such depictions of alcohol consumption in popular programmes may precipitate increased drinking among young viewers. The association of attractive lifestyles or characters with drinking may encourage viewers, especially young ones, to believe that alcohol goes hand in glove with being wealthy and successful. Through such associations, it has been argued, alcoholic drinks may be perceived in a more attractive light. Although it has been shown that many television programmes contain extensive portrayals of alcohol use, empirical evidence concerning the effects of such material on actual alcohol consumption is inconclusive.

Effects of programme portrayals

Research into the depiction of alcohol consumption in television programmes derives largely from the United States and covers the past quarter of a century. A small number of studies have been conducted in other countries, including the United Kingdom and Australia. Early studies in the USA covered relatively small samples of programmes and revealed that mainstream television programmes contained anything from one to three acts of drinking an hour.[36] These scenes were divided equally between actual drinking events and talk about drinking. Rates of drinking and related behaviour or verbal references to drink could vary dramatically across different types of programme. Quiz and game shows might contain less than one such incident an hour on average, while soap operas might average between eight and nine such incidents.[37] During the late 1970s, the rate of occurrence of alcohol consumption portrayals on American television increased significantly, especially in peak-time fictional programming.[38]

In the context of the possible influences of drinking portrayals on television, however, the nature of drinking behaviour is probably more important than simply how much of it is shown. What kinds of examples of drinking are shown? Generally, drinking was depicted most often as a social activity, consumed on its own among friends. Secondly, it was depicted as a supplement to eating, taken over a meal. Thirdly, it was depicted in connection with business discussions. Drinking alone was relatively rare, as were incidents of drunkenness and of motor-vehicle accidents associated with being over the limit.[39]

Drinking portrayals on television did not always result in positive outcomes for those involved. While many of the consequences of drinking were benign, others were not. Unwanted effects included: strained relationships with spouses, family members, friends, bosses and co-workers; danger to self where drinkers put their own health and safety at risk; harm to others, including involvement in crime and violence, or accidents with cars or other machinery; embarrassment or a hangover; and loss of status to the drinker such as loss of spouse, friendships or job.[40]

There has been some indication that the subtle messages about drinking carried by programmes may be incompatible with accepted cultural norms or standards of public health. Among the problem portrayals are: characters turning to drink to face a crisis or escape from tension; failure to disapprove strongly enough of alcohol abuse; inability of characters to decline a drink; and the absence of consequences of alcohol abuse which are known to occur in real life.[41]

British research covering two weeks of peak-time television broadcasts on the four major television channels found that approximately two-thirds of programmes monitored contained some visual or verbal reference to alcohol, while actual consumption of alcohol was portrayed in nearly one-third of the programmes.[42] Most of the images of alcohol appeared in fictional programmes, with soap operas having the highest frequency of alcohol portrayal. Fictional programmes in general depicted over three scenes per hour showing characters drinking alcohol, while in soap operas this average increased to over five acts of drinking per hour. Two out of every three drinks consumed by a soap character contained alcohol. Thus, in programmes which attracted the largest audiences, alcohol was the single most prominent drink consumed. Drinking in these programmes was generally dealt with as a natural part of everyday life, which featured especially in the context of social interaction with others. There was little portrayal of excessive consumption or alcohol abuse, nor was alcohol consumption associated with accidents, violence or ill-health. Drinking was most likely to take place in a pub, bar, restaurant or other public drinking location, while around one in three drinking portrayals took place in the home. Drinking was rarely shown taking place at work.

What evidence is there that television programmes can affect young people's propensities to consume alcohol? The handful of published studies which address this question break down into correlational surveys, which examine relationships between television viewing and alcohol consumption, and experimental research, in which groups of youngsters are subjected to controlled exposure to programmes before being given opportunities to drink.

In one correlational survey, Tucker investigated the extent to which adolescents classified as light (less than two hours' viewing a day), moderate (two to four hours a day) or heavy (more than four hours a day) television viewers differed regarding alcohol use and the extent to which any association between reported viewing and drinking behaviours were mediated by demographic factors.[43] Nearly 400 adolescent males were questioned about their television viewing and drinking habits. Results showed that heavy viewers reportedly consumed more alcohol than did lighter viewers. This applied even when the effects of demographic differences in drinking and viewing had been controlled.

Two further studies investigated the impact of portrayals of drinking in programmes under controlled conditions. One study found that children aged 8 to 11 years who were shown the television programme *M*A*S*H* were subsequently more likely to choose an alcoholic drink over water as the beverage most appropriate for serving to 'parched' adults, compared with children who had watched the same episode with drinking scenes deleted or children who did not watch the programme at all.[44]

In another controlled experiment, 10- and 11-year-old children were randomly assigned to groups in which some of them were shown videotaped television programmes featuring leading characters who consumed alcoholic drinks. Immediately after viewing the programmes, the children completed alcohol attitude scales and a questionnaire in which they estimated how likely it was that they would drink in the future. There was only one apparent effect of watching a programme featuring drinking. Boys who watched a television actor drinking were more likely than boys who did not see such a portrayal to say that the good things about alcohol are more important than the bad things.[45]

Some of the latest evidence has indicated that portrayals of alcohol consumption in programmes may influence pre-teenage children's expectations that they too, one day, will drink alcoholic beverages, but only if they identify strongly with such television portrayals and if their parents also drink. Television's influences in this context only occur within the context of other potential influences in the child's life. Parental role models and a favourable attitude towards alcohol consumption in the child's own family appear to be key factors here. Merely seeing drink being consumed on television and enjoyed for its taste did not provide sufficient conditions for children to say that they would expect to take up drinking themselves.[46]

In Britain, research has been carried out among teenagers, aged 12 to 17 years, to find out if television influences their images of drinking and their beliefs and practices concerning alcohol.[47] The research comprised a survey supplemented by a series of focus groups. An assumption was made at the outset that any contribution television might make to young people's alcohol consumption propensities would take the form of gradual socialisation over a long period of time rather than in terms of short-term changes in behaviour contingent upon exposure to specific individual programmes.

The teenagers were divided into three groups: those who never drank, those whose last drink was more than a week ago, but less than three months ago; and those who had had a drink during the last week. Recency of drinking did not differ by gender, but age differences did emerge, with older teenagers being more likely to claim recent drinking. Taking out the effects of gender, age and social class upon drinking recency, there was little evidence that amount of reported television viewing had any relationship with drinking. There was no evidence to substantiate the view that television viewing contributed independently to frequency of drinking alcohol. However, with increased age, teenagers viewed less and drank more. As the teenagers grew older and socialised away from home more often, their television viewing reduced.

Effects of advertising

Evidence for the possible effects of television advertising for alcoholic drinks upon children's and teenagers' interest in alcohol consumption derives principally from correlational surveys. This research has explored the extent to which alcohol advertising affects the level of alcohol consumption among young people and the roles various orientations to advertising play in the influence that such advertising might have.

The evidence for television advertising effects upon adolescents' drinking behaviour has been equivocal. American research among teenagers aged between 13 and 17 found no significant relationship between reported exposure to television advertising for alcoholic drinks and the level of consumption of such drinks. This relationship was not true for all teenagers, however. Those who were motivated to pay careful attention to such advertising because they thought they might learn something from them about how to behave in different social situations, were found to be potentially more susceptible to advertising's influences. Advertising for alcoholic drinks was also found to be more influential among teenagers, who turned to such advertising to fantasise about certain desired lifestyles. Even when motivated to watch advertising, however, its influence was still relatively trivial.[48]

Another American study found that drinkers aged 12 to 16 years, or those who intended to drink alcohol when older, were more likely to have seen beer, wine and spirits commercials on television.[49] The relationship between reported exposure to television advertising for alcoholic drinks products and current or intended consumption of these products, however, was relatively strong in respect of spirits consumption, more modest in the case of beer, and weak in relation to wine consumption. One weakness of this study was that the direction of causality was never clearly established. Thus, the relationships observed might indicate that heavier drinkers among the teenagers interviewed were more motivated to watch commercials for drinks products rather than that the exposure to advertising led to their drinking more.

Although relationships between exposure to advertising and the consumption of alcoholic drinks have not been conclusively demonstrated by correlational surveys among young people, other evidence has suggested that the impact of advertising on children's or teenagers' propensities to drink may operate in much more subtle ways.

British research among children aged 10 to 16 years has examined the advertisements youngsters said they liked or disliked.[50] The findings suggest that advertisements for alcoholic drinks become increasingly salient and attractive over the years from 10 to 14. Although 10-year-olds rarely mentioned advertisements for alcoholic drinks when talking about favourite television commercials, older children tended to do so increasingly often. Children's perceptions of the characteristics of drinkers changed as they grew older, tending to become less 'moralistic' and more positive and more differentiated as they approached their mid-teens.

There were also consistent developmental trends in their descriptions of liked and disliked qualities of advertisements and of the symbolism in commercials for alcoholic drinks. Whereas the 10-year-olds' comments tended to be tied to what is specifically shown in commercials, the older children tended to go beyond this and alluded to much more complex imagery, much in the same way as adults have been found to do. For example, 14- and 16-year-olds tended to see lager and beer commercials as promoting masculinity, sociability and working-class values, and certain of the more stylish and sophisticated alcoholic drinks advertisements (e.g., Bezique and Martini) were perceived to present attractive qualities, especially to teenage girls.

These observations raise an important question about the way in which advertisements may indirectly influence under-age potential drinkers. Much of the controversy about whether advertising for alcoholic drinks should be more strongly controlled revolves around the issue of whether it influences volume sales or whether, as the industry claims, it reflects brand-switching strategies.[51] Despite the claim that the target market at which these advertisements are aimed consists of young adult drinkers, the finding that they also contain attractive images which appeal to younger teenagers carries implications for a possible role they might play in the development of positive attitudes towards alcoholic drinks and drinking behaviour.

SMOKING

The role that television might play in influencing children and teenagers to take up smoking is an important issue because cigarette smoking has been recognised as the most important single preventable cause of death in modern society.[52] Smoking has been established as a major cause of cancer, heart disease, emphysema and complications during pregnancy.

Smoking is not commonly depicted on television. American research indicated that, on prime-time US television, only 11 per cent of male characters and 2 per cent of females smoked.[53] Advertising for tobacco products on television in many countries, including the United Kingdom, has been banned. What is the evidence for a television influence where child and adolescent smoking is concerned?

There is far more research on the impact of advertising than that of programmes. The advertising-related research varies in terms of whether it has attempted to measure direct or indirect effects of advertising upon young people's attitudes to smoking and smoking behaviour. Research among children and adolescents has indicated that advertising may affect their ability to name brands.[54] Brand awareness, however, may not necessarily indicate actual smoking behaviour or an inclination to begin smoking at some point in the future. Teenage smokers in Australia have been found to be significantly better at identifying cigarette advertisements than non-smokers.[55]

In Britain, children aged 9 to 13 years were found to be attracted to certain cigarette advertisements and enjoyed looking at them. One view is that this initial attraction to advertising for cigarettes may lead to positive impressions developing about smoking among young people. Children who could name a favourite cigarette advertisement exhibited significantly greater support to the claimed 'positive values' of smoking, such as looking tough, looking grown up, calming nerves, giving confidence and controlling weight.[56] Among children who smoked, however, only a minority smoked the brand they named as their favourite advertisement, with many expressing no brand loyalty. If brand loyalty existed, the taste of the cigarette was the main reason given for choosing it, not the advertising.

Going beyond the measurement of brand awareness, some studies of the impact of cigarette advertising have focused upon young people's attitudes toward the advertisements themselves. Attitudes toward television advertising for cigarettes, however, has been found to be less influential than whether best friends and peer groups favour smoking.[57] Teenage smokers have been found to hold generally more favourable opinions about cigarette advertising than non-smokers, which is seen by some researchers as sufficient evidence of a reinforcing effect of cigarette advertising upon smoking.[58]

Research on the effect of exposure to cigarette advertising on smoking behaviour consists principally of studies in which teenage smokers have been asked if they feel that their behaviour has been in any way shaped by advertising, and investigations in which independent measures of exposure to advertising messages have been statistically related to the reported smoking behaviour. While teenage smokers have been found to attribute their own smoking behaviour in part to the influence of advertising,[59] no consistent evidence has emerged that levels of exposure to cigarette advertising on television is linked directly to smoking behaviour among teenagers.[60]

Another approach to establishing whether cigarette advertising has any influence on smoking among children and teenagers has been to examine the impact of controls over tobacco advertising in different countries. For example, in countries such as Norway and Finland, there is restrictive legislation banning all cigarette advertising. In other countries, such as

Australia, United Kingdom and the United States, cigarette advertising on television is banned, though certain other media advertising is allowed. In yet other countries, such as Hong Kong and Spain, cigarette advertising is permitted across all media.

Two kinds of comparisons have been made to investigate the impact of restrictive legislation:

- those between smoking prevalence before and after cigarette advertising bans were implemented in particular countries; and
- between smoking prevalence in countries with and without advertising restrictions.

The evidence for an effect of bans on cigarette consumption from both these sources has failed to substantiate any impact of advertising restrictions in terms of reducing smoking levels. Much of this work has focused upon adult consumption of cigarettes. Two major international studies among children and teenagers, however, failed to produce evidence that restrictive legislation on cigarette advertising on television (and in other media) had any noticeable effect upon cigarette consumption levels among young people.[61]

Another area of concern, in addition to standard forms of advertising, is the sponsorship of televised events by tobacco manufacturers. According to some critics, this coverage can function as advertising for cigarette brands and may influence the smoking behaviour of children and young people. There is some suspicion that this alternative form of cigarette advertising could encourage children to take up smoking. As to whether televised sports events sponsored by cigarette manufacturers actually influence children and teenagers in this way, little evidence has so far emerged. According to one researcher, who examined this question among British children aged 11 to 15, sponsored sports events can increase brand awareness and can create a firm association in children's minds between the cigarette brand and the sport being sponsored.[62] This finding was subsequently replicated in a follow-up survey of teenagers in England.[63] Whether or not the awareness engendered by such sponsorship encourages children to take up smoking themselves, however, has not yet been fully demonstrated.

IMAGES OF DRUGS

Although images relating to drinking and smoking are common on television, images relating to illicit drugs and drug abuse are relatively rare. There are, however, numerous commercials for over-the-counter pharmaceutical products that tend to extol their benefits and offer rapid solutions to ailments. There has been concern about the possible effects images in programmes and advertising relating to legal and illicit drugs might have upon young people's attitudes towards drugs and their use.

Studies of television output have indicated that illicit drug use/abuse is rare on entertainment programming.[64] Research on prime-time American television network programmes during the early 1970s identified fifty-six programmes which contained any references to drugs. On average, there was one programme about drug use being broadcast every nine days. Forty of these programmes presented drug use as a solitary activity, with heroin the most frequently used drug. The consequences of drug use were generally negative, both personally and socially, with unpleasant repercussions appearing long after the original experience.

Later analyses of general-entertainment television output in the United States found that illicit drug use appeared rarely. When it did occur, it was shown in a context of abuse and generally evoked unfavourable reactions. Drug abuse occurred most often in dramas and action-adventure programmes, where drug use was usually followed by arrest and legal, rather than physical or psychological, consequences.[65] Other American research confirmed the general pattern of rare depictions of drug abuse.[66]

Research on the impact of television portrayals of drug abuse is rare. It divides between studies of television's legitimate promotion of proprietary drugs, and depictions of illicit drugs and drug-taking. Research into the effects on young viewers of images of drug-taking in programmes has been rare. Recent British research has indicated that children may exhibit sophisticated opinions about dramatic portrayals of drug abuse.

Qualitative research among children in London has been used to explore their attitudes towards the way the theme of drug-taking was covered by a popular children's drama serial set in a school environment, *Grange Hill*. This storyline followed the involvement with drugs of one of the serial's resident characters, a 15-year-old boy. While this character was depicted obtaining certain pleasure from drug-taking initially, the longer-term deterioration of his health and life provided a major focus and had the most profound impact upon pre-teenage children and teenagers who watched this drama. Young viewers exhibited a sophisticated and varied array of opinions about this storyline. Even though the series showed the drug-taker being sent away and trying to get over his drug problem, the children interviewed still felt that it encouraged young people to take drugs. They believed that the programme could have done more to show young viewers why they should not take drugs and how to stop if they get started. It was felt that the storyline had, on balance, depicted drug-taking as a dangerous thing to do, with negative consequences which outweigh any short-term pleasures. There was a concern, however, that susceptible young viewers might still have had the idea to take drugs implanted in their heads by such a storyline.[67]

Studies of advertising have indicated some relationships between exposure and drug use among children and teenagers. There is little indication that children are strongly disposed toward usage of proprietary drugs from viewing commercials for these products. Certain perceptions of the world may be influenced by this advertising. For example, as their level of exposure to televised advertising for medicines increases, children aged 10 to 12 years have been found to perceive that people are sick more often, worry about getting sick, approve of medicine, and are more likely to report that they feel better after taking medicine.[68] Elsewhere, 8- to 13-year-old children's beliefs about the frequency with which people suffer from various health problems (e.g. headaches, stomach upsets) appeared to be unaffected by their apparent level of exposure to televised medicine advertising.[69]

Although the use of illicit drugs is depicted relatively infrequently on television drama programming, advertising of proprietary drugs is fairly commonplace during peak viewing hours. Concern has been voiced that the use of illicit drugs may be linked to the use of standard proprietary drugs. Is there any evidence that television advertising for proprietary drugs is linked to their use, and in turn to the use of illicit drugs?

To investigate this question, Milavsky and his colleagues conducted a five-wave panel study with teenage boys, in which they examined the relationship between the boys' exposure to drug advertising on television and their intended or actual use of proprietary and illicit drugs.[70] They found that viewing of drug advertising exhibited a weak relationship with the boys' reported use of proprietary drugs. Additionally, an inverse correlation was found between viewing these advertisements and the reported use of illicit drugs – both marijuana and narcotics. Finally, although an attitude of readiness to use proprietary or illicit drugs was linked to their actual level of use, this disposition was not related to the boys' exposure to drug advertising on television. Thus, no evidence emerged that drug advertising led teenage boys to take illicit drugs. While sensing evidence for the development of what the authors called a 'pill-pushing' culture, television did not appear to play a significant role in the formation of this attitude.

CONCLUSION

The 1990s has witnessed a drive toward healthy living which increasingly places emphasis upon the responsibility of the individual to take control of his or her health and well-being. Regular exercise, a balanced diet that is low in fat and sugar, moderate alcohol consumption and no smoking – although not guaranteeing a lifetime free of illness – represents a pattern of behaviour that will go a long way towards ensuring that individuals are not storing up problems for themselves in later life. These patterns of healthy behaviour need to be instilled in young people so that healthy lifestyles become a natural part of everyday living. Television, along with other major mass media, may have a part to play in getting this message across.

Unfortunately, its critics claim that television all too often presents images which encourage unhealthy practices among children and teenagers.

Nutritional messages in programmes and advertisements apparently promote consumption of sugared snack foods rather than fresh fruit and vegetables. The idea of a balanced diet is superseded by portrayals of characters eating whatever comes to hand.

Consumption of alcohol, though healthy in moderation for adults, is regularly portrayed without sufficient emphasis being given to the potential dangers of overconsumption. Commercials for alcohol products are often among the most popular advertisements rated by young people and may, according to some researchers, create a climate in which the attractions of alcohol are established early on among youngsters before they are legally old enough to drink. While alcohol consumption may therefore be actively cultivated by television, according to some observers, rather less effort is made to warn about the dangers of alcohol when consumed to excess.

Concerns about smoking have led to bans on tobacco advertising on television in many countries, although it is unclear that such steps have made much difference to smoking levels among young people. Depictions of the use of harder drugs on television have tended to be rare and generally show the negative consequences of consumption in the longer term.

Despite the allegations levelled against the medium by its critics, many accusations about the nature and significance of television's effects on children's health-related attitudes and behaviour go beyond the research evidence. There can be little doubt that television role models may draw children's attention to the attractions or otherwise of certain types of food, drink and other substances. Singling out the specific influence of television upon children's eventual behaviour from the range of other factors in the home and social environment which play a part in shaping health-related orientations, however, has proven difficult. Whatever the status of television in terms of its actual impact upon how children and young people behave, clearly an abundance of messages and images on television illustrating the advantages of healthy lifestyles and the potential problems associated with unhealthy habits is the desirable goal for material targeted at an age group that generally believes it is invulnerable.

Chapter 11

Does TV affect school performance?

We began this book by highlighting some of the general concerns that are continuously expressed about the *effects* of television on the young. Much of the criticism is inevitably directed at the effect the medium may well be imposing on children's educational development.

For children to achieve their full potential at school, two factors come into play. They not only need to develop the basic skills, such as reading, writing and numeracy, to perform the tasks expected of them but also the motivation to want to acquire those skills. Television has been accused of hindering both these things – but what is the true picture?

Children with different intellectual capabilities have been found to approach television in different ways. Researchers have noted, for instance, that gifted children differ from non-gifted children in respect of their use of television. Gifted children may watch television for two hours less each day than other children during their pre-teenage years. The patterns over time of television consumption, however, differ among gifted and non-gifted children, with one particularly interesting difference. With non-gifted children, viewing gradually decreases from preschool through primary school to secondary school. With gifted children, viewing drops from preschool to early school years, but then increases again during adolescence.[1]

Preschool gifted children are more likely to watch educational programmes (e.g., *Sesame Street*, *Mr Rogers' Neighbourhood* and *The Electric Company*) than cartoons and other commercial programming. In addition, they are more likely to watch these programmes more regularly than non-gifted children.[2]

Such differences in the use of television do not provide an explanation for children's level of giftedness. Given that children of varying intellectual abilities do exhibit marked differences in their television viewing patterns, however, it does open up the possibility that its impact upon what and how they learn could also vary. The more discriminating diet of gifted children may reveal a more considered and selective approach to the medium, which might engender more effective learning. The less selective pattern of viewing typically adopted by the less gifted child may reflect a more relaxed attitude towards the medium, which is less conducive to learning. On this reasoning, one would expect a knowledge-gap to open up between the gifted and non-gifted as a function of their respective approaches to television. The question which remains to be answered is whether television makes non-selective young viewers mentally lazier, or whether it impedes the development of certain crucial cognitive skills.

TELEVISION AND MOTIVATION

First, can television affect motivation? And if so, is it to do with the amount of viewing or types of programmes viewed, and does the child's own personality and home environment interact with either of these?

One suggestion is that watching television has become such a popular pastime that many children have little time left over to practise and acquire one of the most essential of the basic skills – *reading* – and because television offers them a daily fare of differing narrative discourses, they lack the incentive to learn in the first place. In other words, television comes to displace reading.

One explanation of this displacement effect is that television replaces reading because both activities satisfy similar needs, and television offers the most attractive package. Thus, during the pre-television era, children (and adults) sought diversion of excitement through reading light fiction, thereby practising their reading skills – even comic books provide some reading practice. In contrast, television provides entertainment with a minimum of effort on the child's part. The hours that used to be spent reading are now taken up by television viewing. But how true is this statement? What is the real relationship between the amount of television viewing and reading habits?

Research has indicated that the amount of time, on average, children devote to viewing television tends to increase steadily during primary-school years until it reaches a peak of between three and five hours daily by the age of 12. Furthermore, as television comes to play an increasingly prominent part in the life of the child, the amount of time spent reading seems to decrease.

Early studies conducted during periods when television was just being introduced in various parts of the world generally reported significant displacements of comic book reading[3] and book reading.[4] But many of these studies also included intelligence testing as part of the research and there is some indication that IQ, and not television viewing, could account for differences in reading levels.

Hilde Himmelweit and her colleagues observed that the impact of the introduction of television in the United Kingdom on book reading was most marked for children of average intelligence. Brighter pupils were not affected much, while the less intelligent read little anyway. With time, television seemed to stimulate an interest in book reading – particularly of books whose stories had been televised or which were linked in some way to television programmes.[5] Wilbur Schramm and his co-writers made a similar study of media usage among children in a number of North American communities, including towns with and without television. They concluded that the reading of books, newspapers and quality magazines was not affected by television, but the reading of comics and pulp magazines was reduced with the introduction of television.[6]

A third study, in Australia, also produced similar results. John Murray and Susan Kippax studied 5- to 12-year-olds in three Australian communities: No-TV (no television), Low-TV (one channel – the public channel with a mandate to provide educational programming for use in schools) and High-TV (the public channel and a commercial channel).[7]

Their research produced the findings shown in Table 11.1, based on reported estimates given by the children themselves.

Table 11.1 Children's reading levels in communities with and without television

	Books (per week)	Comics (per week)`
No-TV children read	1.08	5.84
Low-TV children read	1.61	3.91
High-TV children read	1.85	2.76

Source: Murray and Kippax, 1978

It seems that, although High-TV children spent less time reading, it was their *comic* reading that was significantly reduced when compared with the No-TV group. In fact, their reading of books, which could be described as 'quality' reading, proved to be higher than both of the other groups.

Much of the research so far, then, is inconclusive when considering the amount of television watched and its likelihood either to encourage or to discourage good reading habits. Some studies, however, have attempted to examine the relationship in more detail, in taking account of children's programme preferences and how this might interact with their attitudes and ability to learn.

For example, a Japanese study examined 10- to 11-year-olds' analytical abilities and thinking styles in relation to programme preferences. Children who preferred informational programmes were deemed to be more analytical and reflective in their thought process, approaching problems in a considered and logical manner. Those who preferred fictional entertainment were categorised as impulsive; that is, they were more likely to tackle problems in a random, intuitive fashion. In fact, when the same children were tested a year later it was also found that this preference for commercial programming was related to an increase in impulsivity, particularly amongst girls. However, it is possible that these children were predisposed to become more impulsive anyway and there is no indication as to whether other causal factors such as home environment, parental rearing practices and so on were taken into account.[8]

Nevertheless, these results have been supported by more recent findings in the United States. A group of American researchers looked at relationships between television viewing preferences and reading habits among children in the same age range as the Japanese sample.[9] Information concerning the youngsters' behaviour at home and in school was obtained from parents and teachers. Among these children, those who spent more time reading tended to be the ones with higher IQs and highly educated fathers, but who also watched fewer fantasy violent-action programmes such as *The Incredible Hulk*, *The Six Million Dollar Man* and *Wonder Woman*. Children who were rated by their teachers as the most imaginative also tended to be those who viewed fewer of these fantasy, all-action shows. Even among children who were only moderate viewers of television anyway, reading habits were influenced by the types of television programmes watched. Regular viewing of action-adventure shows, and also of game and variety shows, usually meant less time spent reading. And it seems that television's more realistic, and often violent, adult action-dramas are not to blame here. Very few of these children watched what the writers called 'hard-core' violent programmes, such as *Starsky and Hutch* and *Hawaii Five-O*. Instead, it seems that programmes featuring fantasy, superhuman characters and fast-moving action sequences, which children generally find highly enjoyable, have come to replace adventure books, comics and other popular children's reading matter as a source of entertainment and satisfaction of their fantasy needs. This is not to say that there is no cause for concern, though; after all, passive viewing of fantasy television content does not stimulate the active, imaginative mental processes essential for advanced intellectual growth.

TELEVISION, COGNITIVE DEVELOPMENT AND THE ACQUISITION OF SKILLS

If passive viewing does not stimulate children's imagination, can it actually harm the development of their creative, analytical and linguistic abilities?

Reading, for instance, requires and encourages mental effort on the part of the reader to examine carefully the context in which a word is used or to consult a dictionary to find out its meaning. Further, difficult or discriminating passages may encourage the reader to draw upon his or her own experiences, memories or fantasies to add meaning to the written material. According to some experts, however, most commercial television programmes essentially train children passively to sit and watch rather than actively to think and do. The cognitive growth of the child depends very much on how often and to what extent his or her imagination is exercised.[10]

Make-believe play is one of the most important ways in which preschool children learn about their environment. It can help children to develop a large vocabulary, it may play a role in development of sequencing or ordering of events, and it may foster concentration. Children can mimic the utterances or behaviours of fantasy television characters, but popular programmes broadcast on public and commercial networks rarely offer the opportunity for the child to engage in the kind of creative imaginative play that is essential for advanced cognitive development. For one thing, the pace of commercial television programming may be too rapid for children effectively to assimilate the words, ideas and images it contains.

One important aspect of a child's imagination development is the extent to which he or she daydreams. There are contradictory opinions about how television affects children's propensity to daydream. The reduction hypothesis postulates that television's inherent presentational characteristics inhibit children's daydreaming. This may happen because television presents children with ready-made visual images and, unlike when reading books or listening to radio, they get no practice in imagining for themselves what the scene of the action looks like.[11] Television also presents fantasies produced by others which can be consumed by children with little mental effort.[12] Finally, television's tempo allows children no time to daydream while watching.[13]

The stimulation hypothesis postulates that television viewing can encourage specific types of daydreaming through programme content. Hence, young viewers who frequently watch certain types of television programming tend to daydream more often about themes that correspond to the ones covered by the programme.[14] The stimulation hypothesis, for example, predicts that frequent viewing of violent programmes results in increased daydreaming about action heroes and aggressive themes.[15]

It is known that a variety of environmental stimuli can evoke daydreams, especially when these stimuli stir our emotions or correspond to our current concerns.[16] Research among children in The Netherlands has indicated that when children watch programmes with non-violent themes, more positive, pleasant and childlike forms of daydreaming are stimulated. In contrast, watching programmes with violent themes can increase the frequency of daydreaming about action-hero and other more violent themes. Watching violent programmes may also serve to inhibit more positive forms of daydreaming, while watching non-violent programmes may also have a similar effect on more violent daydreaming themes. The latter effect, however, has not been demonstrated unequivocally.[17]

A further concern is that regular viewing of television may have an adverse effect on the intelligence of the young viewer. There is certainly ample evidence that child TV watchers exhibit lower intelligence scores compared with non-watchers,[18] which has resulted in the charge that viewing television lowers the IQ. But, on taking a closer look at some of the studies, it soon becomes clear that these kinds of accusations are based on oversimplified interpretations of the results. For example, correlations between children's scores on intelligence tests and their reported TV viewing do not prove a causal connection. In fact, extensive research in ten communities in the USA and Canada revealed that high intelligence was positively related to regular viewing up to the age of 11, and it is not until after this age that the opposite effect occurs. In this particular study, the brighter children, who were motivated to do well academically as well as participate in a wide range of leisure activities, tended to reduce their viewing by the time they reached their mid-teens. However, the duller ones, who also displayed less interest in both school and alternative pursuits, had increased their viewing.[19]

This particular finding has not yet been fully explained. One hypothesis could be that most TV programmes are matched to the interests and abilities of bright, younger children, who then outgrow them. At the same time, the less bright youngsters become more dependent on television for both stimulation and entertainment, as it seems to offer material at an intellectual level with which they can cope.

Further evidence has emerged from another American study by Michael Morgan and Larry Gross, who examined relationships between amount of television viewing and intelligence and reading comprehension scores for over 600 children, aged between 11 and 14 years, at a New Jersey public school.[20] Among this sample, children with lower IQs again tended to watch more television than those with higher IQs. But, while children with lower IQs also exhibited poorer reading skills, when the effect of IQ difference was controlled, a significant negative relationship still remained between amount of viewing and reading performance. Although suggestive, these latter results are not unequivocal because there are still two possible explanations for the observed relationship. It is possible that television viewing impedes development of reading skills; but it could equally be the case that children with reading problems turn to television as an alternative source of gratification and amusement.

Two further studies which took account of other environmental factors in conjunction with television are also worth considering. The first examined the development of reading skills by means of a TV diary kept for the child by the parent and information about parental disciplinary practices and household routines.[21] Good reading comprehension among middle-class children by the time they reached 7 or 8 years of age was predicted best not only by fewer hours of television watching during preschool years but also by a more orderly household routine with more hours of sleep, the self-description of mothers as resourceful and curious about the world, and the use of democratic rather than authoritarian parental disciplinary practices. Among working-class children, however, television viewing during preschool years was associated with better school performance, along with having a mother who reports herself as curious and imaginative. Television emerged, therefore, as just one out of a number of features of the home environment that are important to the child's reading development.

The second study concerned itself with the development of children's writing skills, seen by educationalists as a natural progression from reading. A sample of 11- to 15-year-olds, 102 in total, were asked about their viewing habits and preferences, parental restrictions in relation to these, their reading habits and their after-school activities.[22] Parents were also given a questionnaire asking similar questions to confirm children's answers. Writing ability, in terms of skills and creativity, was then tested by asking each child to write a story about an imagined situation. Each piece of work was then scored for grammar, spelling, punctuation, sentence construction and idea development.

According to the results, writing ability correlated significantly and positively with the number of books read per month, parents' level of education and parental interest. Degree of parental interest was judged by use of a scale which combined items concerning: restriction of viewing by parents, whether the parent read to the child when the child was younger, and whether the parents watched and discussed programmes with the child. Writing ability correlated both significantly and negatively with television viewing hours. In other words, the more TV the children said they watched, the worse their writing ability. This still held true irrespective of the number of books they said they needed or the degree of parental encouragement, although these were also powerful predictors of writing ability. Of course, this study does not establish the direction of causality. The question still remains: does television viewing cause poor writing skills or do poor writing (as well as reading) skills cause children to watch more television anyway?

Survey evidence can demonstrate degrees of association between television viewing patterns and educational performance; but, in order to understand the mechanisms underlying the possible adverse effects the medium might have upon academic achievement, it is necessary to get closer to the way in which these effects work in practice. A different approach has been adopted by some researchers who have attempted to manipulate the circumstances under which television might actually impede tasks related to educational development. If children have the television on while doing their homework, for example, will it prove so much of a distraction that they will be unable to do it properly?

Research conducted with teenagers and young adults has shown that performance on spatial problem-solving tasks and memory and comprehension for a passage of prose tends to be poorer when reading and problem-solving are carried out with a television set playing in the background than when done in silence.[23] This television interference effect, demonstrated under experimental conditions, corroborates the more descriptive, correlational evidence that poorer educational performance is associated with television viewing. Mental work done in the presence of television, when the set is switched on, may be distracted by parallel input from the set. Television may affect not simply the quantity of intellectual activity, but also the quality of that activity.

Up to this point, this chapter has sought to examine the possible detrimental effect of television on children's education. Obviously, many other studies could have been cited, but the overall picture remains the same; there still seems no definite proof that television alone can hinder children's scholastic achievement. But what about television's potential for *improving* school performance? It is to this question that we turn our attention next.

TELEVISION AS AN INSTRUMENT OF EDUCATION

International research has indicated that the extent to which teachers themselves use educational television in school varies significantly from one country to the next. One recent survey reported a range from a high of 84 per cent of teachers in Canada to a low of 37 per cent in Norway, who used television as an educational tool. In Sweden, it was noted that the use of television in primary schools fell from 80 per cent in 1968 to 40 per cent in 1987. There were many reasons for this decline, but the principal factors were often inconvenient broadcasting times, questionable relevance of programmes to the curriculum, and teachers' teaching styles.[24]

Elsewhere, availability of equipment has often been a barrier to the use of educational television.[25] Some writers have noted that this should be a weakening factor, given the widespread ownership of video recorders by schools in modern industrialised societies.[26] Availability of television sets and VCRs may not simply be a function of their presence in the school, however. There are other factors which affect availability, such as whether the equipment can be easily moved around the school, whether certain classrooms have the electrical sockets with which to power up the equipment, and whether or not the equipment is locked away at night for security reasons and the keyholder is available to unlock it.[27]

The scheduling problem is a real one. In some countries, programmes are transmitted at inconvenient times for schools. One solution to this problem is to repackage programmes on video. This was done with the American production *3-2-1 Contact*, designed for elementary-school use. In repackaging this science series for schools, it was necessary both to edit the programme so that it was more narrowly focused to supply background information about its science content and to produce support materials with more guided instruction about how to use the series as an educational resource.[28]

Used with care, television can provide a valuable instructional tool in certain circumstances. Research in British primary schools, for example, indicated that educational television could provide a valuable resource to aid the development of language and reading skills.[29] The American series *The Electric Company* was shown to be of special value for underprivileged pupils.[30] A study of the Israeli series *No Secrets* demonstrated the importance of professional mediation for learning from television among children from culturally deprived homes.[31]

Educational television has also shown itself to be a good tool for extending the curriculum by introducing topics that normally do not fall within the province of separate curriculum subjects, such as learning how to learn, critical thinking, creativity, self-expression, communication skills, altruistic values and behaviour.[32]

Although educational television is not used by many schools as an integral component of the curriculum, other programmes designated as 'educative' have also been produced for home consumption. In the United Kingdom perhaps the most well known of these have been *Play School*, recently replaced by *Playbus* and aimed at the preschool child, and *Blue Peter* for the older viewer. Both of these attempt to provide information for children in an entertaining manner. In the United States, one of the most active and productive groups involved in the development and production of both educational and educative television has been the Children's Television Workshop. This group has produced a number of children's television series on which experienced television producers, educationalists and researchers work together to create programmes designed to achieve specific goals with carefully identified, target child audiences. A great deal of effort is expended in formative research and consumption to ensure that the educational messages get across. Feedback is obtained regularly from young viewers both to pilot programmes and during the production of the actual series itself, as a running check on what children find appealing and what is being understood or misunderstood.[33] In this way, appropriate changes can be made wherever necessary. Two of the most successful programmes, *Sesame Street* and *The Electric Company*, have been produced specifically for younger viewers.

Sesame Street

One of the best-known productions to grow out of this 'marriage' of the creative programme-making process, research feedback from the audience and consultation with professionals in education is *Sesame Street*. At the outset, the aim of the programme was to help prepare children for school, and in particular to provide special assistance to children from disadvantaged homes and neighbourhoods. It was intended that the show would not simply teach young children factual knowledge, but also enhance their abilities to think for themselves.

These global objectives were to be achieved through a range of specific functions served by each programme. Tuition would be provided in the recognition and use of letters, numbers and geometric forms. Mental processes concerned with ordering, classifying and identifying relationships between objects and events were to be exercised. Information was provided about natural environmental phenomena in the world; social skills training and understanding of the need for social rules were also given some attention.

Before the first series went on air, a staff of formative researchers spent eighteen months pre-testing elements and segments designed to be included in *Sesame Street*. This procedure continued to form an essential part of the production process. The research effort invested in the design of *Sesame Street* has been matched by that concerned with assessing the impact of the series. During the first two years the series was broadcast, learning from the programme was assessed by the Educational Testing Service (ETS). Achievement in eight areas of cognitive development stressed by the programme was evaluated: body parts, letters, forms, numbers, relational terms, sorting, classification and puzzles. In later years, as the programme came to stress pro-social and affective dimensions more frequently, other tests have been derived to evaluate their impact.[34]

An early publication reported the ETS research from the first year of *Sesame Street* on 943 children, 731 of whom were classified as disadvantaged. Improvements in relevant abilities, skills and areas of knowledge were found to be directly related to the extent to which children viewed the programme, with younger children achieving more than older ones. There were also family differences between children who responded well to the programme and those who did not. Parents of high learners were more likely than parents of low learners to be educated and to talk to their children about *Sesame Street*. The parents of low learners tended to be less optimistic about their children's schools and teachers, but all high–low learner comparisons had insufficient numbers of subjects for conclusive interpretation. Nevertheless, the general conclusion after the first year was that the series had an educational impact for other areas of cognitive development contained within the programme.[35]

More detailed research was carried out at the end of the second year of transmission, with similar results.[36] This second wave of assessment also revealed that children viewing for the second year performed better on more difficult tasks than first-time viewers. This finding seems to support the educational viewpoint that children need constant repetition and to be able to build on existing knowledge to understand new concepts. The second-year viewers also displayed significantly more positive attitudes towards school and race of others than did viewers who had seen only the first season and summer of *Sesame Street*. Teachers who were unaware which pupils had seen the show prior to entering school ranked viewers higher than non-viewers on seven criteria, with attitude towards school and peer relationships reflecting statistically significant differences. Other writers were not so convinced about *Sesame Street's ability to teach children unaided. There was some indication, for instance, that viewing alone was not sufficient to produce widespread significant changes, but needed to be reinforced by encouragement to watch and to think about what was seen.*

Sesame Street has been broadcast in the original English language version in more than forty countries outside the United States, including Canada, the Caribbean, Europe, Africa, the Far East, and Australia and New Zealand. Many countries enter co-production arrangements for *Sesame Street* and foreign individual cultural requirements. Such arrangements have been made with Spain, Holland, Germany, France, Latin America, Brazil, Kuwait, Sweden and Israel.

The first foreign language versions with local adaptations were in 1972: *Plaza Sesamo* in Mexico City and *Vola Sesamo* in Brazil. *Plaza Sesamo* was the occasion of extensive, carefully controlled examination of viewers' cognitive achievement; in many ways the findings replicated those of the American studies, with regular viewers scoring significantly higher than non-viewers in all the areas examined. Education gains to impressive levels have also been measured among viewers of *Sesame Street* in other countries, for example in Chile and in Israel. In Israel, co-watching by mothers increased enjoyment and learning; in Chile, heavy viewers of the show did better on almost all areas.[37]

Sesame Street was the first mass-audience educational programme and still maintains the largest number of young viewers. Each week in the United States in 1980–1981 *Sesame Street* reached 78 per cent of all 2- to 5-year-olds within range of its signal, with its signal coverage estimated as 92 per cent of all US television households. *Sesame Street* was the flagship of the 'education by entertainment' or 'learning can be fun' perspective, the facilitator and product of a rare synthesis of art and science to serve the cause of education, and the pioneer in the use of a child-oriented magazine format with a variety of special production techniques to educate (e.g. animation, word balloons and the Muppets).[38]

The Electric Company

The Electric Company (TEC) was designed by the Children's Television Workshop to increase reading skills among primary-school children (aged 6 to 10 years). The reading skills emphasised were symbol and sound analysis and meaning. The show had a magazine format and a variety of entertaining and attention-grabbing production techniques.

Formative research for *The Electric Company* provided a number of innovative techniques and critical insights about learning from television. Pre-production research measured the appeal of characters by eliciting children's responses to photographs in identifying the main characters, and by asking them to describe the role of the character in the programme, and rank characters on appeal by means of sorting photographs. The children were also asked to recall why they liked or disliked characters in attempts to distinguish between reactions to programmes and photographs.

Appealing attributes or production techniques were identified through observations of young viewers' eye contact with the television screen while particular segments of the programme were being shown. This was done using a time-lapse camera technique. Formative testing was employed to improve the ability of segments to encourage children to read aloud from the screen. A coding system was devised to describe all programme segments by defining attributes related to appeal (type of humour, theme, characters) and to comprehension (e.g. manner of presenting print, pace, density, or instructional content).

Each of these elements was further broken into components (e.g. humour included sight gags, incongruity, puns, whimsy, parody). Comprehension was evaluated using eye-movement recording, a stop tape technique, free verbal reports, test analytic procedures and group observation. Eye movement recording determined whether the viewer was attending to relevant aspects of the segments. Some elements that were found to be positively related to visual attention were integration of print with action, dynamic presentation of print, and animated format, while negative elements were print in the lower quarter of the screen, distracting action and rapid presentation of segment material.[39]

The stop tape technique was the most frequently used method of comprehension testing for *The Electric Company*. Children were shown individual *Electric Company* programme elements, and the presentation was interrupted at predetermined points to question the viewers about what had happened, had not happened or would happen. The group observation technique operated under the assumption that comprehension is related to viewers' active participation, relating spontaneous verbal responses to the show to programme attributes.

After the second season, Children's Television Workshop (CTW) researchers monitored and videotaped visual, verbal and behavioural classroom responses to programming transmitted from the Children's Television Workshop, which remotely controlled the pan, zoom and focus of the camera in the classroom. Through a transmitter, CTW staff members asked children questions before and after the showing. With the programme viewed by the children superimposed in a corner of the CTW monitor, a continuous record of both stimuli and responses was available.[40] It was subsequently reported that the programme produced significant positive effects on reading among children in grades one to four (aged 5–9 years), with the largest improvements among first-graders. Overall, gains for viewers over non-viewers were noted for seventeen of the nineteen reading skills tested. Children who viewed for the first season only displayed similar reading gains to those who also watched for the second season. For those who watched for the two seasons, it seemed that seeing both series was only a little better than seeing one. No differences in effects were noted for viewing in black and white versus colour. No effects were found for amount of home viewing, attitudes of children towards school or reading, attitudes of teachers towards children or reading performance of children. However, some parents, in particular those of first-grade viewers, appeared to reveal positive attitudes towards the educational benefits of the programme and seemed more confident that their children were achieving average levels or above in reading than were the parents of non-viewers of similar ages.[41]

It seems, then, that both of these American programmes appear to have promoted gains in educational ability amongst young children. However, as made evident by the *Sesame Street* research, it is doubtful if significant learning occurs from solitary viewing of an individual programme. The children who achieved most appeared to be those who received encouragement from an adult, enabling them to discuss what they had seen, thus reinforcing the educational 'message' contained within the programme.

The UK experience

In the UK a similar picture emerges, although research on individual series, such as *Sesame Street*, has been far more limited. A survey of school teachers in the early 1990s found that a wide range of educational programmes were endorsed as being useful classroom material. In general, though, only a small percentage of teachers endorsed any individual programme or series. Just two programmes were mentioned by more than 6 per cent of primary or secondary teachers: *Look and Read* and *Words and Pictures* (14 per cent and 12 per cent of primary teachers respectively). The main reasons why teachers felt programmes to be useful were when programmes formed the basis for follow-up discussion, were perceived as interesting and stimulating in their own right, were presented in an attractive manner, and linked in with specific classroom or project work. Programmes were criticised principally on the basis of poor presentation, lack of fit to current coursework, and not being geared to a specific age group.[42]

A study of the use of educational programmes in the 1980s, with particular reference to the programme *Look and Read*, also points to the need for some kind of adult reinforcement if children are to achieve positive learning from television. In this particular study, teachers who stated their commitment to the programme and maximised the educational opportunities it offered reported significant gains in reading ability. They pointed out that educational television appeared to be most successful if children themselves perceived that the content of the programme and the follow-up work was particularly real and relevant to them. In this study, successful planning by teachers frequently gained a corresponding response from the pupils; that is, they became more willing to observe, criticise and query if the teachers displayed a similar attitude towards broadcast material.

Look and Read aimed to help 7- to 8-year-olds, still at the 'emergent' reading stage, to become more skilled at both the process of reading and abstracting meaning from the text. Like *Sesame Street*, it used cartoon figures and songs to emphasise specific language points, but as a later pilot study carried out in the mid-1980s revealed, it was rare for a child to grasp the 'message' unaided, even though some teachers involved in the study were convinced that the phonic information had been understood.[43]

Part of the problem in the UK seems to be that, although the producers of educational programmes publish booklets advising teachers of the kinds of follow-up work that can be carried out in schools, the take-up of this advice is limited. For educational television, as it is used in schools in the UK, to be effective, teachers need to be committed to its use and incorporate it as an integral part of the curriculum. Teachers are rarely given advice in the use of educational television either during their initial training or by subsequent in-service training provision; instead they are expected to adopt and adapt individual programmes to suit their children's needs as best they can. It is not surprising, then, that teachers rarely admit to their own feelings of insecurity in this area.

A study carried out by Hurst in 1981 maintained that the main disincentives for using television, expressed by teachers themselves, tended to be technical (that is, they had insufficient knowledge of video usage), or to do with timetabling restrictions and locality/availability of the television and video recorder. Many teachers believed that children watched too much television at home and that it was therefore bad in principle for them to view in school. It was felt that a surfeit of television could encourage passivity or laziness in children and that teachers who used television too frequently could perhaps be shirking their responsibilities. The attitudes revealed in this survey also highlighted the general lack of awareness in teachers as to the real potential of educational television.[44]

More recent research with teachers in Britain has revealed that opinions towards television have shifted. Used constructively, television is regarded by many teachers as a potentially useful tool and source of educational material which can provide important content, not available through any other form, from which children can benefit. Programmes produced especially for schools tend to receive a generally favourable reception, although some productions are regarded as better than others.[45]

Teachers themselves have been found able and willing to offer quite specific suggestions concerning how programmes could be improved. One approach has been to invite teachers to view editions from particular schools' series in their entirety and to evaluate the programme on a minute-by-minute basis while watching it using an electronic push-button system. Afterwards, the programme is played back to the teachers with their ratings superimposed on a screen over the picture in graphical form. Any sudden shift in level of liking or disliking could then be further examined to explore the reasons for it.

One study applied this technique to obtain mathematics teachers' opinions about two schools maths programmes, *Videomaths* and *Square One Maths*. *Videomaths* was produced by a British company, Central Television, and was the most heavily used of all mathematics series in British primary schools over its five-year run, which began in 1988. *Square One Maths* was first transmitted in 1992 after being developed by the Children's Television Workshop. The electronic response measure, coupled with a group discussion afterwards, represented a powerful technique for enabling teachers to identify strong and weak spots in each programme. It yielded an index of the general perceived usefulness of these two programmes to teachers of mathematics and also enabled teachers to pinpoint specific points which they thought worked well or should be omitted.[46]

CONCLUSION

As the first part of this chapter showed, there is no definite proof that television alone can hinder the educational achievements and school performance of individual children. In fact, it now seems likely that, used sensibly, and with the right encouragement from both parents and teachers alike, it can help to enhance the learning process. However, as the next chapter reveals, many parents rarely get involved with programmes that their children watch, so that many of today's youngsters are unlikely to be receiving the necessary input to make learning from television a real possibility.

Chapter 12

How can parents influence children's viewing?

One recurring cosy picture of domesticity, frequently reinforced by the medium itself, is of the 'nuclear' family gathered together in front of a flickering screen, enjoying an entertaining evening's viewing. But how often do whole families sit together in this way, particularly in today's society where the traditional set-up of two parents, one of whom (usually the woman) chooses to stay at home and adopt a nurturing role, is becoming more of a rarity?

Modern child-rearing practices have resulted in young people being far more independent and less malleable than previous generations, which is reflected in the manner in which they strive to make their own decisions about when and what they watch on television. But at what point do parents step in and interfere with this decision-making process? Is it only when bedtime approaches or do parents make value judgements about the programmes themselves and act accordingly? Researchers have attempted to investigate both these questions.

VIEWING DECISIONS WITHIN THE FAMILY

There is a wide range of factors that can influence the ways in which different families establish their viewing habits. As research has shown, the matter of what to watch on television can be the scene of some conflict in the home. When more than one member of the family wants to take over a television set for different reasons, there may be long arguments as to who gets to watch their preferred programme. In these days of multi-set homes, one might imagine that conflicts would be reduced or more quickly resolved, but this may not always be the case if it is the best set in the house which is being strongly competed for.

When they are very young, children's viewing is influenced significantly by what and when their parents view, particularly where the main TV set is concerned. However, children are much more likely to watch with other children than with an adult.[1] As children get older, they spend less and less time viewing with their parents.[2] The precise pattern of coviewing, however, does depend upon the nature of the programming being viewed. There may be much more coviewing by parents and their children for programmes aimed at a general audience. On those occasions, children and their parents may view together at least two-thirds of the time, while with programmes aimed especially at children, coviewing may fall to no more than a quarter of the time.[3]

Idiosyncratic family viewing patterns and rule-based controls over the use of the television set do exist and can be important mediators of the impact of television on children.[4] However, decisions over how the set is used, by whom and under what circumstances, can vary a lot. For example, one family may not exert as much control over what the children watch as another; although parents may often claim to take care over what they allow younger members of the family to watch, this may well be far removed from what actually happens in practice. Added to this, in these days of two- and three-set households, and unnecessary numbers of sets in children's bedrooms, parents may not always know when or what their children are watching. Should the parents be out, youngsters are then free to watch whatever they like.

We can begin by taking a look at some early research on family television watching. Some of the evidence suggests that families behave democratically and take joint decisions on which programmes they will watch, but this pattern may well be restricted to certain hours of the day. For example, a joint decision may be taken as to what to watch at night, when presumably the family are most likely to be gathered together as a group in front of the set, but during the day it is more likely for individual family members to assume control of the set. This early evidence also shows that children were more likely than their parents to be happy with programmes selected by the family.[5]

Another study found that, in family households, wives were the most likely to select shows at night, with general agreement or husbands tying for second place in the decision-making. Children were invariably in the minority, with only one out of seven decisions being left to them. This study also showed that, in families where the education level of either one or both parents was high, there was more likelihood of programmes being selected by general agreement instead of more authoritarian measures.[6]

Steven Chaffee and Albert Tims observed in 1976 that programme selection is partly dependent on other members of the family who are watching.[7] In a study of about 200 junior and senior high-school students, a relationship was found between the presence of others and the type of programme viewed. Brothers and sisters were often present for humorous shows, parents were more likely to be present for aggressive and 'real' shows, for example, news programmes. It is not known whether children adapt their viewing to who is present or whether they seek certain kinds of company for certain shows. George Comstock noted that viewers often watch programmes that are selected by someone else in the family,[8] although much viewing is non-selective anyway and viewing is often determined by channel loyalty and inheritance of audiences from one programme to another. But the picture can get highly complex when families decide to watch television. A focus group study undertaken by the Corporation for Public Broadcasting in 1974 revealed that programme selection decisions are often complicated interpersonal communication activities involving intra-family status relations, temporal context, the number of sets available and rule-based communication conventions within the household.[9]

One Canadian researcher found that choosing which programmes to watch did not always lead to family togetherness. Mothers were found to dominate fathers when they disagreed over which TV shows to watch, even though fathers were generally perceived by members of the family to be in charge of the set.[10] This finding was corroborated by James Lull, who observed that fathers were regarded by other family members as the most influential person in family discussions about which shows to watch. In general, fathers, mothers and older children (13–18 years) were more likely than younger children to get their own way in choosing what the family should view.[11]

Another observation which underlined the father's dominance was that they were less likely to ask others before changing channels. Trained monitors spent two days observing families watching television and then returned on the third day to conduct interviews with each family member. Observers actually joined in other family activities so that the main purpose of the study was less obvious.[12] Ninety-three families were observed, of which seventy-four were two-parent families, which formed the focus of the study. Fathers were named most often as the person or one of the persons who controlled the selection of television programmes. Children and mothers were more likely to regard fathers in this way than were the fathers themselves. Fathers believed that their spouses or partners were more responsible than any other single person or specific combination of individuals for determining the choice of programmes. Overall, however, family members were just as likely to say that one of the children, rather than the mother, decided what was viewed on the main television set. Children often perceived themselves, or one of their siblings, as the primary controller of the set. Family consensus was another procedure that was mentioned.

These perceptions were supported only in part by the observed instances of control of the main television set that were documented by the researchers who lived with families. Observers noted who turned the set on, who changed the channel and who turned the set off. They also noted whether or not these actions were undertaken with any discussion of what would be viewed. The observations indicated that fathers controlled more programme decisions than any other single family member or combination of family viewers. They were more than twice as likely as their female partners to do so. Further, they acted alone in more than 90 per cent of these decisions. One of the children was next most likely to turn the set on, turn it off or change the channel. Children were responsible for 30 per cent of these actions (compared to 36 per cent of their fathers) and they were also extremely likely to do so without discussion (93 per cent of the time acting alone).

Mothers were observed to be far less involved in the actual manipulation of the set than were either their husbands (or live-in partner) or children. They were the initiators of only 15 per cent of these actions. They were far less likely than either fathers or children to negotiate action alone. Three-quarters of all set alterations were made by one family member – mostly without observable negotiations.

This observation study conflicts with the earlier research, which cites the mother as the person who makes most of the viewing decisions, implying that people's self-reported behaviour is often in direct opposition to what they actually do in practice.

INFLUENCE OF FAMILY COMMUNICATION PATTERNS

Another source of influence to which mass communication researchers have given increasing significance is the manner in which parents communicate with each other and how this interacts with the way in which the television set is used in the family home. One assumption here is that children are socialised into particular styles of television viewing as one consequence of the prevailing climate of parental control and disciplinary practices in the home.

Early studies of the media use of children suggested that youngsters learn patterns of television viewing through imitating their parents.[13] More recently, however, other researchers have pointed out that this modelling explanation may be an oversimplification of how children's viewing behaviours develop. It fails to take into account the role of other factors such as the common social class of parents and children which might account for the similarities in their respective viewing patterns, quite apart from direct copying by one of the other's television-related habits. And another possibility is that the child's viewing behaviours may sometimes influence those of parents, thus giving rise to a reversal of the initial hypothesis.[14]

We have already seen that the evidence for the implementation of direct control over children's viewing by parents is equivocal. The notion of a sphere of influence which operates in a less direct fashion through the climate of parent–child interactions has produced evidence that the family can affect the amount and type of television viewing indulged in by children.

This social interaction view puts forward the idea that children's viewing behaviours are shaped and controlled by norms and values concerned with the conduct that generally occurs in the family context. Attempts to investigate the significance of interpersonal relationships between family members for the development of certain patterns of media use have derived from research by Steven Chaffee and his colleagues, beginning in the early 1970s.[15]

According to this perspective, parent–child communication patterns are among the most persuasive influences in child socialisation and development. Parental values and norms need not be transmitted directly, however, in order to have an impact. It is not simply the existence of certain rules within the home that matters; the way in which they are applied is equally important. Chaffee and two colleagues, Jack McLeod and Daniel Wackman, developed a two-dimensional model of family communication patterns, labelled *socio-orientation* and *concept-orientation*. In a socio-oriented family setting, parents encourage their children to maintain a harmonious climate of personal relationships, to avoid arguments, anger and any form of controversial expression or behaviour. In a concept-oriented family, children are invited to express their ideas and feelings, even if they are controversial, and to challenge the beliefs of others.[16]

These patterns of family communication are known to be associated in part with social class. Thus, the socio-oriented climate is more characteristic of working-class families, while concept-orientation is more typical of middle-class families.[17] But the effects of family communication patterns are not believed to be wholly explicable by social class alone.[18] Although the above class differences in orientations do exist, they are not strong, and the orientations themselves have relationships with cognitive processes which are more than simply an outcome of social class.[19]

Another interesting question was whether families were either socio-oriented types or concept-oriented types, or whether they could be a little bit of both. Further research showed that these two orientations were positively correlated, but only to a slight extent.[20] Nevertheless, it emerged that it was possible to develop a fourfold typology by dichotomising families at a halfway point along each dimension. This gave rise to the following four family types:

- *Laissez-faire* families, in which neither socio- nor concept-orientation were strongly emphasised. This meant that there was little parent–child communication of any sort, and the child instead was influenced more by friends and peer groups outside the home.
- *Protective* families, in which only socio-oriented relations were emphasised, with little impetus provided to the child from parents to develop a broad-minded thoughtful outlook on the world.
- *Consensual* families, in which both socio- and concept-orientation were encouraged. In this context, the child was encouraged to take an interest in

what was going on in the world but to avoid taking up controversial positions and disturbing the internal harmony of the family.

• *Pluralistic* families, in which only concept-orientation was stressed, and where the child was encouraged to be exploratory, to challenge existing norms and values, though again without disrupting family harmony.

A Swedish study of adolescents' use of television in the family context reported that at a basic level of analysis low concept- and high socio-orientation in the family were associated with heavy television viewing by adolescents in the household. Family communication patterns, however, did not stand up as significant predictors of young people's television viewing in the presence of multiple statistical controls for social class and other socialisation variables such as parental attitudes towards television.[21]

James Lull observed that both socio-oriented (emphasis on harmony and agreement) and concept-oriented (emphasis on dissent and expression of opinion) dimensions were related to uses of television as a resource for the accomplishment of interpersonal objectives in the home. That is, television can be used to create occasions when family members come together as a unit; it can act as a source of mutual interest and conversation. The socio-oriented families watched more television and were more likely to use it to reach these interpersonal objectives. Concept-oriented families saw television as not being useful to them as a social resource, although they did use it for transmission of values and exercising authority.[22]

Lull examined patterns of how families talked to and got on with each other in relation to specific television-linked attitudes and activities. Family members answered questionnaire items designed to determine the degree to which they were 'concept-' or 'socio-'oriented. Concept-oriented families were those who valued the presentation of personal points of view on issues under discussion and did not discourage disagreement or arguments about these issues. Socio-oriented homes, on the other hand, were characterised by an environment where social harmony was prized and children were told to repress expression of ideas if it would cause friction in the home. Some interesting differences were found in how these families watched television.

First, the overall amount of television viewing carried out in these households was negatively associated with concept-orientation and un-correlated with socio-orientation. That is to say that, on the whole, concept-oriented families watched less television than socio-oriented families. However, satisfaction with the family's selection of television programmes was not related to either concept- or socio-orientation scores. However, sensitivity to others' preferences when choosing programmes was stronger among concept-oriented families and weaker among socio-oriented ones. Second, selective viewing was more typical of concept-oriented families than it was of socio-oriented families. Concept-orientation was negatively associated with watching programmes that were not selected by the individual or watching 'television' instead of particular shows. Socio-orientation was unrelated to both of these indices. Third, concept-oriented families were less likely to be satisfied with television as a form of family entertainment. Socio-orientation was linked with more arguments over the selection of television programmes, while concept-orientation scores were not thus correlated. Concept-orientation related to fewer such developments.

It seems, then, that concept-oriented families are more likely to be selective in their viewing, switching on only for specific programmes rather than out of habit; they are also more considerate of other people's viewing habits. This more responsible attitude towards television, in which the content of programmes is given due consideration, presumably influences children's responses to the medium and possibly results in a higher degree of critical awareness.

Parental disciplinary styles can affect how children respond to television, but these may work in different ways for boys and girls. Some parents may control their children through power assertion, while others do so through love withdrawal. The former tends to emphasise physical punishment and coercion and has been found to be especially predictive of aggressive behaviour in children.[23] A love-withdrawal disciplinary style has been found to be connected with a general lack of parental control or involvement in their children's viewing, and children in such households tend to be heavy viewers. Power assertive families, in contrast, contain children who were better able to distinguish reality from fantasy on television, and have a better knowledge of production techniques and how television works.[24]

Boys and girls responded differently to parental mediation of television viewing, when it did occur. Boys, whose parents took a greater interest in their viewing, exhibited greater understanding of television, while for girls parental involvement in viewing appeared to have less influence. While there was some indication that the boys studied on this occasion had a better understanding of television than did girls, there was also some suggestion that girls may have reacted differently to particular styles of parental discipline. While both boys and girls benefited to some extent from increased parental interest in their television habits, boys responded better both to love-withdrawal and power assertion techniques of discipline.[25]

OTHER PEOPLE'S INFLUENCES ON CHILDREN'S USE OF TV

Parents and other people can both influence children's television viewing behaviour. They may influence how much children watch television generally or, more specifically, affect what types of programmes children watch. This in turn can control the impact television has on children by limiting the extent to which they watch certain types of programmes. In addition, the strength of impact of particular TV shows can be affected by parental intervention.

The influence of others on viewing behaviour can operate through two mechanisms. First, direct intervention with a child's viewing may occur when parents lay down rules about television watching or encourage or discourage in explicit terms the watching of particular kinds of programmes or amounts of television.

For example, parents may limit children's viewing to a set number of hours per day or impose an early bedtime, thus restricting the viewing of 'unsuitable' material. Perhaps they insist that youngsters watch only programmes that are produced specifically for children, or ones that are perceived to have educational content.

Second, influence from parents may be less direct and without specific intent, whereby parents provide models of viewing which are matched by their offspring. As already pointed out, if parents themselves are both selective and critical when viewing television, this kind of behaviour might well rub off on their children. However, young people, particularly when reaching adolescence, also respond to peer pressure and are more likely to insist on watching material their parents might well regard as unsuitable if the majority of their school friends are allowed to watch it.

PARENTS' CONCERN AND AWARENESS

A good deal of survey evidence shows that parents are concerned with the violent and sexual content of television, although this concern is extended by only some of them to worry about the amount of time their own children spend watching television.[26] One reason for this lack of worry is that parents may underestimate their child's viewing time and may not realise the extent of the violent content of what they watch.

Bradley Greenberg has found that children gave estimates of their own viewing time that were twice as great as those given by their mothers when estimating how much time their children devoted to viewing. This finding has since been repeated and extended. For instance, there is some suggestion that mothers report more rules, higher levels of watching with their children, and lower estimates of the child's susceptibility to TV advertising compared with the child's own responses on these questions.[27]

There is also some evidence that mothers may not recognise the extent of their child's response to television content. Children tend to perceive more violence in the same set of television programmes than their mothers do.[28] Furthermore, mothers apparently underreport their children's fright reactions to scary television programmes and movies and also the extent to which they intervene to control what their children watch or to explain programmes to their youngsters.[29]

There is even more evidence which casts doubt on how much influence parents exert over their children's viewing. One major survey asked a question of parents with children at home under the age of 15: 'Are there any rules or regulations in your home about when and what the children watch, or do you let them make their own decisions?' While 41 per cent said they had definite rules, 30 per cent said they had no rules at all. Another 6 per cent said they made an effort to control their children's viewing, but did not go so far as to say they had definite rules. Even though an attempt was made here to balance the wording of the question, there was probably still some bias towards giving rules as a socially desirable response. Among the rules mentioned were those relating to hours when viewing is permitted; duties, such as homework or chores, which must be done first; programme-specific rules relating to prohibitions on watching particular programmes; and supervision while watching other programmes. Mothers (31 per cent) and fathers (29 per cent) were more or less equally likely to mention rules governing circumstances of viewing; while mothers (38 per cent) were more likely than fathers (30 per cent) to mention programme guidance.[30]

One form of programme control was conspicuously small. In the same sample that designated 'violence' the number one irritant, only about 5 per cent specifically mentioned some attempt at regulation in this regard. More significant still, this figure was not substantially higher among those parents who actually cited violence as a disadvantage (about 7 per cent, compared to 5 per cent of those who did not).

On the whole, few relationships were observed between the disadvantages the parents cited and the controls they mentioned. For instance, those who worried about television's interference with chores or other activities were only slightly more likely to mention appropriate limitations on the circumstances under which children can watch (14 per cent vs 12 per cent).

A few years later, this 1960s survey was followed up by a new survey at the beginning of the 1970s among children aged 5–6, 11–12 and 15–16 years, and their parents. When questioned, 27 per cent of 11- to 12-year-olds and 38 per cent of 15- to 16-year-olds said their parents never complained about their television watching. When complaints were received, they fell usually into one of three categories, in which concern was expressed about watching too much television, watching too late, and about the types of programmes watched. When asked directly if their parents exhibited any control over their television viewing, over one in three of the 11–12s and 15–16s felt that they either currently were, or in the past had been, under a limit. Mothers of the youngest children interviewed in this survey said that the form of control they used more often with their youngsters was supervision of programme selection. Mothers of girls reported more control than did mothers of boys. Very little use of the television to keep the child occupied or indoors was reported.[31]

Later research found that parents were unlikely to control the quantity or the character of viewing, although there are certain restrictions in some families. These restrictions tend to decline sharply as children reach their teens. Some 39 per cent of 11- to 12-year-olds and 18 per cent of 15- to 16-year-olds reported rules about the time spent watching television. Mothers were more likely to report rules, with 69 per cent of the mothers of 11- to 12-year-olds and 31 of the mothers of older children reporting rules about viewing. In both cases, however, rules about television viewing were much less prevalent than rules about other things.[32]

What about parental guidance in connection with specific programmes? One study reported that 6- to 12-year-olds were likely to say that parents control, but do not guide, their television watching in the sense of telling them what and what not to watch.[33] Another found that both mothers and their children (9- to 14-year-olds) reported very little parental guidance, with 85 per cent of both groups saying 'none' for guidance about specific programmes.[34]

An Australian study measured parental control of children's television viewing by asking parents to list the programmes they considered unsuitable viewing fare for their youngsters. Parents who were unable to specify either a particular programme or programme type were assumed to be non-discriminating in relation to their child's viewing. It emerged that parental knowledge regarding the potential harm of commercial television did not necessarily lead to a reduced amount of such viewing by children.[35]

Parents were also asked to specify the extent to which the television viewed by their preschool-age children in the past week was selected by a parent, siblings or the preschoolers themselves. The finding here was that preschoolers who selected their own television had higher viewing rates. Parental attitudes to television were important, too. Children who were heavy users, or who watched proportionately more of commercial stations, had parents who were less likely to express concern over the negative side effects of watching television. Such children also tended to have parents who perceived less need to control their child's use of the medium.

American researchers have asked parents about their encouragement of television as well as their limiting of its use. Many parents were found to encourage children to watch particular programmes that they considered educational or good entertainment for children. Such encouragement apparently reflects selectivity on the part of parents, which is not the reverse of regulation of viewing.[36]

Further results revealed that programme content, rather than time of broadcast, is the most common reason given for parental restrictions and encouragement. These American parents were more apt to encourage viewing because they saw positive value in the content rather than because of the time of day. Similarly, these parents were more likely to prohibit viewing on the basis of the content than to put time restrictions on children. They valued educational programmes and 'specials' prepared for children. Violence, sexual content and frightening content were often reasons for restrictions. However, on balance, most parents considered much of television to be innocuous.

PARENTAL INFLUENCES ON THE IMPACT OF TELEVISION

The questions regarding the actual form that mediation assumes in families, as well as how much mediation of child viewing is done, have not been comprehensively answered. When parents are surveyed, they may report that family talk about television frequently takes the form of approval ('This is a good programme') or disapproval ('You shouldn't be watching this rubbish') and at times comments may dissolve into what researchers call 'para-language' ('Ugh!').[37] This evaluative criticism, coupled with general evaluative comments regarding the positive and negative aspects of the medium in general, comprise a frequently cited form of mediation. Another form that mediation may take is interpretation, where siblings explain the characteristics of television programmes to younger children, or when parents explain the conventions of programme production to their children.[38] Parents also report that they comment about the morality of characters and their suitability as role models.[39]

A third category of mediation is rule-making and discipline. Parents report that they intervene in children's viewing by limiting viewing and enforcing bedtimes, prohibiting or encouraging specific programmes or, in extreme cases, removing television from the home.[40] There are indications that parents also actively discourage the imitation of television portrayals by their children, attributing a host of undesirable child behaviours to television.[41]

Parents can have an impact on what their children take from television, although few parents actually become involved in, or exercise control over, their children's consumption, interpretation and use of television information. When parental intervention is used – through, for instance, discussion about programmes – it can be influential on the child. However, while some parents may forbid their children from viewing certain 'adult' or 'offensive' programmes, set bedtime limits on viewing, or make comments on the nature of the content being viewed, the majority tend not to participate in their child's television viewing. The most common form of control seems to take the form of rules about how late to watch, but even that kind of intervention may be neither widespread nor consistent. Watching with children can be effective in influencing what they view, but a great deal of the time children watch unsupervised.

There is evidence too that parents can be induced to exert guidance on their children's television viewing. A leading market researcher, Gordon Heald, posted TV guides to a sample of parents over a six-week period.[42] A significantly greater proportion of the experimental groups reported receiving their parents' positive and negative recommendations about programmes than of a control group who were not mailed guides. Unfortunately, there is no indication of the extent to which parental recommendations influenced the children's viewing of programmes. Other researchers, however, have found that, even when supplied with an external source of information about the negative impact of television on children, the majority of parents may be unlikely to participate in their children's television viewing behaviour to any significant degree.[43]

Although these investigations indicate that few parents establish explicit rules and practices regarding television, they fail to take into consideration other forms of social interaction that might have an impact on children's learning from the medium.[44] It is possible that more implied or global forms of mediation exist in the household. Parental disciplinary practices, for example, may also serve to mediate what and how children learn from television. Research elsewhere has demonstrated that disciplinary practices are related to children's social behaviour in general.

This issue has been explored by attempting to specify some of the conditions under which children's modelling of antisocial television portrayals was minimised and maximised. Enduring parental styles of discipline and behaviour towards each other and their children should mediate the degree to which children acquire and express antisocial predispositions modelled after television offerings. In practice, children with mothers who primarily discipline with reasoning and explanation seem to be less affected by antisocial television content.[45]

Another consideration is the role of parental disciplinary practices on children's learning of pro-social behaviour from television. Television contains as much pro-social behaviour as antisocial behaviour. There is evidence that mothers who discipline by acts or threats of physical punishment or the deprivation of material objects or privileges tend to be less likely to be aware of, or to learn from, television's pro-social portrayals than children whose mothers engage in other forms of discipline.[46]

What are the mediating effects of parental disciplinary practices on television's impact on their children? Do styles of parental discipline make a difference to children's television viewing patterns? One researcher looked at two modes of parental discipline which were labelled *induction* and *sensitisation*. Induction techniques include the use of reasoning, explanation and appeals to the child's pride and achievements, and exert little external power over the child. Parents who engage in this form of discipline typically point out to the child why one course of action may be better than another for the child's well-being or because of effects on others.

Sensitisation techniques are basically punitive, threatening children with negative consequences – material or emotional – unless the children behave as their parents wish. External rewards or threat or removal of such rewards are characteristic of this mode of discipline.[47] Abelman obtained information about disciplinary patterns from parents, and about television viewing habits, programme preferences and how well or badly their children generally behave. The results indicated that inductive discipline – a style which encourages the development of some internalised standard of morality and behaviour – tends to have a positive impact on children's pro-social behaviour and viewing of programmes whose characters are generally well-behaved, as well as a negative impact on children's viewing of programmes containing violence. Sensitising discipline would seem to contribute to the overall amount of television viewing as well as children's preference for disruptive, uncivilised ways of resolving disagreements with others and violence-containing television programmes.

It was also found that the disciplinary style used by their mothers has a greater impact on the way children resolve arguments and disagreements than does the disciplinary style employed by fathers. Mothers may also have more influence over children's television viewing. Regardless of whether fathers are sensitising or inductive, children from households whose mothers are inductive are more likely to react to conflict in a pro-social manner and expose themselves to a greater amount of pro-social television content.

Parental mediation of children's viewing may influence children's level of understanding of television. American researchers have found that, although the child's intelligence is important to his or her ability to follow programmes, clear parentally imposed rules about television, strong discipline and a generally light viewing diet were also significant factors associated with children showing better comprehension of TV plots and clearer distinctions between fantasy and reality on television. Children whose parents exerted a certain degree of control over the use of television exhibited better awareness of production techniques and what they signified.[48]

Researchers in the United States attempted to distinguish the different types of parental guidance which seem to exist. Three principal types emerged:

- *restrictive guidance*, which involves imposing restrictions on the child's amount of viewing (e.g. setting special hours during which the child is allowed to watch) and on the material watched (e.g. forbidding the viewing of certain programmes);
- *evaluative guidance*, which involves discussing programmes with the child for the deliberate purpose of helping the child to evaluate the meaning (e.g. explaining the meaning of television advertisements), morality (e.g. pointing out bad things actors are doing) and characterisation of programme content (e.g. explaining television people are not real);
- *unfocused guidance*, which involves non-specific guidance methods such as coviewing with the child and talking to the child about programmes. In contrast to evaluative guidance, unfocused guidance is not necessarily motivated by parents' desires to mediate children's television experiences.

Parent–child coviewing and discussions about programmes may occur primarily because parents and children enjoy the same programmes rather than because parents are concerned that their children get the most good and the least bad from their viewing experiences.[49] More recently, these parental guidance types were also found to exist among Dutch parents. Here, demographic differences were found in the extent to which different styles of mediation were applied. The use of unfocused guidance, for example, was greatest in families with relatively few children, possibly because parents in smaller families have more time to watch television together with their children and to discuss programmes. It is also understandable that parents who are themselves heavy viewers more frequently use unfocused guidance, because parents who spend a lot of time in front of the screen have more opportunity to watch together with their children and therefore to discuss programmes with them.[50]

PRACTICAL ADVICE FOR PARENTS

Various publications have now been introduced that can act as a guide to those parents who would really like their children to become more critical viewers. Unfortunately, there is no indication as to whether the activities suggested in some of these books have any degree of success when transferred to the home environment. For example, M. R. Kelley's *A Parent's Guide to Television* provides a detailed list of aggregated activities that parents can encourage their children to do in response to a wide range of television genres from soap operas to documentaries.[51] Some of these activities, however, appear to replicate those of the classroom: for example, writing programme reviews or imaginary news forecasts, interpreting new vocabulary or making up bar charts to display information collected from the screen. It seems doubtful if many children could be persuaded to carry out these tasks at the end of a busy school day. Furthermore, how many parents would be willing to supervise these kinds of activities on a regular basis?

Perhaps Laurene Krasny Brown's advice in *Taking Advantage of Media* would be more useful, particularly in the light of the research findings outlined earlier in this chapter.[52] As she points out, if parents adopt responsible attitudes towards their own viewing – that is, they are seen to be making informed decisions as to when and what to watch – they can act as role models for their children. At any rate, parents should try to discourage children from indulging in long hours of solitary viewing, by sitting with them when possible and demonstrating that they value opinions the children might have about individual programmes. By encouraging discussion about televised material, parents can then help their offspring to clarify and interpret not only character behaviour and narrative structure, but also examples of biased information and stereotyping. Children might then approach the medium in a more serious fashion. These kinds of positive attitudes within the home, as well as the exertion of some kind of reasonable control over amount and content of viewing, might then not only assist in making children more critical viewers but also more resistant to any potential harmful effects. More structured activities, such as those outlined by Kelley, are probably better left to educationalists, who, as we shall see in the next chapter, are now beginning to adopt a more active role as far as children and television are concerned.

Chapter 13

How can schools influence children's viewing?

Throughout this book, we have tried to describe not only the manner in which children watch television but also the ways in which they attempt to make sense of it. It seems from the research so far that there might well be a need to educate young viewers to become more intelligent consumers of television. One way of achieving this could be through specially designed courses which can be taught to children in the classroom. As they grow older, children become more sophisticated about television and learn its conventions. Through natural viewing experiences, children develop a better understanding of television content, becoming able to make finer distinctions between programmes and more sophisticated and critical judgements about them. With further guidance from adults – parents and teachers alike – who discuss programmes with them, children's understanding of television can be further enhanced and the way they use television can be substantially modified.

Educators are becoming increasingly aware of the role that television can play as an educational medium.[1] Making the most of television in this context, however, may also depend on the extent to which the medium can be used effectively both by teachers and students.[2] This means that users of television must have the necessary skills to obtain the maximum learning benefit from television. The need for television literacy is seen as an objective which will be achieved not simply through a process of natural osmosis, but through the implementation of properly constructed programmes of tuition and training.

While parents can play an important role in moderating television's influences or enhancing the benefits it can have for children, much of the evidence would suggest that few parents bother to make this kind of effort on behalf of their children. Attention has therefore moved on to the role which schools might play. In-school intervention strategies aimed at teaching children to become critical, responsible consumers of television are seen as one answer to this problem.

TELEVISION IN SCHOOLS

Much early research on the role and utilisation of television in schools in the United Kingdom was stimulated by the Independent Television Authority (ITA) which established a Schoolteacher Fellowship Scheme in 1967. Under this scheme practising teachers were given an opportunity to take a year out to undertake a project of their own choosing about the relationship of television to education. This research programme continued under the auspices of the ITA's successor, the Independent Broadcasting Authority (IBA) as the IBA Fellowship Scheme which subsumed an expanded brief to sponsor research conducted by academic researchers as well as teachers into wider issues linking television and education. The Fellowship Scheme ran for seventeen years and had a marked influence on educational broadcasting policy.[3]

The ITA Teacher Fellowships in the late 1960s described viewing conditions in most schools as being less than ideal, and in many cases as being 'abysmal'.[4] Although the standards of programmes produced specifically for schools have improved, viewing conditions and technical facilities continue to represent major difficulties, impeding the effective implementation of television in the school context.[5]

In the early days of schools television in Britain, following its launch in 1957, there were fears that it would be used only to keep children quiet and give teachers a break. There was perceived to be a risk that children would become little more than 'passive viewers'. This opinion still prevails today. Yet, while television should not be seen as a substitute for teachers, it is increasingly acknowledged to be a potentially useful supplement to standard teaching methods. More and more schools, at primary and secondary levels, own television sets and video-recording equipment. Further, growing numbers of teachers are willing to recognise that such equipment has a place in education.[6] The key question, however, is whether formal education has a role to play in cultivating a certain approach, among children, to watching television.

THE MEDIA EDUCATION DEBATE

The notion of 'media education' as an academic discipline in its own right has had a far from smooth passage through history. The need for media education has been acknowledged at different times over the past twenty-five years, but has not, until recently, shown signs of becoming established. The perceived importance of media education has stemmed not simply from public anxieties about allegedly harmful effects of television on children's intellectual, moral or social development, but also from a recognition of a need within media industries for trained personnel. Traditional media education in Britain has tended, however, to focus upon critiques of media output and on the predominant ideologies which underpin its production, rather than offering a vocational training regime tailored to the needs of media organisations.[7]

Enquiries into the skills requirements of media industries during the 1980s began to emphasise the need for a form of media education which would offer vocational or 'pre-vocational' training, thus contributing towards the establishment of a richer skills base on which media industries could draw. This new perspective was not universally welcomed by media educators, who feared that such a strong emphasis on practical training would reduce the critical, theoretical aspects of traditional courses, which were seen as central to a comprehensive and balanced media education.[8]

Despite the critics, new courses in media have proliferated in Britain at GCSE and A level, and at BTEC and City and Guilds levels. The study of media institutions already forms a key component of media studies at GCSE and A level and even occurs in media education at primary level.[9] In addition to these formalised qualifications, other courses in practical aspects of media have been offered via schemes designed to provide access opportunities to underprivileged young people to whom formal training might not otherwise be offered.[10]

One of the core problems with all these developments in media education has been the lack of dialogue between educators and industry. To be most effective, it is essential that courses in media education meet the needs of media industries. What kinds of academic and professional training do media industries require of potential employees? What balance should be struck between the theoretical or critical aspects of media courses and their professional or vocational training components? A dominance of 'critical' approaches is unlikely to satisfy industry needs.[11] Nevertheless, an approach heavily weighted towards vocational training may fail to provide a well-rounded education, which, be it taught at school or college level, ought to be expected of an established academic course. Real progress, of benefit to all concerned, is only likely to be achieved once media educators and media industries manage to transform their traditional mutual suspicion into a climate of mutual trust, cooperation and understanding.

Media educators have resisted the notion of media teaching as merely a form of training in technical skills. Nonetheless, media syllabuses have increasingly incorporated substantial elements of practical training in media production. The practical aspects of media training have been seen to allow opportunities for self-expression among young people, thus contributing to their personal growth as well as enhancing their critical understanding of the media.[12] It can bring out of themselves those pupils who have difficulty with other forms of learning, leading to improvement in social and communication skills.[13] Taking part in the physical production of media output can assist in the critical analysis of different types of media content, such as television programmes, thus enhancing media literacy skills among young viewers.[14]

THE POTENTIAL SIGNIFICANCE OF TELEVISION LITERACY

The past twenty years have witnessed a growing effort to teach children to understand the television medium. In the United States, which is probably ahead of any other country in this field, a number of school curricula have been developed that incorporate teacher-taught lessons, specially provided documentary and instructional programmes, practical assignments in the actual use by students themselves, and audiovisual and other technical equipment to produce their own television programmes.[15]

Evidence is accumulating to suggest that such curricula are welcomed by teachers and pupils, and that these educational projects produce changes in awareness of specific aspects of television, such as how programmes and advertisements are made, and of more global aspects of the medium, such as the economics and politics of the TV industry, the influence television can have on intellectual development, and social attitudes and behaviour.[16]

Despite the upsurge in interest in school-based television literacy courses, many researchers in this area have focused on issues such as television violence. It is usually intended that, through enhanced understanding of television, children will become more critical and discerning viewers and less vulnerable to harmful television effects. Other forms of social behaviour which might be influenced by television have not attracted the same degree of research attention or effort. Most of the intervention projects have either ignored the pro-social potential of certain types of mainstream television content and have instead prepared specially produced programming for instructional purposes,[17] or served to mediate and control the negative impact of mainstream television's antisocial content on children's behaviour.[18] The overriding and traditional desire to negate the alleged impact of television's antisocial content has all but blinded individuals from considering the pro-social elements contained within the same material they condemn.

Teaching about television is considered by many television researchers to be one of the most important practical developments of the 1980s and 1990s, and one that needs to be continued, expanded and improved in the coming years. Our initial intention, then, is to look at the broad theoretical perspectives from which television literacy projects were derived.[19]

PERSPECTIVES ON TEACHING TELEVISION

The notion of critical skills directing the processing of information is an old one. The application of these skills to information presented via a particular medium – as in critical reading skills, listening skills or television viewing skills – is an acknowledgement that the medium of presentation is an integral part of the message. It also implies that there are elements of grammar, syntax, symbols and meaning which are medium-specific and which presumably can be taught. Television literacy curricula have derived from four principal theoretical perspectives only, whilst others have attempted to achieve instructional objectives specified by two, three or all four perspectives. James Anderson of the University of Utah,[20] a leading authority on the development of television literacy curricula, has labelled the four theoretical stances:

- Impact mediation or intervention
- Goal attainment
- Cultural understanding
- Visual literacy

Impact mediation or intervention

This perspective derives from the experimental research that has been concerned with the effects of the mass media. This research has typically assumed that different types of media content can have different effects on the way individuals behave subsequent to their exposure to it. Perhaps the best example of this is the belief that violent television leads to subsequent viewer aggression, even though the results of behavioural effects research have not indicated consistent one-to-one relationships between certain types of television content and later behaviour changes among viewers. Nevertheless, one line of thought is that an appropriate television literacy curriculum can help students to recognise portrayals of undesirable social behaviour and to distinguish these from the portrayals of desirable conduct.

The aim is to teach young viewers to realise that certain forms of TV conduct are acceptable in real life, and that others are not. It is explained to children, for instance, that unacceptable behaviours, such as violence, are often added to programmes as ingredients designed to enhance the entertainment value of fictional storylines. However, they are not to be taken as examples to be copied or used as justification for similar conduct by the children themselves.

The main goal of curricula derived from the impact mediation perspective, therefore, is to control the influence of television and ensure that, through teaching children to make full and proper interpretations of portrayals, only socially appropriate lessons are learned from the events it portrays.

Goal attainment

This perspective derives from an area of research and theory known as use- and gratifications. Instead of looking at the effects of television on viewers, this research model examines the reasons why people use television, some of which have been outlined in Chapter 2.

Instructional curricula within this perspective focus children's attention on their motives for viewing television. Next, they help children develop standards by which television viewing can be evaluated as the most appropriate method of satisfying their needs – social, emotional, intellectual and so forth. Finally, tuition is designed to encourage students to make careful and selective decisions about television usage, and to manage the amount of viewing they do. The idea is to teach children to become more critical consumers of television, and to realise that there may be other, more profitable, ways of spending one's time than sitting in front of the TV screen.

Cultural understanding

Television is an aspect of the culture in which it is produced, and it conveys the dominant values, beliefs and attitudes of that culture. Instructional frameworks deriving from this perspective attempt to convey the fact that television is simply an element of the culture. At the same time, however, television often exaggerates or distorts aspects of the sociocultural milieu out of which it is born, and the images it conveys may not always be entirely faithful reflections of social reality.

One area of concern, relating to TV's impact on children, is that the medium tends to depict various social groups – women, old people and ethnic minorities in particular – in relatively traditional and demeaning roles, and that such portrayals cultivate stereotypes and negative attitudes about these groups among young, impressionable viewers. These effects can be counteracted by making children more aware of how television can, through its statistical representation or by the characteristics it attributes to certain social groups, distort the way things are in the real world.

Visual literacy

This perspective focuses on the production techniques of television programmes, and in this respect contrasts with the cultural understanding model which emphasises the nature of the content of television. According to this approach, understanding television is founded in knowledge of the way programmes are made. This includes an awareness of the various ingredients of programmes, development of a concept or theme, writing of scripts, shooting film or videotape, recording and matching of narrative to visuals. An underlying assumption is that the impact of a programme may be determined as much by its technical quality as by its content. Special camera and editing effects are given particular attention and learning is evaluated in terms of students' abilities to describe and appraise specific techniques. This perspective usually includes a strong practical teaching element, in which students are taught how to handle technical equipment and produce different kinds of programmes for themselves.

These perspectives are not so distinct in their procedures and divergent in their aims as to be mutually incompatible, and much of the television literacy curricula that have now emerged incorporate elements from all four. But how successful have some of these televised literacy projects been, and what indications do they provide as to the value of educating children to become more TV literate?

TELEVISION LITERACY IN THE UNITED STATES

Much of the work on television literacy has been conducted in the United States, although this has still been on a limited scale. Many of the studies were stimulated by parent–teacher association interaction with parents, educators and network officials about the negative consequences of television on children's lives. Different television literacy curricula have had different emphases. Some have emphasised management of viewing, whilst others have focused on teaching children about the techniques of television as a means of innovation against possible harmful effects of watching certain types of television content (e.g. violence).[21]

One of the most comprehensive studies has been carried out by the Yale Family Television Research and Consultation Centre, which received funding from the ABC network. The researchers developed a series of eight lessons for use in elementary schools to teach children to understand television and to capitalise on their interest in this medium in conjunction with reading, writing and discussion skills. The study was carried out in a school system near a large city and replicated twice in the same state.[22]

After many improvements in the videotapes and teachers' guides had been made, it was tested on a larger sample in ten school districts in cities scattered throughout the United States. An additional curriculum was also developed for kindergarten, first- and second-grade children (ages 4, 5 and 6 respectively), and subsequently tested in one community. This was a refinement of the elementary-school curriculum but geared to younger children and emphasised more non-verbal activities.

The curriculum was designed to teach children the following things:

- to understand the different types of television programmes – news, documentaries, variety, game shows, situation comedies, dramas, etc.;
- to understand that programmes are created by writers, producers, directors, etc., and that they use actors and props;

- to understand how television works in terms of simple electronics;
- to distinguish fantasy from reality on the screen, and to be aware of and able to recognise camera techniques and special effects;
- to learn about the purpose and types of advertisements, including public service announcements and political broadcasts;
- to understand how television influences feelings, ideas, self-perceptions and identification;
- to become aware of television as a source of information about the world – and to become aware of the ways in which stereotypes are presented;
- to help children to be more critical of violence on television; to become aware that television rarely shows someone recovering from an act of violence or the aggressor being punished; and to understand the distinction between verbal and physical aggression;
- to use these lessons within a language arts framework so that children can gain experience in using correct grammar and spelling; writing letters; abstracting ideas, critical thinking, expressive language, and oral discussion and reading.

The first study ran an experimental and a control group; in order to evaluate the impact of the curriculum, pre- and post-tests and follow-up tests were used which included questions relating to the eight topics being taught. These topics were: Introduction to Television; Reality and Fantasy on Television; Camera Effects and Special Effects; Commercials and the Television Business; Identification with Television Characters; Stereotypes on Television; Violence and Aggression; and How Viewers Can Influence Television.

Results indicated that children in the experimental school showed a greater increase in knowledge about television than those in the control school. Differences were greatest between the two groups in the measures of knowledge and understanding of special effects, commercials and advertising. The children in the experimental school also learned more lesson-related vocabulary words and showed more improvement in their ability to identify videotaped examples of camera effects and special effects than did children in the control school.

Tests were also run to find out if the knowledge gained from the curriculum could be generalised to another situation – tests were on new material involving the area of special effects. Results demonstrated that the children could transfer their learning to the new situation, and indeed understood camera techniques and special effects when used in different shows from the ones used in the lessons. After this initial development, a follow-up study was conducted with a refined curriculum. Children aged 4–9 years took part, with lessons taught once a week. Modified materials were used for the youngest children, whose lessons included more play activities, puppets and so on.

Results for kindergarten (4-year-olds) through second grade (6-year-olds) indicated that at each level there was clear evidence of improvement in understanding the material covered in the curriculum. Particularly strong effects were found for the children's learning about camera techniques, the nature of editing, and the distinction between reality and fantasy characters.

In another important study it was found that young children were able to learn the contents of television literacy curricula and to apply them in discussions about television reality, but such learning did not seem to mediate television's impact on social attitudes. In a project begun originally in 1974, Dorr and her colleagues were concerned with modifying the effects of entertainment television via the cultivation of critical viewing skills in children.[23] This research was broken down initially in terms of a number of objectives. The first was to decrease the extent to which children perceived fictional television programmes as real. The second was to increase children's tendencies and abilities to compare television content with information from other sources. The third aim was to diminish the credibility children ascribed to television through teaching about the industry's economic goals, about production and about other legitimate sources of information. The final aim was to teach children to apply the knowledge they gained from the first three areas to the evaluation of television content.

To incorporate these four areas, two curricula about television and one control curriculum about social reasoning were used. All three curricula had separate versions for kindergarteners (aged 4) and for second- (aged 6) and third-graders (aged 7–8). They were designed to be taught to small groups of boys and girls in six one-hour lessons; they involved viewing audiovisual material, group discussion, drawing, role-playing, games, and commentary by the teacher.

Most emphasis was placed on games and role-playing, since these were effective ways to engage the children and to make the lessons concrete, and all curricula attempted to use analogies from the children's own experiences. The two television curricula used segments of programmes taped off-air to teach, illustrate and test informally the achievement of each lesson's goals.

The first television curriculum (the 'industry' curriculum) was designed to teach children about the production of entertainment programmes and the industry's economic system. Children were to learn eight facts, four about television production and four about broadcast economics, and apply them to reasoning about the reality/fantasy of entertainment programming. The eight facts were:

- plots are made up;
- characters are actors;
- incidents are fabricated;
- settings are often constructed;
- programmes are broadcast to make money;

- money for programmes comes from advertisers' purchasing airtime;
- ads are to sell products to the viewer;
- audience size determines broadcaster income.

The second television curriculum (the 'process' curriculum) was designed to teach children processes and sources for evaluating television content. Children were to learn four facts, three about television programmes and one about sources for judging television realism, and apply them in reasoning about the reality/fantasy of entertainment programming. The four facts were:

- entertainment programmes are made up;
- entertainment programmes vary in how reliable they are;
- viewers can decide how realistic they find entertainment programmes;
- television content may be evaluated by comparing it to one's own experience, asking other people, and consulting other media sources.

In this curriculum most of the effort was devoted to teaching children about the sources available to them to evaluate television content. Teaching about realism of entertainment programmes was less extensive here than in the industry curriculum. Moreover, while the process curriculum emphasised the extent to which programmes vary in their realism, the industry curriculum emphasised only their lack of realism.

The control curriculum on 'social reasoning' was designed to teach children role-taking skills. Children were to learn that other people have their own perspectives and feelings which matter in interactions with others, and that one can learn about them by asking, observing, talking with others, and trying out different interaction strategies. Children were expected to use this information in reasoning about social dilemmas common to them.

The children were pre-tested and the curricula were taught for two weeks. About three days after the last class, the children were tested on reality–fantasy judgements of entertainment content and knowledge of television production, industry economics and number of known sources for evaluating the reality of television. The children also viewed a half-hour episode of *The Jeffersons*, judged to present mildly uncomplimentary views of Blacks. About seven days later, the children were further tested, interviewed about reality/fantasy of television in general, of one of their favourite programmes and about the episode of *The Jeffersons* they saw.

The results showed that young children can, in as short a time as six hours, learn much about television and alternative sources of information, and can apply that information when asked to reason about the reality of television content. The two curricula each in their own way helped young children to understand better and evaluate television content. Each was effective for both kindergarteners and second- or third-graders. Improvement was more likely to be in areas where children do not have to engage in much reasoning. The study found that children can learn more about the television medium and how to evaluate it, and can apply that knowledge in discussing its contents.

Another study explored the effectiveness of an instructional film about television advertising, which was designed to reduce children's susceptibility to commercial appeals.[24] Here the researchers were interested in the possibility that children might be taught how to process and evaluate all commercials in a more 'adult', rational way. They conducted two studies: the first used an instructional film called *The Six Billion Dollar Sell*, a five-minute film designed for classroom use. Children (aged 9, 11 and 13) were split into two groups – one saw the instructional film and the other saw a film unrelated to commercials or persuasion. Immediately after viewing, the children filled out a questionnaire that asked how much they liked the film and how much they felt they had learned from it. It also repeated questions about general attitudes to commercials which had originally been given to them ten days before.

Five days later they watched a videotape with five commercials and answered questions dealing with general issues covered in *The Six Billion Dollar Sell*. The results showed that the children who viewed *The Six Billion Dollar Sell* were more sceptical than children who viewed the control film; this was particularly noticeable with the 9-year-olds.

The second study focused on younger children (aged 7, 8 and 10) and was of similar design. Children saw either one of two educational films (either *The Six Billion Dollar Sell* or one called *Seeing Through Commercials*), or a control film not concerned with advertising. Results showed greater increases in scepticism in the youngest age group, assumed to be more susceptible to commercial appeals due to their immaturity. This was borne out by pre- and post-test data. They, of course, had greater room to move or change.

Broadcasters themselves have also attempted to educate children to become more television-literate. It was in 1978 that NBC took the first steps towards direct industry participation in developing and airing television literacy information. A small number of short segments designed to inform children about some aspects of television were created by NBC and broadcast on Saturday mornings; they were known collectively as *How To Watch TV* (HTWTV).[25]

Television literacy curricula have various ultimate goals. These may include that children will watch less television, that they will watch better television, that they will believe or be influenced by less of what they see on television, and/or that they will be less influenced by the 'bad' things they see on television. Attaining these goals is usually thought to come about by making children aware of their viewing practices, teaching them how and why programmes are produced and broadcast, and helping them to be more analytical and evaluative about programme and advertising content.

The NBC experiments sought only to inform children about some of the illusions that can be created by television, to explain why commercials are broadcast, and to advocate certain desirable practices *vis-à-vis* television viewing patterns and response to commercials.

The HTWTV segments were designed to be inserted into the Saturday morning schedule in the same way that commercials are. Each was therefore self-contained and addressed one idea. Each message lasted thirty seconds and featured a male actor who was the lead in a half-hour 'pro-social' children's programme which NBC had also broadcast. As far as possible, the message was acted out and ended with a visual and audio presentation saying, 'There's a smart way to watch TV.'

Aimee Dorr and her colleagues investigated the impact of this educative material on a group of ninety-five ethnically mixed children in the Los Angeles area. The youngsters were invited to view a selection of children's programmes over a five-day period which included a variety of HTWTV drop-ins.[26]

The children were then asked if they recalled having seen something on television about 'how to watch TV' or a 'smart way to watch TV'. The majority of children believed they had recently seen something about how to watch television. Older children were more likely than younger children to say they had seen it, and boys were more likely than girls to say so. There was greater recall the closer in time to viewing recall was tested. When asked to describe the content of programmes on how to watch television, many could not. Only 62 per cent of those claimed to have seen such programming could actually describe any of the HTWTV content.

Each child was asked about a drop-in just seen, and if he or she could recognise the main point of it; 61 per cent of the children correctly selected the appropriate main idea from among three alternatives. Many more older than younger children, and more girls than boys, were able to select the correct alternative. Younger boys performed no better than chance on this item, and older boys performed only about as well as younger girls. This suggests that the ideas behind HTWTV messages were not communicated very effectively to boys, especially younger boys.

Did the children see these messages as presenting new ideas? Did they think the idea was worth presenting? Sixty-four per cent of children believed they already knew the information in the drop-in they had just viewed. Older more than younger children, and girls more than boys, were likely to feel they already knew it. Many believed they learned something new from HTWTV drop-ins. Overall, 54 per cent of the children who said they did not already know a drop-in's information indicated that they had wondered about it. Also, 81 per cent of all children felt that the drop-ins' information was worth knowing.

Did children see these short messages within programmes as programmes themselves, as commercials, or what? Fifty-one per cent categorised drop-ins as adverts. The remainder were split between seeing them as part of the programme or as something else. The HTWTV drop-ins were a positive contribution to children's television viewing experiences. They presented information which children judged to be worthwhile, whether or not they believed they already knew it, and adults certainly judged the information to be beneficial for children.

An attempt to redress the balance following a criticism of television literacy research made earlier was represented by a course developed in the mid-1980s in the United States which was designed to enhance the salience of pro-social material within programmes among children. The children under investigation were aged 10 to 12 years. The course ran for three months and its primary aim was to get children consciously to review their own television viewing.[27]

This in-school 'critical receivership skills' curriculum was found to be effective in enabling children to recall more of the factual content of programmes. Before the course, the children exhibited moderate levels of awareness that some programmes contained mainly antisocial content, others mainly pro-social content, and yet others a mixture of the two. Following the course, there was a reduction in children believing that 'few' programmes contained pro-social material. Having completed the course, more children explained the appearance of violence in programmes in terms of genre demands or plot requirements. There was a marked increase, especially among the younger children, in the belief that fictional television characters were 'made up' rather than real.

Further research with this television literacy course revealed that children who participated in it gained more accurate perceptions of how much pro-social material could actually be found in mainstream television programmes, and were better able to identify various forms of pro-social behaviour within these programmes. The course improved children's abilities to identify altruism, empathy, cooperative behaviours, sympathy and sharing behaviour, when they occurred on screen.[28]

EXAMPLES OF TV LITERACY PROJECTS IN BRITAIN

So far there has been little in the way of continuous and systematic assessment of the efficiency of teaching television in the classroom, even though in recent years a series of publications have emerged under the IBA's Educational Fellowship Scheme, and several television series for schools have been produced on the subject of television. In his book *Teaching About Television*, Len Masterman proposed a television studies curriculum for schools and colleges which aimed to achieve specific television literacy goals. Whilst this book is a mine of very good ideas for TV literacy curriculum development, it did not go on to report examples of their practical implementation and educational usefulness in the classroom.[29]

Nevertheless, more recently, particularly with the advent of new examinations for 16-year-olds (the GCSE) in the late 1980s, media studies is gradually becoming an acceptable component of the secondary-school curriculum. These courses invariably include a section on television and attempt to combine critical analysis and theory with practical work. The current National Curriculum Orders for English also recommend that children aged 5 and upwards should be given the opportunity to examine the ways in which different forms of media construct texts. However, there has been no attempt formally to assess children's understanding of different media as part of the national testing programme of English at ages 7, 11 and 14. Even at age 15–16, media studies is still an optional subject and is not an integral part of the core curriculum. In practice, this means that GCSE media studies is often seen as an 'easy' option and is frequently chosen by the less able students as an appropriate area of study.

One early practical attempt to teach television was made by Edward Buscombe, who piloted a number of experimental courses on television during the 1973–1974 academic year in several schools and colleges of further education in and around London.[30] One course, for example, consisted of three class periods per week for six weeks, in which 14-year-old boys at a London comprehensive school examined the content of a television series in detail. The chosen series was *Kung Fu* and, because no video-recording equipment was available, the teacher had to rely on the boys watching the programme in their own time at home.

A second course was developed in a different school, similar to the above in that it focused on the genre of TV series, but with the additional advantage that available video-recording equipment meant that programmes could be watched in class. This course was for two periods a week over ten weeks and examined events in programmes and attributes of leading characters, their lifestyles, personal histories, attitudes towards sex, violence, crime, money and so on. Essay exercises were set at regular intervals, based on specific topics of classroom discussion about the series under examination. Other courses in schools and colleges where facilities were even better included practical exercises in making programmes. Buscombe believed that pupils and students gained something from each of these courses, although he stressed that they were experimental and did not look at or attempt to teach the same things. An amalgam of these courses would probably bring most benefits, and even then there were many television topics he did not cover. However, Buscombe's effort at the time represented a very important initiative.

During the mid-1980s, in Britain, a further attempt was made to explore the best ways to teach with or about television. The Television Literacy Project reported a pilot study for a course taught to 14- to 15-year-old children, aimed at explaining television production techniques and approaches, and at evaluating critically television news broadcasts and drama. The course involved analysis of specific broadcasts and the planning, preparation and production of video programmes by the pupils themselves. Detailed course evaluation, by careful pre- and post-testing of experimental and control groups, demonstrated clear improvements of the children's understanding of those aspects of television on which tuition was given.[31]

This initial study was designed to develop, test and eventually further refine a course that would teach children to understand better how television is made and to become more critical in the way they watch programmes. The course gave equal emphasis to teaching about the practical problems of television production and to cultivating more active and critical thinking about programmes. In addition to the efficacy of the course as it stood, the researchers hoped to gain experience from this exercise which would serve as a pilot for the development of a more detailed and extensive course in the future.

Broadly, the aims of the course were to improve children's awareness on a number of specific topics:

- To understand techniques of production and the meanings conveyed by certain types of camera work such as cuts, fades and zooms; awareness of special effects and what they signified.
- To become more aware of different settings and contexts and to distinguish between realism and fantasy in programmes on television.
- To improve understanding of the news on television and to think more carefully about the value and credibility of the news; news was considered as a form of entertainment as well as information and thought was given to why television news tends to stress certain kinds of events and depict them in a certain way.
- To evaluate the portrayals of characters and events in television dramas more critically and to consider how they compare with people and events in the real world.

In all, forty-two 14- to 15-year-old pupils from a single school on Humberside took part in this pilot exercise. Twenty-six children were selected for the experimental group (who were taught the course) and sixteen were allocated to the control group (who were not taught about television in class). While the former were taught about television, the latter were given normal English lessons which involved reading and essay-writing exercises on non-television topics. Half of each group were boys and half were girls.

The course lasted eight weeks and was taught in English lessons. During six weeks there were six forty-minute classroom periods per week. Another week was devoted to a field trip on which pupils made their own video-recordings. During the eighth week of the course, school examinations meant that only two forty-minute classroom periods were available. Pupils on the course spent about half their time on practical exercises, making their own news and drama programmes with video-recording equipment, and the other half discussing television in general or particular programmes from which extracts were viewed in class. The children also completed three pieces of written work on discussion topics about different aspects of television.

Both experimental and control groups were given tests on their understanding of drama on television and of news on television before the course began, and re-tests on both topics after completion of the course. Experimentals and controls were tested at the same time. The tests were constructed, marked and check by a team of teachers from the school. In the drama tests and re-tests, both groups were shown a fifteen-minute excerpt from two television dramas, not seen by any of them before. Tests probed children's memory and understanding of the plot of each programme, perceptions of how realistic the setting appeared to be, and impressions about the characters and their lives. In the news tests, both groups saw an edited network television newscast recorded several days earlier from a lunchtime bulletin, which none of the children would have seen because they were all at school at the time of transmission. Questions probed recall and comprehension of the news stories in the bulletin.

Results showed that the scores of children in the experimental group improved substantially from initial to final tests of television drama and television news, whilst the scores of the controls improved slightly for news and fell for drama. On the initial drama test there were no significant differences between experimental and control group children, while on the final test, the former performed significantly better than the latter. On the initial news test, control group children actually performed better than the experimentals, while on the final test their positions were reversed, as the children who had undergone the television literacy course were able to remember and understand more than were those children who had not taken the course.

Thus, in a relatively short spell of lessons lasting only two months, it was possible to enhance teenage children's understanding of television and their abilities to learn from it.

However, very little appears to have been done for the younger age group. Most activities carried out with primary-school children (aged 5 to 11) seem to depend on the interests of individual teachers. The British Film Institute attempted, during the early 1990s, to redress this imbalance, with support from the (then) Department of Education and Science, and set up a working party to examine the possibility of introducing a standardised media studies curriculum for younger children. A small group of enthusiastic and committed teachers has designed and tested various methods of introducing media studies to younger children, but this seems to be in a fairly haphazard and unstructured way, making no provision for any kind of formal assessment to be applied.

In extending the Television Literacy Project, Paul Kelley has described courses in television literacy developed for young children aged 5 to 10 years.

Separate courses were developed for 5- to 6-year-olds and for 9- to 10-year-olds. In each case, the course involved watching and discussing television, as well as practical video work.[32]

Testing 5- to 6-year-olds proved a considerable problem. Open-ended discussion with individuals or small groups seemed to work best, but questions of standardisation and scoring of responses were difficult. There was little doubt that the children learned from the course, but the difficulties of testing very young children meant that it was not practical to test more than a few. With the older children, testing was easier because written tests could be used. Even here, though, there were limitations, because some children could not respond very effectively or always do themselves justice in written tests.

Following these two pilot studies, two more larger-scale studies were run with 9- to 10-year-olds and 11- to 12-year-olds. All groups were given pre- and post-tests. These tests examined comprehension of television, as well as ascertaining facts about usual media use. The course involved the children in viewing and discussing programmes and practical work with video equipment. The course itself ran for six weeks and early evidence indicated that it had produced improvements among the children on it in levels of television comprehension.

Television's own attempts to help children

As in the United States, beginning in the late 1970s there were several notable television series in Britain, produced by the broadcasting industry itself, that attempted to improve young people's understanding of television. Accompanying each series was a booklet, published by the television company concerned, in which synopses were provided of each programme and questions raised by it, and around which classroom lessons or written exercises could be built. One series examined the influence of television, and two looked at the inner structure and production process of television. *Viewpoint 2* was a series of four programmes produced by Thames Television in 1979 about the mass media and the way different groups of people – notably young people, Blacks, workers and those out of work – are represented in them. The aim of the series was to get young viewers to think more carefully about the media images of different social groups and to consider whether these images are often accurate or unreliable, and whether media portrayals might influence public attitudes and beliefs. In 1978, Yorkshire Television produced a series of eight programmes called *Looking at Television*, which examined a number of different aspects of television – measuring the audience, the historical development of the TV industry, the production of drama, regional programming, light entertainment and the news, the role of advertising in TV, and future developments in the industry.

Later (September–October 1983), Thames Television transmitted five programmes on *Understanding Television* as the first unit of the 1983–1984 series of *The English Programme.* The aim of this unit was to introduce school children to aspects of television with which they may not hitherto have been familiar. Topics covered included how programmes are constructed and the production process, the history of broadcasting in Britain, audience research and how its findings may influence programme-making and scheduling, and future technological developments in the television industry.

Each of these television productions and publications illustrates the efforts of the industry to enhance young people's understanding of television, and to encourage and sponsor research in curriculum develop-ment. Unfortunately, there is very little evidence emanating from the United Kingdom that these various television literacy curricula have been 'field'-tested and found feasible and successful in real school situations.

In The Netherlands, Dutch researchers have reported educational effects of a six-part schools television series designed to encourage children aged 10 to 12 years to become more discriminating consumers of violent television crime series. The series was made by the Dutch School Television Corporation and was broadcast nationwide, being seen in 3,500 primary schools (35 per cent of all Dutch primary schools).[33]

The main objective of this course was to reduce the level of the perceived realism of television violence by making children more aware of the unrealistic nature of dramatised violence and of the salient differences between violence on television and violence in real life. The course chose to focus specifically upon the depiction of crime and police in fictional TV drama. Cartoons and fantasy programmes for children were not used in this study because it was felt that by the age of 10 to 12 children were already aware of the purely fictional or fantasy nature of such programmes.

The justification of much of the violent activity on the part of the 'good guys', as seen in excerpts from television programmes, was called into question by explaining, among other things, that real-life police officers and private detectives are only permitted to use violence in very exceptional circumstances. The schools broadcasts also encouraged children to take a more critical stance on the justification of violent acts in general by presenting evidence of the serious nature of real-life violence as opposed to violence as depicted on television. To this effect, children were confronted with recorded interviews with

- police officers who had actually shot someone in the line of duty, and who related the deep impression this event had made on them;
- victims of violence who talked about the physical and, especially, the emotional effects they had suffered as a result of their experience; and
- a medical doctor who discussed the medical consequences of various types of violent acts.

Commentary by real police officers and private detectives on excerpts from crime programmes, pointing out the differences between film and real life, was used to make clear the unrealistic nature of many violent films.

The television series was accompanied by a workbook which had six chapters, each corresponding to one of the six episodes in the series. The material in the workbook was designed to reinforce and further develop points made in the programmes. The text was interspersed with questions and assignments. A teachers' manual was also produced to help with student supervision.

The evaluation of the project involved ascertaining the subjective impressions of teachers and students as well as more objective tests of learning from it. The latter included questions about the police, police work, crime, and comparisons between fictional depictions and real-life facts. Teachers and students reacted positively to the schools television projects; it was found enjoyable and informative. The lessons produced a significant reduction in the level of realism children attributed to fictional television crime series, as well as an increase in knowledge of the issues covered.

A further study was carried out to examine the educational effects of a further six-programme schools television series in The Netherlands designed to teach children aged 10 to 12 years that television news broadcasts give a selective and thus incomplete impression of the world.

Three measures were used in evaluating the success of the schools television project:

- the amount of information acquired from the project ('knowledge');
- proficiency in recognising the choices that have been made in the putting-together of a news item ('news viewing skills'); and
- credence given to television news ('credibility of TV news').

Subjective reactions to the TV series and the project were also ascertained.

Results indicated that the schools television series led to an increase in children's knowledge of the selection processes involved in the production of news programmes, and an increase in children's proficiency in recognising the moments of selection in news items. However, the television series did not result in a more critical attitude towards the news or to a decrease in the level of credibility children attributed to television news broadcasts. The reason for this finding was that the series showed that the makers of news programmes are conscious of the selective processes involved in making news programmes and do their utmost to make the choices in the most responsible way possible. As a result, the series may have unintentionally created the impression that the problem of selectivity can be satisfactorily solved.[34]

CONCLUSION

Concern about the impact of television on the lives of children has existed since broadcasts began. For a long time the predominant assumption was that television acted upon young viewers whose behaviours and outlook on life were changed through constant passive exposure. However, there is a growing awareness now that television can be turned to educational advantage as a tool for instruction, a source of information about the world and as a subject in its own right. Furthermore, children's natural interest in television may function as a powerful motivating force which can facilitate rapid learning about the medium itself and encourage youngsters to practise other skills in reading, writing and critical thinking, which they normally face up to only with reluctance.

It is easy enough to join those who criticise television for its destructive social and intellectual influences; but rather more imagination and effort is required to use the medium for its socially and educationally constructive value. Let us hope that schools do not shy away from this challenge.

Chapter 14

Making the best of television

Television is an inescapable part of family life – and this means of children's lives, too. We have presented a broad overview of what is known about children's use of television, their understanding of what it broadcasts, and of the impact that it has (or is often assumed to have) on their lives. The television environment has undergone a period of rapid and unprecedented change in the last ten years. The potential range of influences that television might have upon young viewers has expanded as the medium itself has evolved. As the television market has become a more competitive place, with more channels competing for viewers, the notion of centralised regulation of broadcast output has become increasingly problematic. Technological advances in communications and the marriage of television to the computer, in particular, means that more and more control over reception is passing to the consumer.

Public discussion about children's relationship with the small screen has been dominated over the years by the supposed harm it does to them. The daily press regularly abounds with stories which report on adverse influences of television portrayals of violence, sex, drinking, drug-taking and affluence in programmes, and of uncontrolled consumerism in advertisements. Television has been accused of encouraging children and teenagers to become more aggressive, to begin drinking under age, to use bad language, and to adopt sexist and racist points of view. Television is also seen as undermining the educational development of young people through cultivating mental passivity and laziness and by keeping children up too late.

While it may be true that the overindulgence with television, as with most other things, can bring problems, it is equally true that when it is used properly and constructively television can have many positive influences on young viewers. All too often, these influences are ignored or underplayed simply because they fail to make such good news copy compared with stories about its supposed negative effects.

Television can provide children with a breadth of experiences, not all of which can in any way be construed as bad. Indeed, television can bring to children knowledge and other personal benefits which may be unavailable to them through any other source. People who dwell on the negative side of television fail to do the medium justice in terms of identifying and elaborating the role it actually plays in children's lives.

Moreover, the arrival of interactive entertainment technology has brought with it opportunities for viewers to take more active control over the nature of the experiences they can glean through their television sets. We are already beginning to witness early examples of the kinds of enhanced entertainment forms such technologies can deliver. Interactive game shows allow viewers at home to compete on an equal footing with contenders in the studio. In the near future, viewers will be able to select, on a personal basis, the particular camera angle from which they wish to watch sports events. Even more exciting notions are now emerging, such as the virtual reality newsroom which does not simply render viewers direct eyewitnesses of events as they happen, but places them at the centre of the action, from which they have a three-dimensional viewpoint and herald television experiences unlike any ever dreamed of twenty years ago.[1]

Despite the opinions held by its critics, television is not invariably bad for children. In the past ten years, the balance of opinion has been redressed at least in part by evidence that emphasises some of the good things that can happen to children contingent upon their sensible use of television.[2] In its more interactive form, television has been shown to have the potential to help children with the development of important intellectual skills. Despite the concern about the prevalence of violence themes, video games, for example, have been found to improve children's spatial skills[3] and their logical and strategic planning skills.[4] Boys seem to benefit especially from playing video games, although both sexes show improvement in certain intellectual skills which appear to be exercised by playing video games.[5]

Television can and does influence children. Its effects can be either good or bad, depending on how the medium is used. Either way, television's effects on youngsters are rarely simple or direct. For a start, television's influences can occur at a number of levels. It can affect children's knowledge, beliefs and values; it can produce shifts in attitudes or feelings about things; and it can cause certain courses of action and changes in patterns of behaviour.

What children get out of television, however, can depend crucially on what they bring to it. Children do not simply sit passively and watch the images displayed before them on the screen, absorbing anything that is presented without question or interpretation.[6] Instead, they often actively select what to watch to satisfy particular needs or moods, and they place their own meanings on programming and advertising content. Some programmes may indeed wash over children, leaving behind no clear trace of having been viewed. Others may have a profound impact on them, perhaps shifting a belief about or in something, or radically altering a particular view of the world. In the case of most programmes, however, their influence falls somewhere in between these two extremes, with the precise nature and strength of television's impact being determined and limited by the reasons children have for watching at all, and by their understanding and interpretation of what was shown.

The effects of television on children can also depend on what kinds of programmes they are watching. Another important factor is how the programmes are made. Some programmes are designed to inform and educate, while others are made principally to entertain. Programmes do not always sit comfortably in these convenient categories, though. Nor do they always or necessarily attract viewers by their major functions. Entertainment programmes may excite, enthral, amuse and in other ways move their audiences, but they may also cultivate awareness of certain aspects of life, influence beliefs and values, or provide insights into how to deal with personal and social problems. In addition to their entertainment function, therefore, these programmes also have an educational impact. This educational impact may be perceived by viewers who turn to such programmes not simply to be entertained but also because they believe they can learn something of personal value from them. Television's fictional narratives often contain elements of truth or insights into everyday reality which viewers – young and old – can pick up on and recall at some later date for their own use where relevant or appropriate.

Programmes that are made to inform may also need to be entertaining in order to win and maintain their audience. In peak-time television in the United Kingdom, the schedules regularly feature magazine shows whose principal aim is to inform or advise the public about social and consumer issues (e.g. holidays, gardening, health and medical matters), together with the latest news about scientific and technological developments. These programmes, which often contain film reports as well as studio anchors, employ entertainment formats, visual effects and background music. The popularity of such television series may often be put down to their production qualities as much as to the value of the information they provide.

It is becoming increasingly well established that children can learn from all kinds of television programmes, including ones not ostensibly designed to inform or educate. They may learn about science from studio-based magazine programmes, whether these are made especially for children or for the general audience. In addition, though, factual information can be picked up even from television game shows. There are two learning effects associated with these programmes. First, active participation in a question-and-answer quiz format can lead young viewers to strengthen what they know already through the rehearsal invoked by answering a question posed to the contestants in the show. Second, new facts can be learned from the correct answers given to questions either by the contestants or by the compère when the contestants themselves are unable to give the correct reply.[7]

Young viewers soon learn to make up their own minds about programmes. They learn to distinguish between different categories of programming by genre and in terms of the kinds of functions different programmes have. Children come to recognise that some programmes are good for entertainment reasons and others are good as sources of learning – but learning which touches on issue of importance to them.

Although broad distinctions can readily be made by children between 'reality' or factual programmes and fictional or 'make-believe' programmes, there are subtler shades of realism where confusions can still arise. Children may not automatically believe everything they see in contemporary dramas, for instance, but sometimes preconceived ideas about aspects of the real world may be shifted, albeit temporarily, by credible dramatised events which run counter to their beliefs. Thus, British pre-teen and teenage children's opinions about women police officers were altered by convincing dramatic television portrayals of fictional female police officers being competent in positions of authority.[8]

There is an accumulating body of academic research evidence, some of which has been reviewed in this book, which demonstrates the very positive learning potential of television. This learning function can be implemented throughout all stages of childhood with appropriate programming for different age-bands. Studies carried out among preschool children in the United States using programmes such as *Sesame Street*, and in Britain with *Play School* and *Rainbow*, show that children can and do learn many valuable lessons from such television – particularly when they watch with other people like their mothers or older children. Young children can benefit most from television if parents, or other adults watching with them, discuss what they have seen.

Schools can also play their part. Educationally oriented programmes, when carefully integrated into a structured course framework involving input from other source materials, can have an influential teaching impact. It is essential, however, that television is used in a controlled and systematic fashion, rather than in a haphazard, hit-and-miss sort of way, in order to be effective in a formal educational context.

At the same time as drawing attention to the good effects of television, a more considered and cautious appraisal is needed of the so-called bad effects of the medium. Without diminishing the very genuine concern that exists among some critics about the possible harms of television, we believe there is a tendency to make television a scapegoat for some of society's ills. Television is often unjustifiably accused of misleading children on very flimsy evidence and a very poor understanding of how young viewers respond to programmes.

The research on the effects of television violence, for example, is voluminous, but far from conclusive. It might be argued that where there is doubt caution should prevail. We would not dispute this. We would point out, though, that the broadcasters in the United Kingdom already implement comprehensive codes of practice on the portrayal of violence on television, and these codes are made known to programme makers. Furthermore, we cannot see that it is of benefit to anyone to distract attention from the significant causes of social violence by unreasonably laying the blame at the door of television. Nevertheless, it is important to be as clear as possible about what sensible advice can be gleaned from the existing research evidence to enable effective codes of practice to be put in place which protect the interests of viewers while not placing unreasonable or unworkable constraints on programme makers.

Recent times have seen a shift in the tempo of the debate on the other side of the Atlantic. In the United States, there is now a general acceptance of the conclusion that television violence does cause harmful effects by increasing individual levels of aggressiveness in children and serving up examples of antisocial conduct which young viewers readily copy. Rather than continuing to debate whether or not television violence has any effects, therefore, attention has moved on to a consideration of what to do about this established social problem. This has led to a renewed focus on the cataloguing of violence in programme output, but with special reference to the nature of the violence shown, rather than simply its overall amount.[9] The context in which portrayed violence occurs is seen as being central because audience research has repeatedly shown that viewers make perceptual distinctions between on-screen violent incidents primarily in terms of the setting or context in which they occur.[10]

Critics of television often point to the considerable research literature on the effects of television violence. The fact that there is a great deal of research on the effects of television violence does not necessarily make the case stronger. Research techniques commonly employed by researchers in this field can be questioned for the robustness and veracity of the findings they produce. Research which takes place under artificial conditions may have doubtful relevance to what happens between children and television in reality. Even when children's use of television and the impact it has upon them has been studied under real-world conditions, shortcomings on the part of respondents to supply accurate or complete information about their viewing and other social habits may often undermine the validity of the research findings.

Looked at in a broader context, studies of children's aggression, and its relationship with television viewing and upbringing, suggest that family lifestyle, local neighbourhood, school and peers are more influential than television programmes. Television can show children how other people, including 'bad' people, behave, but it cannot bring them up to be good or bad. Indeed, television may show that bad behaviour is something not to be copied or to be proud of. There is evidence that, far from wanting to imitate 'bad examples', children can become quite moralistic and disapproving of televised bad behaviour.[11]

Intellectually, television watching can stimulate conversational skills, cooperation with other children, imaginative play, the development of logical inferences, the understanding of stories and insight into (and sympathy with) other people's human dilemmas. Adults can encourage this learning. The study of television in school can introduce children to complex literary concepts of plot and style, persuasive techniques and critical appraisal through a medium that is both accessible and interesting to them. These benefits do not all happen by accident or good luck; however, they can be cultivated and controlled. We must learn how to use television to enjoy its full benefits, and we must teach our children to do likewise.

We are already witnessing an accelerating expansion in the number of television channels available to the public, especially via cable and satellite transmissions. The shift from analogue to digital transmissions will mean that many more television channels will be available over the existing terrestrial wavebands. What will all this growth mean for viewers? Increased public anxiety about this development stems not only from worries about what it will mean for the quality and diversity of broadcasting, but also from the ways in which it will affect children. Will they spend more time watching the box? Will they be exposed more often to material that is unsuitable for them? Will increased interactivity in the use of the TV set present greater risks of addiction to the medium, as some researchers have already hinted at for arcade video games?[12]

Regarding the questions about amount of viewing and suitability of broadcast material, we can probably be reassured by the fact that children do not use television haphazardly, but selectively. And they do not accept impassively everything that is shown to them in programmes; instead they learn to question and discriminate. These faculties can be strengthened through teaching management of viewing and critical television literacy. Children's understanding of television can also be aided by the attention of parents to what their offspring watch. The role and responsibilities of parents, especially with very young children, will become even more important as the range of home entertainment options available to children continues to grow. With this help, children can become careful and sensible users of television who recognise its positive qualities and eschew its negative ones.

References

PREFACE TO THE SECOND EDITION

1 *The AGB Cable and Satellite Yearbook 1995*, London: BARB/Taylor Nelson AGB plc, 1995.
2 *Television: The Public's View 1994*, London: Independent Television Commission, 1995.
3 Gunter, B., Sancho-Aldridge, J. and Winstone, P., *Television: The Public's View – 1993*, London: John Libbey, 1994.

1 WHAT IS THE NATURE OF CHILDREN'S VIEWING?

1 Anderson, D. R. and Burns, J., Paying attention to television, in J. Bryant and D. Zillmann (eds), *Responding to the Screen: Reception and Reaction Processes* Hillsdale, NJ: Lawrence Erlbaum Associates, 1991 (pp. 3–25); Morley, D., *Family Television: Cultural Power and Domestic Leisure*, London: Comedia, 1986; Gunter, B., Furnham, A. and Lineton, Z., Watching people watching television: what goes on in front of the TV set?, *Journal of Educational Television*, 1995, 21(3), 165–191.
2 Svennevig, M. and Wynberg, R., Viewing is viewing is viewing... or is it? A broader approach to television research, *Admap*, 1986, May, 267–274.
3 Bechtel, R. B., Achelpohl, C. and Akers, R., Correlates between observed behaviours and questionnaire responses on television viewing, in E. A. Rubinstein, G. A. Comstock and J. P. Murray (eds), *Television and Social Behaviour*, vol. 4, *Television in Day-to-Day Life: Patterns of Use*, Washington DC: US Government Printing Office, 1972.
4 Anderson, D. R., Alwitt, L. F., Lorch, E. P. and Levin, S. R., Watching children watch television, in G. Hale and M. Lewis (eds), *Attention and Cognitive Development*, New York: Plenum, 1979.
5 Schramm, W., Lyle, J. and Parker, E. B., *Television in the Lives of Our Children*, Stanford, CA: Stanford University Press, 1961.
6 Levin, S.R. and Anderson, D. R., The development of attention, *Journal of Communication*, 1976, 26(2), 126–135.
7 Anderson, D. R. and Levin, S. R., Young children's attention to *Sesame Street*, *Child Development*, 1976, 47, 806–811.
8 Independent Television Commission, *Viewing of Cable Channels on the Increase*, London: Independent Television Commission news release, 23 December 1995.

9   Gunter, B., Sancho-Aldridge, J. and Winstone, P., *Television: The Public's View in 1993*, London, John Libbey, 1994.
10 Wober, J. M., The extent to which viewers watch violence containing programmes, *Current Psychology: Research and Reviews* special issue, B. Gunter (ed.), *Violence on Television*, 1988, 7(1), 43–57.
11 Ibid.
12 Himmelweit, H. T., Oppenheim, A. N and Vince, P., *Television and the Child: An Empirical Study of the Effects of Television on the Young*, London: Oxford University Press, 1958.
13 Gunter, B. and Greenberg, B. S., Media-wise, *Times Educational Supplement*, 10 October 1986.
14 Brown, J. R., Cramond, J. K. and Wilde, R. J., Displacement effects of television and the child's functional orientation to media, in E. Katz and J. Blumler (eds), *The Use of Mass Communication: Current Perspectives on Gratifications Research*, Beverly Hills, CA: Sage, 1974; Williams, T. M. (ed.), *The Impact of Television: A National Experiment in Three Communities*, New York/London: Academic Press, 1986.
15 Robinson, J. P., Television and leisure time: yesterday, today and (maybe) tomorrow, *Public Opinion Quarterly*, 1969, 33, 210–222.
16 Himmelweit et al., op. cit.
17 Bechtel et al., op. cit.
18 Kubey, R. and Csikszentmihalyi, M., *Television and the Quality of Life: How Viewing Shapes Everyday Experiences*, Hillsdale, NJ: Lawrence Erlbaum Associates, 1990.
19 Maccoby, E., Television: its impact on school children, *Public Opinion Quarterly*, 1951, 32, 102–112.
20 Coffin, T., Television's impact on society, *American Psychologist*, 1955, 10, 630–641.
21 Weiss, W., Effects of the mass media of communications, in R. Lindzey and E. Aronson (eds), *Handbook of Social Psychology*, vol. 5, *Applied Social Psychology*, Reading, MA: Addision Wesley, 1969, 77–195.
22 Himmelweit et al., op. cit.; Hornik, R. C., Out-of-school television and schooling: hypothesis and methods, *Review of Educational Research*, 1981, 51, 199–214.
23 Himmelweit et al., op. cit.; Schramm et al., op. cit.
24 Brown et al., op. cit.
25 Himmelweit, H.T. et al., 1958, op. cit.
26 Medrich, E. A., Raizen, J. A., Rubin, U. and Buckley, S., *The Serious Business of Growing Up*, Berkeley: University of California Press, 1982.
27 Murray, J. P. and Kippax, S., Children's social behaviour in three towns with differing television experience, *Journal of Communication*, 1978, 28, 19–29.
28 Williams, op. cit.
29 Selnow, G. A. and Reynolds, H., Some opportunity costs of television viewing, *Journal of Broadcasting*, 1984, 28(3), 315–322.
30 Muntz, D. C., Roberts, D. F. and Van Vuuren, D. P., Reconsidering the displacement hypothesis: television's influence on children's time use, *Communication Research*, 1993, 20(1), 51–75.
31 Gunter and Greenberg, op. cit.

2 WHY DO CHILDREN WATCH TV?

1 Gunter, B. and Svennevig, M., *Behind and in Front of the Screen: Television's Involvement with Family Life*, London: IBA/John Libbey, 1987.

2 Lin, C. A., Modelling the gratification-seeking process of television viewing, *Human Communication Research*, 1993, 20, 224–244.

3 Conway, J. C. and Rubin, A. M., Psychological predictors of television viewing motivation, *Communication Research*, 1991, 18, 443–463.

4 Katz, E., Blumler, J. and Gurevitch, M., Utilisation of mass communication by the individual, in E. Katz and J. Blumler (eds) *The Uses of Mass Communications: Current Perspectives in Gratifications Research*, Beverly Hills, CA: Sage, 1974.

5 Herzog, H., What do we really know about daytime serial listeners?, in P. F. Lazarsfeld and F. Stanton (eds), *Radio Research 1942–3*, New York: Duell, Sloan & Pearce, 1944.

6 Schramm, W., Lyle, J. and Parker, E. B., *Television in the Lives of our Children*, Stanford, CA: Stanford University Press, 1961.

7 Greenberg, B. S., Viewing and listening parameters among British youngsters, in R. Brown (ed.) *Children and Television*, London: Collier Macmillan, 1976.

8 Rubin, A., Television usage, attitudes and viewing behaviours of children and adolescents, *Journal of Broadcasting*, 1977, 21, 355–369; Rubin, A., Television use by children and adolescents, *Human Communication Research*, 1979, 5, 109–120.

9 Greenberg, op. cit.

10 Dembo, R. and McCron, R., Social factors in media use, in Brown, op. cit.

11 Greenberg, op. cit.

12 Gunter and Svennevig, op. cit.; Gunter, B., Sancho-Aldridge, J., and Winstone, P., *Television: The Public's View in 1993*, London: John Libbey, 1994.

13 Maccoby, E. E., Television: its impact on schoolchildren, *Public Opinion Quarterly*, 1951, 15, 421–441.

14 Gantz, W. and Masland, J., Television as babysitter, *Journalism Quarterly*, 1986, 63(3), 530–536.

15 Howitt, D. and Cumberbatch, G., The parameters of attraction to mass media figures, in Brown, op. cit.

16 Johnsson-Smaragdi, V., *TV Use and Social Interaction in Adolescence: A Longitudinal Study*, Stockholm: Almqvist and Wiksell International, 1983.

17 Himmelweit, H. T., Oppenheim, A. N. and Vince, P., *Television and the Child: An Empirical Study of the Effects of Television on the Young*, London: Oxford University Press, 1958.

18 Ibid.

19 Freedman, J. and Newston, R., The effect of anger of preference for filmed violence, paper presented at the annual conference of the American Psychological Association, Chicago, September 1975.

20 Goldstein, J. H., Preference for aggressive movie content: the effects of cognitive salience, unpublished manuscript, Temple University, Philadelphia, 1982.

21 'Gunter, B., Do aggressive people prefer violent television?, *Bulletin of the British Psychological Society*, 1983, 36, 166–168.

22 Dominick, J. F. and Greenberg, B. S., Attitudes toward violence: the interaction of television response, family attitudes and social class, in G. A. Comstock and E. A. Rubinstein (eds), *Television and Social Behaviour*, vol. 3, *Television and Adolescent Aggressiveness*, Washington, DC: US Government Printing Office,

1972; McIntyre, J. J., Teevan, J. J. and Hartnagel, T., Television violence and deviant behaviour, in Comstock and Rubinstein, op. cit.; McLeod, J. M., Atkin, C. K. and Chaffee, S. J., Adolescents, parents and television use: adolescent self-report measures from Maryland and Wisconsin samples, in Comstock and Rubinstein, op. cit.

23 Atkins, C., Greenberg, B. S., Korzenny, F. and McDermott, S., Selective exposure to televised violence, *Journal of Broadcasting*, 1979, 21, 5–13.

24 Zillmann, D., Hezel, R. T. and Medoff, N. J., The effect of affective states on selective exposure to televised entertainment fare, *Journal of Applied Social Psychology*, 1980, 10(4), 323–339.

25 Schramm et al., op. cit.

26 Boyanowsky, E. O., Film preferences under condition of threat: whetting the appetite for violence, information or excitement?, *Communication Research*, 1977, 4, 133–144.

27 Sparks, G., The relationship between distress and delight in males' and females' reactions to frightening films, *Human Communication Research*, 1991, 17, 625–637.

28 Sparks, G., Developing a scale to assess cognitive responses to frightening films, *Journal of Broadcasting and Electronic Media*, 1986, 30, 65–73; Zillmann, D., Transfer of excitation in emotional behaviour, in J. T. Cacioppo and R. E. Petty (eds), *SocioPsychophysiology* (pp. 215–240).

29 Zillmann, D. and Bryant, J., Affect, mood and emotion as determinants of selective exposure, in D. Zillmann and J. Bryant (eds), *Selective Exposure to Communication*, 1985, Hillsdale, NJ: Lawrence Erlbaum Associates (pp. 157–190); Sparks, G. And Spirek, M. M., Individual differences in coping with stressful mass media: an activation-arousal view, *Human Communication Research*, 1985, 15, 195–216.

30 Johnston, D. D., Adolescents' motivations for viewing graphic horror, *Human Communication Research*, 1995, 21(4), 522–552.

31 Oliver, M. B., Adolescents' enjoyment of graphic horror: effects of viewers' attitudes and portrayals of victims, *Communication Research*, 1993, 20, 30–50.

32 Medoff, N. J., Selective exposure to televised comedy programmes, *Journal of Applied Communication Research* 1982, 10(2), 117–132.

33 Zillmann, D., Mood management: using entertainment to full advantage, in L. Donohew, H. E. Sypher and E. T. Higgins (eds), *Communication, Social Cognition and Affect*, Hillsdale, NJ: Lawrence Erlbaum Associates, 1988 (pp. 147–171).

34 Zillmann, D., The experimental exploration of gratifications from media entertainment, in K. E. Rosengren, L. A. Wenner and P. Palmgreen (eds), *Media Gratifications Research: Current Perspectives*, Beverly Hills, CA: Sage, 1985 (pp. 225–239).

35 Zillmann, D., The logic of suspense and mystery, in J. Bryant and D. Zillmann (eds), *Responding to the Screen: Reception and Reaction Processes*, Hillsdale, NJ: Lawrence Erlbaum Associates, 1991 (pp. 281–303).

36 Masters, J. C., Ford, M. E. and Arend, R. A., Children's strategies for controlling affective responses to aversive social experience, *Motivation and Emotion*, 1983, 7, 103–116.

3 HOW DO CHILDREN WATCH TV?

1 Svennevig, M., *The Viewer Viewed*, paper presented to ESOMAR, Seminar on Research for Broadcasting Decision-Making, Amsterdam: ESOMAR, 1987.

2   Svennevig, op. cit.; Gunter, B., Furnham, A. and Lineton, Z., Watching people watching television: what goes on in front of the TV set?, *Journal of Educational Television*, 1995, 21(3), 165–191.

3   Anderson, D. R. and Lorch, E. P., Looking at television: action or reaction?, in J. Bryant and D. R. Anderson (eds), *Children's Understanding of Television: Research on Attention and Comprehension*, New York: Academic Press, 1983.

4   Gunter et al., op. cit.

5   Singer, J. L., The power and limitations of television: a cognitive-affective analysis, in P. H. Tannenbaum (ed.), *The Entertainment Functions of Television*, Hillsdale, NJ; Lawrence Erlbaum Associates, 1980.

6   Anderson, D. R. and Levin, S. R., Young children's attention to *Sesame Street*, *Child Development*, 1976, 47, 806–811.

7   Anderson and Lorch, op. cit.

8   Calvert, S. L., Huston, A. C., Watkins, B. A. and Wright, J. C., The relation between selective attention to television forms and children's comprehension of content, *Child Development*, 1982, 53, 601–610; Alwitt, L. F., Anderson, D. R., Lorch, E. P. and Levin, S. R., Pre-school children's visual attention of television, *Human Communication Research*, 1980, 7, 52–67; Welch, A. and Watt, J. H., Visual complexity and young children's learning from television, *Human Communication Research*, 1982, 8, 133–145.

9   Singer, op. cit.

10 Hollenbeck, A. R. and Slaby, R. G., Infant visual responses to television, *Child Development*, 1979, 50, 41–45.

11 Anderson and Levin, op. cit.; Carew, J. V., Experience and the development of intelligence in young children at home and in daycare, *Monographs of the Society for Research in Child Development*, 1980, 45, 1–89.

12 Alwitt et al., op. cit.; Anderson and Levin, op. cit.; Calvert et al., op. cit.

13 Collins, W. A., Children's comprehension of television content, in E. Wartella (ed.), *Children's Communicating: Media and Development of Thought, Speech, Understanding*, Beverly Hills, CA: Sage, 1979.

14 Singer, op. cit.; Singer and Singer, *Television, Imagination and Aggression: A Study of Pre-schoolers*, Hillsdale, NJ: Lawrence Erlbaum Associates, 1981; Tower, R. B., Singer, D. G., Singer, J. L. and Biggs, A., Differential effects of television programming on pre-schoolers' cognition, imagination and social play, *American Journal of Orthopsychiatry*, 1979, 49, 265–281.

15 Anderson, D. R., Lorch, E. P., Field, D. E. and Saunders, J., The effects of TV programme comprehensibility on pre-school children's visual attention to television, *Child Development*, 1981, 52, 151–157.

16 Lorch, E.P., Anderson, D.R. and Levin, S.R., The relationship of visual attention to children's comprehension of television, *Child Development*, 1979, 50, 722–727.

17 Anderson et al., op. cit.

18 Anderson and Lorch, op. cit.

19 Huston, A. C. and Wright, J. C., Children's processing of television: the informative functions of formal features, in J. Bryant and D. R. Anderson (eds), *Children's Understanding of Television: Research on Attention and Comprehension*, New York: Academic Press, 1983.

20 Anderson and Lorch, op. cit.; Huston and Wright, op. cit.

21 Anderson, D. R., Alwitt, L. F., Lorch, E. P. and Levin, S. R., Watching children watch television, in G. Hale and M. Lewis (eds), *Attention and Cognitive Development*, New York: Plenum, 1979.

22   Anderson and Lorch, op. cit.
23   Boeckman, K. and Hipfl, B., Children's TV viewing habits and family context, paper presented at the International Television Studies conference, London, July 1988; Timmer, S. G., Eccles, J. and O'Brien, K., How children use time, in F. T. Juster and F. P. Stafford (eds), *Time, Goods and Well-Being*, Ann Arbor: Institute for Social Research, University of Michigan, 1985 (pp. 353–382).
24   St Peters, M., Fitch, M., Huston, A. C., Wright, J. C. and Eakins, D. J., Television and families: what do young children watch with their parents?, *Child Development*, 1991, 62, 1409–1423.
25   Steiner, G. A., *The People Look at Television*, New York: A. Knopf, 1963; Lyle, J. and Hoffman, H. R., Children's use of television and other media, in E. A. Rubinstein, G. A. Comstock and J. P. Murray (eds), *Television and Social Behaviour*, vol. 4, *Television in Day-to-Day Life: Patterns of Use*, Washington, DC: US Government Printing Office, 1972.
26   Anderson and Lorch, op. cit.
27   Bechtel, R. B., Achelpohl, C. and Akers, R., Correlates between observed behaviour and questionnaire responses on televison viewing, in Rubinstein et al., op. cit.
28   Gunter et al., op. cit.
29   Anderson, D. R., Levin, S. R. and Lorch, E. P., The effects of TV programme pacing on the behaviour of pre-school children, *AV Communication Review*, 1977, 25, 159–166.
30   Wright, J. C. and Huston, A. C., The information processing demands of television and 'media library' in young viewers, paper presented at the Annual Meeting of the American Educational Research Association, New York, March 1982.
31   Huston and Wright, op. cit.
32   Anderson and Lorch, op. cit.
33   Wright, J. C., Calvert, S. L., Huston-Stein, A. and Watkins, B. A., Children's selective attention to television forms: effects of salient and information production features as functions of age and viewing experience, paper presented at the Meeting of the International Communication Association, Acapulco, Mexico, 1980.

4 HOW WELL DO CHILDREN FOLLOW AND UNDERSTAND TV?

1   Anderson, D. R. and Lorch, E. P., Looking at television: Action or reaction?, in J. Bryant and D. R. Anderson (eds), *Children's Understanding of Television: Research on Attention and Comprehension*, New York: Academic Press, 1983; Huston, A. C. and Wright, J. C., Children's processing of television: the informative functions of formal features, in Bryant and Anderson, op. cit.
2   Alwitt, L. F., Anderson, D. R., Lorch, E. P. and Levin, S. R., Pre-school children's visual attention to attributes of television, *Human Communication Research*, 1980, 7, 52–67.
3   Collins, W. A., Interpretation and inference in children's television viewing, in Bryant and Anderson, op. cit.
4   Rydin, I., *Information Processes in Pre-School Children I.I. The Tale of the Seed*, Stockholm: Swedish Broadcasting Corporation, Project no. 72–7–114, 1976.
5   Collins, W. A., Learning of media content: a developmental study, *Child Development*, 1970, 41(4), 1133–1142; Collins, W. A., The developing child a viewer, *Journal of Communication*, 1975, 25(4), 35–44; Collins, W. A., Wellman,

H., Keniston, A. and Westby, S., Age-related aspects of comprehension and inference from a televised dramatic narrative, *Child Development*, 1978, 49, 389–399.

6 Collins et al., op. cit.

7 Collins, Learning of media content, see note 5; Collins, Interpretation and inference, see note 3; Collins et al., op. cit.; Newcomb, A. F. and Collins, W. A., Children's comprehension of family role portrayals in televised dramas: effects of socioeconomic status, ethnicity and age, *Developmental Psychology*, 1979, 15(4), 417–423.

8 Collins, Interpretation and inference, see note 3; Collins, W. A. and Wellman, H., Social scripts and developmental changes in representations of televised narratives, *Communication Research*, 1982, 9(3), 380–398.

9 Clifford, B., Gunter B. and McAleer, J., *Television and Children: Programme Evaluation, Comprehension and Impact*, Hillsdale, NJ: Lawrence Erlbaum Associates, 1995.

10 Collins et al., op. cit.

11 Newcomb and Collins, op. cit.

12 Gross, L. and Jeffries-Fox, S., What do you want to be when you grow up, little girl?, in G. Tuchman, A. Daniels and J. Benet (eds), *Hearth and Home: Images of Women in the Mass Media*, New York: Oxford University Press, 1978.

13 Fernle, D. E., Ordinary and extraordinary people: children's understanding of television and real-life models, paper presented at the Society for Research in Child Development Biennial Meeting, Boston, MA, April 1981.

14 Dorr, A., No shortcuts to judging reality, in J. Bryant and D. R. Anderson (eds), *Children's Understanding of Television: Research on Attention and Comprehension*, New York: Academic Press, 1983.

15 Ibid.

16 Fernle, op. cit.

17 Hawkins, R. P., The dimensional structure of children's perceptions of television reality, *Communications Research*, 1977, 4(3), 99–320.

18 Dorr, op. cit.

19 Ibid.

20 Ibid.

21 Rarick, D. L., Townsend, J. E. and Boyd, D. A., Adolescent perceptions of police: actual and as depicted in TV drama, *Journalism Quarterly*, 1973, 50, 438–446

22 Clifford et al., op. cit.

23 Leary, A., Wright, J. C. and Huston, A. C., Young children's judgement of the fictional/nonfictional status of television programming, paper presented at the biennial meeting of the Society for Research in Child Development, Toronto, Canada, 1985.

24 Greenberg, B. S. and Reeves, B., Children and the perceived reality of television, *Journal of Social Issues*, 1976, 32, 86–97; Huesmann, L. R., Lagerspetz, K. and Eron, L. D., Intervening variables in the TV violence–aggression relation: evidence from two countries, *Developmental Psychology*, 1984, 20(5), 746–755.

25 Dorr, op. cit. (pp. 199–220); Wright, J. C., Kunkel, D., Pinon, M. and Huston, A. C., Children's affective and cognitive reactions to television coverage of the space shuttle disaster, paper presented to the biennial meeting of the Society for Research in Child Development, Baltimore, MD, 1987.

26 Dorr, A., Kovaric, P., Doubleday, C., Sims, D. and Seidner, L. B., Beliefs about the realism of television programmes featuring families, paper presented at the

annual meeting of the American Psychological Association, Los Angeles, CA. 1985.

27 Flavell, J. H., Flavell, E. R. and Kortmacher, J. E., Do young children think of television images as pictures or real objects?, *Journal of Broadcasting and Electronic Media*, 1990, 34, 399–419.

28 Wright, J. C., Huston, A. C., Reitz, A. L. and Piemyat, S., Young children's perceptions of television reality: determinants and developmental differences, *Developmental Psychology*, 1994, 30, 229–239.

29 Calvert, S. L., Television production feature effects on children's comprehension of time, *Journal of Applied Developmental Psychology*, 1988, 9, 263–273; Wilson, B. J., Children's reactions to dreams conveyed in mass media programming, *Communication Research*, 1991, 18, 283–305; Wright et al., op. cit.

30 Dorr, op. cit.

31 Potter, W. J., Perceived reality in television effects research, *Journal of Broadcasting and Electronic Media*, 1988, 32, 23–41; Wright et al., Young children's perceptions, see note 28.

32 Wright et al., Young children's perceptions, see note 28.

33 Cantor, J. and Wilson, B. J., Modifying fear responses to mass media in preschool and elementary school children, *Journal of Broadcasting*, 1984, 28, 431–443; Wilson, B. J., Hoffner, C. and Cantor, J., Children's perceptions of the effectiveness of techniques to reduce fear from mass media, *Journal of Applied Developmental Psychology*, 1987, 8, 39–52.

34 Huston, A. C., Wright, J. C., Alvarez, M., Truglio, R., Fitch, M. and Piemyat, S., Perceived television reality and children's emotional and cognitive responses to its social content, *Journal of Applied Developmental Psychology*, 1995, 16, 231–251.

35 Field, D. E., Child and parent co-viewing of television: relationships to cognitive performance, doctoral dissertation, University of Massachusetts, Amherst, 1987 (*Dissertation Abstracts International*, 1988, 48, 2799B–2800B); Rubin, A. M., Age and family control influences on children's television viewing, *Southern Speech Communication Journal*, 1986, 52, 35–51.

36 Haefner, M. J. and Wartella, E. A., Effects of sibling co-viewing on children's interpretations of television programmes, *Journal of Broadcasting and Electronic Media*, 1987, 31, 153–168.

37 Alexander, A., Ryan, M. S. and Munoz, P., Creating a learning context: investigations of the interactions of siblings during television viewing, *Critical Studies in Mass Communication*, 1984, 1, 345–364.

38 Wilson, B. J. and Weiss, A. J. ,The effects of sibling co-viewing on preschoolers' reactions to a suspenseful movie scene, *Communications Research* 1993, 20(2), 214–245.

39 Reeves, B. and Lometti, G., The dimensional structure of children's perceptions of television characters: a replication, *Human Communication Research*, 1979, 5, 247–256.

40 Dorr, A., Graves, S. B. and Phelps, E., Television literacy for young children, *Journal of Communication*, 1980, 30(3), 71–83.

41 Collins, Interpretation and inference, see note 3.

42 Dorr, op. cit.; Collins, Interpretation and inference, see note 3.

43 Collins, W. A. and Westby, S., Moral judgements of TV characters as a function of programme comprehension, paper presented at the Society for Research in Child Development Biennial Meeting, Boston, MA, April 1981.

5 DOES TV IMPROVE CHILDREN'S KNOWLEDGE?

1 Gunter, B., *Poor Reception: Misunderstanding and Forgetting Broadcast News*, Hillsdale, NJ: Lawrence Erlbaum Associates, 1987.
2 Ibid.
3 Robinson, J. P. and Levy, M. R., *The Main Source*, Beverly Hills, CA: Sage, 1985.
4 Moss, R., Jones, C. and Gunter, B., *Television in Schools* London: John Libbey, 1991.
5 Langham, J., *Teachers and Television: A History of the IBA's Educational Fellowship Scheme*, London: John Libbey, 1990.
6 Lesser, G. *Children and Television: Lessons from 'Sesame Street'*, New York: Random House, 1974.
7 Ball, S. and Bogatz, G. A., *Reading with Television: An Evaluation of 'The Electric Company'* (2 vols) Princeton, NJ: Educational Testing Service, 1973.
8 Sproull, N. L., Ward, E. F. and Ward, M. D., *Reading Behaviours of Young Children Who Viewed 'The Electric Company'*, New York: Children's Television Workshop, 1976.
9 Bryant J., Alexander, A. and Brown, D., Learning from educational television programmes, in M. J. A. Howe (ed.) Learning from Television: Psychological and Educational Research, London: Academic Press, 1983 (pp. 1–30).
10 Mielke, K. W. and Chen, M., Making contact: formative research in touch with children, in *CTW International Research Notes*, New York: Children's Television Workshop, 1980.
11 Mielke, K. W. and Chen, M., Formative research for *3-2-1*: methods and insights, in M. J. A. Howe (ed.), *Learning from Television: Psychological and Educational Research*, London: Academic Press, 1983 (pp. 31–55).
12 Clifford, B. R., Gunter, B. and McAleer, J. L., *Television and Children: Program Evaluation, Comprehension and Impact*, Hillsdale, NJ: Lawrence Erlbaum Associates, 1995.
13 Ibid.
14 Ibid.
15 Chaffee, S. H., McLeod, J. M. and Wackman, D. B., Family communication patterns and adolescent political participation, in J. Dennis (ed.) *Socialisation to Politics*, New York: Wiley, 1973; Greenstein, F. I., Political socialisation, in *International Encyclopaedia of the Social Sciences*, vol. 1b, New York: Macmillan, 1968.
16 Gunter, op. cit.
17 Dominick, J. R., Television and political socialisation, *Educational Broadcasting Reviews*, 1972, 6, 48–56.
18 Conway, M. M., Stevens, A. J. and Smith, R. G., The relation between media use and children's civic awareness, *Journalism Quarterly*, 1975, 8, 240–247.
19 Furnham, A. and Gunter, B., Political knowledge and awareness in adolescents, *Journal of Adolescence*, 1983, 6, 373–385.
20 Atkin, C. and Gantz, W., Television news and political socialisation, *Public Opinion Quarterly*, 1978, 42, 183–197.
21 Cairns, E., Hunter, D. and Herring, L., Young children's awareness of violence in Northern Ireland: the influence of Northern Irish television in Scotland and Northern Ireland, *British Journal of Social and Clinical Psychology*, 1980, 19, 3–6.

22   Cairns, E., Television news as a source of knowledge about the violence for
     children in Ireland: a test of the knowledge-gap hypothesis, *Current
     Psychological Research and Reviews*, 1984, 3, 32–38.
23   Ibid.
24   Drew, D. and Reeves, B., Children's learning from a television newscast,
     Communication Research, 1980, 7, 121–135.
25   Drew, D. and Reeves, B., Children's learning from a television newscast,
     Journalism Quarterly, 1984, 61, 83–88.
26   Furnham, A. and Gunter, B., Sex, presentation mode and memory for violent
     and non-violent news, *Journal of Educational Television*, 1985, 11, 99–105.
27   Brand, J. E. and Greenberg, B. S., Effects of television news and advertising in
     the classroom: the impact of *Channel One*, Paper presented at the International
     Communication Association annual conference, Miami, Florida, 21–25 May,
     1992.
28   Salomon, G., *Interaction of Media, Cognition and Learning*, San Francisco:
     Jossey-Bass, 1979.
29   Meringoff, L. K., Influence of the medium on children's story apprehension,
     Journal of Educational Psychology, 1980, 72, 240–249.
30   Beentjes, J. W. J. and van der Voort, T. H. A., Recall and language use in
     retellings of televised and printed stories, *Poetics*, 1991a, 20, 91–104; Beentjes,
     J. W. J. and van der Voort, T. H. A., Children's written accounts of televised
     and printed stories, *Educational Technology Research and Development*, 1991b,
     39(3), 15–26.
31   Beagle-Roos, J. and Gat, I., Specific impact of radio and television on
     children's story comprehension, *Journal of Educational Psychology*, 1983, 75,
     128–137.
32   Singer, J. L., The power and limitations of television: a cognitive-affective
     analysis, in P. H. Tannenbaum (ed.), *The Entertainment Functions of Television*,
     Hillsdale, NJ: Lawrence Erlbaum Associates, 1980 (p. 51).
33   Salomon, G., Beyond the formats of television: the effects of student
     preconceptions on the experience of televiewing, in M. Meyer (ed.), *Children
     and the Formal Features of Television*, Munich: K. G. Saur, 1993.
34   Ibid.
35   Ibid.
36   Beentjes, J. W. J., Vooijs, M. W. and van der Voort, T. H. A., Children's recall of
     televised and printed news as a function of test expectation, *Journal of
     Educational Television*, 19(1), 5–13, 1993.

6 DOES TV TEACH CHILDREN ABOUT SOCIAL ROLES?

1   Fauls, L. B. and Smith, W. D., Sex-role learning in 5-year olds, *Journal of Genetic
     Psychology*, 1956, 89, 195–217.
2   Gunter, B., *Television and Sex-Role Stereotyping*, London: IBA/John Libbey,
     1986.
3   Dorr, A. and Lesser, G. S. (eds), *Women, Communication and Careers*, Munich:
     K. G. Saur, 1980 (pp. 36–75).
4   Atkin, C. K., Greenberg, B. and McDermott, S., Race and social role learning
     from television, in H. S. Dordick (ed.), *Proceedings of the Sixth Annual
     Telecommunications Policy Research Conference*, Lexington, MA: Lexington
     Books, 1979.
5   Beuf, F. A., Doctor, lawyer, household drudge, *Journal of Communication*, 1974,
     24, 110–118.

6 Frueh, T. and McGhee, P. E., Traditional sex-role development and amount of time spent watching television, *Developmental Psychology*, 1975, 11, 109.

7 McGhee, P. E., Television as a source of learning sex-role stereotypes, in S. Cohen and T. J. Comiskey (eds), *Child Development: Contemporary Perspectives*, Ithaca, IL: Pecork Publishers, 1975; McGhee, P. E. and Frueh, T. Television viewing and the learning of sex-role stereotypes, *Sex Roles*, 1980, 2, 179–188.

8 Morgan, M., Television and adolescents' sex-role stereotypes: a longitudinal study, *Journal of Personality and Social Psychology*, 1982, 43, 947–955.

9 Morgan, M. and Rothschild, N., Impact of the new television technology: cable TV, peers and sex-role cultivation in the electronic environment, *Youth and Society*, 1983, 15(1), 33–50.

10 Morgan, M., Television, sex-role attitudes and sex-role behaviour, *Journal of Early Adolescence*, 1987, 7(3), 269–282.

11 Williams, T. M., *The Impact of Television*, London: Academic Press, 1986.

12 Wober, J. M., Reardon, G. and Fazal, S., *Personality, Character Aspirations and Patterns of Viewing Among Children*, London: IBA Research Paper, 1987.

13 Clifford, B., Gunter, B. and McAleer, J., *Television and Children: Programme Evaluation, Comprehension and Impact*, Hillsdale, NJ: Lawrence Erlbaum Associates, 1995.

14 Johnston, J. and Ettema, J. S., *Positive Images*, Beverly Hills, CA: Sage, 1982.

15 Durkin, K., *Sex Roles and Children's Television*, a report to the Independent Broadcasting Authority, University of Kent, Canterbury, Social Psychology Research Unit, 1983.

16 McNeil, J., Feminism, femininity and television shows: a content analysis, *Journal of Broadcasting*, 1975, 19, 259–269.

17 Glennon, L. M. and Butsch, R., The family as portrayed on television, 1946–1978, in D. Pearl, L. Bouthilet and J. Lazar (eds), *Television and Behaviour: Ten Years of Scientific Progress and Implications for the Eighties*, Rockville, MD: NIMH, 1982; Roberts, E., Television and sexual learning in childhood, in Pearl et al., op. cit.

18 Roberts, op. cit.

19 Ibid.

20 Glennon, L. M. and Butsch, R., *The Devaluation of Working-Class Lifestyle in Television Family Series, 1947–1977*, paper presented at a meeting of the Popular Culture Association, Baltimore, 1977.

21 Ibid.

22 Hines, M., Greenberg, B. S. and Buerkel, N., *An Analysis of Family Structures and Interactions in Commercial television: Project CASTLE*, project no. 6, Department of Communication, Michigan State University, East Lansing, 1979.

23 Greenberg, B. S., Richards, M. and Henderson, L., Trends in sex-role portrayals on television, in B. S. Greenberg (ed.), *Life on Television*, Norwood, NJ: Ablex Press, 1980.

24 Barcus, F. E., *Images of Life on Children's Television: Sex Roles, Minorities and Families*, New York: Praeger, 1983.

25 Thomas, S. and Callahan, B. P., Allocating happiness: TV females and social class, *Journal of Communication*, 1982, 32, 184–190.

26 Buerkel-Rothfuss, N. L., Greenberg, B. S., Atkin, C. K. and Neuendorf, K. A., Learning about the family from television, *Journal of Communication*, 1982, 32, 191–201.

27 Charters, W. W., *Motion Pictures and Youth: A Summary*, New York: Macmillan, 1933.

28 Lambert, W. E. and Klineberg, O., *Children's Views of Foreign Peoples: A Cross-National Study*, New York: Appleton-Century-Crofts, 1967.

29 Bogatz, G. A. and Ball, S., *The Second Year of 'Sesame Street': A Continuing Evaluation*, Princeton, NJ: Educational Testing Service, 1977.

30 Gorn, G. I., Goldberg, M. E. and Kanningo, R. N., The role of educational television in changing intergroup attitudes to children, *Child Development*, 1976, 47, 277–280.

31 Nelson, B., The statement of goals and objectives for *Vegetable Soup*, unpublished manuscript, University of Massachusetts, Amherst, 1974.

32 Mays, L., Henderson, E. H., Seidman, S. K. and Steiner, V. S., An evaluation report on *Vegetable Soup*: the efforts of a multi-ethnic children's television series on inter-group attitudes of children, unpublished manuscript, New York State Department of Education, 1975.

33 Roberts, D. F., Herold, C., Hornby, K., King, S., Sterne, D., Whiteley, S. and Silverman, T., Earth's a *Big Blue Marble*: a report of the impact of a children's television series on children's opinions, unpublished manuscript, Stanford University, CA, 1974.

34 Greenberg, B. S., Children's reactions to TV blacks, *Journalism Quarterly*, 1972, 49, 5–14.

35 Graves, S. B., Racial diversity in children's television: TV's impact on racial attitudes and stated programme preferences, unpublished doctoral dissertation, Harvard University, Cambridge, MA, 1975.

36 Leckenby, J. D. and Surlin, S. H., *Race and Social Class Differences in Perceived Reality of Socially Relevant Television Programmes for Adults in Atlanta and Chicago*, paper presented at the International Communication Association annual convention, Chicago, April 1975.

37 Vidmar, N. and Rokeach, M., *Archie Bunker's Bigotry: A Study in Selection Perception and Exposure*, paper presented at the review meeting of the Eastern Psychological Association, Washington, DC, May 1973.

38 Hartmann, P. and Husband, C., The mass media and recall conflict, *Race*, 1971, 12, 3, also in Cohen, A. and Young, J. (eds), *The Manufacture of News: A Reader*, Beverly Hills, CA: Sage, 1973.

39 Atkin, C. K., Greenberg, B. S. and McDermott, S., *Television and Racial Socialisation*, paper presented at a meeting of the Association for Education in Journalism, Seattle, WA, 1978.

40 Bayton, J. A., Austin, L. J. and Burke, K. R., Negro perception of negro and white personality traits, *Journal of Personality and Social Psychology*, 1965, 3, 250–253; Bronfenbrenner, U., The psychological waste of quality and equality in education, *Child Development*, 1967, 38, 909–925; Jones, J. M., *Prejudice and Racism*, Reading, MA: Addison-Wesley, 1972; Powell, G. J., Self concept in white and black children, in C. V. Willie, B. M. Kramer and B. S. Brown (eds), *Racism and Mental Health*, Pittsburgh, PA: University of Pittsburgh Press, 1973; Spurlock, J., Some consequences of racism for children, in Willie et al., op. cit.

41 Clark, K. B. and Clark, M. P., Racial identification in negro children, in H. Proshansky and Seidenberg, B. (eds), *Basic Studies in Social Psychology*, New York: Holt, Rinehart & Winston, 1955; Greenwald, H. J. and Oppenheim, D. B., Reported magnitude of self-misidentification among Negro children – artifact?, *Journal of Personality and Social Psychology*, 1968, 8, 49–52.

42 Neely, J. J., Heckel, R. V. and Leichtman, H. M., The effect of race of model on imitation in children, *Journal of Social Psychology*, 1973, 89, 225–231.

43 Heckel, R. V., cited in S. B. Graves, Psychological effect of black portrayals on television, in S. B. Withey and R. P. Abeles (eds), *Television and Social*

Behaviour: Beyond Violence and Children, Hillsdale, NJ: Lawrence Erlbaum Associates, 1980.
44 Greenberg, op. cit.

7 DOES TV INFLUENCE AGGRESSIVE BEHAVIOUR?

1 Surgeon General's Scientific Advisory Committee on Television and Social Behaviour, *Television and Growing Up: The Impact of Televised Violence*, Washington, DC: US Government Printing Office, 1972.
2 Pearl, D., Bouthilet, L. and Lazar, J., *Television and Behaviour: Ten Years of Scientific Progress and Implications for the Eighties*, vol. 1, *Summary Report*, Rockville, MD: NIMH, 1982.
3 Centres for Disease Control, *Position Papers from the Third National Injury Conference: Setting the National Agenda for Injury Control in the 1990s*, Washington DC: Department of Health and Human Services, 1991; National Academy of Science, *Understanding and Preventing Violence*, Washington, DC: National Academy Press, 1993; American Psychological Association, *Violence and Youth: Psychology's Response*, Washington, DC: American Psychological Association, 1993.
4 Donnerstein, E., Slaby, R. and Eron, L., The mass media and youth violence, in J. Murray, E. Rubinstein and G. Comstock (eds), *Violence and Youth: Psychology's Response*, Washington, DC: American Psychological Association, 1994, vol. 2; Huesmann, L. R. and Eron, L. D. (eds), *Television and the Aggressive Child: A Cross-National Comparison*, Hillsdale, NJ: Lawrence Erlbaum Associates, 1986.
5 Paik, H., and Comstock, G., The effects of television violence on anti-social behaviour: a meta-analysis, *Communication Research*, 1994, 21(4), 516–546.
6 Huston, A. C., Donnerstein, E., Fairchild, H., Feshbach, N. D., Katz, P. A., Murray, J. P., Rubinstein, E. A., Wilcox, B. L. and Zuckerman, D., *Big World, Small Screen: The Role of Television in American Society*, Lincoln, NB: University of Nebraska Press, 1992.
7 Schramm, W., Lyle, J. and Parker, E. B., *Television in the Lives of our Children*, Stanford, CA: Stanford University Press, 1961; Smythe, D. W., *Three Years of New York Television: 1951–1954*, Urbana, IL: National Association of Education Broadcasters, 1954.
8 Gerbner, G., Violence in television drama: trends and symbolic functions, in G. A. Comstock and E. A. Rubinstein (eds), *Television and Social Behaviour*, vol. 1, *Media Content and Control*, Washington, DC: US Government Printing Office, 1972; Gerbner, G. and Gross, L., Living with television: the violence profile, *Journal of Communication*, 1976, 26, 173–199.
9 Mediascope, Inc, *National Television Violence Study: Executive Summary: 1994–95*, Los Angeles, CA: Mediascope, Inc, 1996.
10 Kunkel, D., Wilson, B. J., Linz, D., Potter, J., Donnerstein, E., Smith, S. L., Blumenthal, E., and Gray, T., Violence in television programming overall: University of California, Santa Barbara study, in *National Television Violence Study: 1994–95 – Scientific Papers*, Los Angeles, CA: Mediascope, Inc, 1996, (pp. I–1 to I–172).
11 Danielson, W., Lasorsa, D., Wartella, E., Whitney, C., Campbell, S., Hadda, S., Klijn, M., Lopez, R. and Olivarez, A., Television violence in 'reality' programming: University of Texas, Austin, study, in *National Television Violence Study: 1994–95 – Executive Papers*, Los Angeles, CA: Mediascope, Inc, 1996, (pp. II–1 to II–55).

12   British Broadcasting Corporation, *Violence on Television: Programme Content and Viewer Perceptions*, London: BBC, 1972; Halloran, J. D. and Croll, P., Television programmes in Great Britain, in Comstock and Rubinstein, op. cit.

13   Gunter, B., and Harrison, J., *Violence on Television in the United Kingdom: A Content Analysis*, London: British Broadcasting Corporation/Independent Television Commission, 1995.

14   British Broadcasting Corporation, op. cit.

15   Van der Voort, T. H. A., *Television Violence: A Child's Eye View*, Amsterdam: Elsevier Science Publishers, 1988.

16   Zillmann, D., Attribution and misattribution of excitatory reactions, in J. H. Harvey, W. Ickes and R. F. Kidd (eds), *New Directions in Attribution Research*, New York: Lawrence Erlbaum Associates, 1978, vol. 2.

17   Berkowitz, L., Some aspects of observed aggression, *Journal of Personality and Social Psychology*, 1965, 2, 359–369.

18   Berkowitz, L., Some effects of thoughts on anti- and prosocial influences of media events: a cognitive-neo-association analysis, *Psychological Bulletin* 1984, 59, 410–427; Berkowitz, L. and Rogers, K. H., A priming effect analysis of media influences in J. Bryant and D. Zillmann (eds), *Perspectives on Media Effects*, Hillsdale, NJ: Lawrence Erlbaum Associates, 1986 (pp. 57–82).

19   Carver, C. S., Ganellon, R. J., Froming, W. J. and Chambers, W., Modelling: an analysis in terms of category accessibility, *Journal of Experimental Social Psychology*, 1983, 19, 403–421.

20   Bandura, A., Vicarious processes: a case of no-trial learning, in L. Berkowitz (ed.), *Advances in Experimental Social Psychology*, New York: Academic Press, 1965, vol. 2.

21   Bandura, A. and Walters, R. H., *Social Learning and Personality Development*, New York: Holt, Rinehart & Winston, 1963; Baron, R. A., *Human Aggression*, New York: Plenum, 1977.

22   Huesmann, R., Psychologial processes promoting the relation between exposure to media violence and aggressive behaviour by the viewer, *Journal of Social Issues*, 1986, 42(3), 125–140.

23   Boyatzis, C. J., Matillo, G. M. and Nesbit, K. M., Effects of *The Mighty Morphin Power Rangers* on children's aggression with peers, *Child Study Journal* 1995, 25(1), 45–55.

24   Drabman, R. S. and Thomas, M. H., Does media violence increase children's toleration of real-life aggression?, *Developmental Psychology*, 1974, 10, 418–421.

25   Osborn, D. K. and Endsley, R. C., Emotional reactions of young children to TV violence, *Child Development*, 1971, 42, 321–331.

26   Linz, D., Donnerstein, E. and Penrod, S., The effects of multiple exposures to filmed violence against women, *Journal of Communication*, 1984, 34(3), 130–147; Linz, D., Donnerstein, E. and Penrod, S., Effects of long-term exposure to violent and sexually degrading depictions of women, *Journal of Personality and Social Psychology*, 1988, 55(5), 758–768.

27   Bandura, op. cit.; Bandura, A., Ross, D. and Ross, S. A., Imitation of film-mediated aggressive models, *Journal of Personality and Social Psychology*, 1963, 66, 3–11.

28   Baron, op. cit.; Kniveton, B. H., Social learning and imitation in relation to TV, in R. Brown (ed.), *Children and Television*, London: Collier Macmillan, 1976.

29   Berkowitz, Some aspects of observed aggression, op. cit.

30   Drabman and Thomas, op. cit.; Osborn and Endsley, op. cit.

31   Gunter, B., Video violence, *Stills Magazine*, 1984 (Feb–Mar), 10, 36–37.

32 Steuer, F. B., Applefield, J. M. and Smith R., Televised aggression and the interpersonal aggression of pre-school children, *Journal of Experimental Child
Psychology*, 1971, 81, 442–447.
33 Parke, R. D., Berkowitz, L., Leyens, J. P., West, S. G. and Sebastian, R. J., Some
effects of violent and non-violent movies on the behaviour of juvenile
delinquents, in L. Berkowitz (ed.), *Advances in Experimental Social Psychology*,
New York: Academic Press, 1977, vol. 10.
34 Dominick, J. F. and Greenberg, B. S., Attitudes towards violence: the interaction
of television exposure, family attitudes and social class, in G. A. Comstock and
E. A. Rubinstein (eds), *Television and Social Behaviour*, vol. 3, *Television and
Adolescent Aggressiveness*, Washington, DC: US Government Printing Office,
1972; McIntyre, J. J., Teevan, Jr. J. J. and Hartnagel, T., Television violence and
deviant behaviour, in Comstock and Rubinstein, *Television and Adolescent
Aggressiveness*.
35 Pearl et al., op. cit.
36 Stipp, H. and Milavsky, J. R., US television programming's effects on aggressive
behaviour of children and adolescents, *Current Psychology: Research and
Reviews*, 1988, 7(1), 76–92.
37 Belson, W. A., *Television Violence and the Adolescent Boy*, Farnborough,
England: Saxon House, 1978.
38 Milavsky, J. R., Kessler, R. C., Stipp, H. and Rubens, W. S., *Television and
Aggression: A Panel Study*, New York: Academic Press, 1982.
39 Eron, L. D., Huesmann, L. R., Lefkowitz, M. M. and Walder, L. O., Does
television violence cause aggression?, *American Psychologist*, 1972, 27, 253–263;
Lefkowitz, M. M., Eron, L. D., Walder, L. O. and Huesmann, L. R., *Growing up
to be Violent: A Longitudinal Study of the Development of Aggression*, New York:
Pergamon, 1977.
40 Freedman, J. L., Effect of television violence on aggressiveness, *Psychological
Bulletin*, 1984, 96, 227–246; Freedman, J. L., Television violence and aggression:
a rejoinder, *Psychological Bulletin*, 1986, 100, 372–378.
41 Huesmann, L. R., Eron, L. D., Lefkowitz, M. M. and Walder, L. O., Stability of
aggression over time and generations, *Developmental Psychology*, 1984, 20(6),
1120–1134.
42 Lynn, R., Hampson, S. and Agahi, E., Television violence and aggression: a
genotype-environment, correlation and interaction theory, *Social Behaviour and
Personality*, 1989, 17(2), 143–164.
43 Bachrach, R. S., The differential effect of observation of violence on Kibbutz
and city children in Israel, in L. R. Huesmann and L. D. Eron (eds), *Television
and the Aggressive Child: A Cross-National Comparison*, Hillsdale, NJ: Lawrence
Erlbaum Associates, 1986; Fraczek, A., Socio-cultural environment, television
viewing and the development of aggression among children in Poland, in
Huesmann and Eron, op. cit.; Sheehan, P. W., Television viewing and its relation
to aggression among children in Australia, in Huesmann and Eron, op. cit.
44 Wiegman, O., Kuttschreuter, M. and Baarda, B., A longitudinal study of the
effects of television viewing on aggressive and pro-social behaviours, *British
Journal of Social Psychology*, 1992, 31, 147–164.
45 Williams, T. M. (ed.), *The Impact of Television: A National Experiment in Three
Communities*, New York/London: Academic Press, 1986.
46 Kaplan, R. M. and Singer, R. D., TV violence and viewer aggression: a re-
examination of the evidence, *Journal of Social Issues*, 1976, 32, 35–70.
47 Duhs, L. A. and Gunton, R. J., TV violence and the childhood aggression: a
curmudgeon's guide, *Australian Psychologist*, 1988, 23(2), 183–195.

48   Andison, F. S., TV violence and viewer aggression: a cumulation of study results 1956–1976, *Public Opinion Quarterly*, 1977, 41(3), 314–331; Hearold, S., A synthesis of 1043 effects of television on social behaviour, in G. Comstock (ed.), *Public Communication and Behaviour*, Orlando, FL: Academic Press, 1986, vol. 1.

49   Paik, H. and Comstock, G., The effects of television violence on antisocial behaviour: a meta-analysis, *Communication Research* 1994, 21(4), 516–546.

50   Gauntlett, D., *Moving Experiences: Understanding Television's Influences and Effects*, London: John Libbey, 1995.

8 DOES TV ENCOURAGE GOOD BEHAVIOUR?

1   Gunter, B., The cathartic potential of television drama, *Bulletin of the British Psychological Society*, 1980, 33, 448–450.

2   Copeland, G. A. and Slater, D., Television, fantasy and various catharsis, *Critical Studies in Mass Communication*, 1985, 2, 352–362; Gunter, op. cit.

3   Biblow, E., Imaginative play and the control of aggressive behaviour, in J. L. Singer (ed.), *The Child's World of Make-Believe*, New York: Academic Press, 1973.

4   Feshbach, S., The stimulating versus cathartic effects of a vicarious aggressive activity, *Journal of Abnormal and Social Psychology*, 1963, 63, 381–385.

5   Feshbach, S. and Singer, J., *Television and Aggression*, San Francisco, CA: Jossey-Bass, 1971.

6   Wells, W. D., Television and aggression: replication of an experimental field study, unpublished manuscript, Graduate School of Business, University of Chicago, 1973.

7   Copeland and Slater, op. cit.; Gunter, op. cit.

8   Noble, G., *Children in Front of the Small Screen*, London: Constable/Sage, 1975.

9   Biblow, op. cit.

10   Gunter, B., Can television teach kindness, *Bulletin of the British Psychological Society*, 1981, 34, 121–124.

11   Bandura, A. and Menlove, F., Factors determining vicarious extinctions of avoidance behaviour through symbolic modelling, *Journal of Personality and Social Psychology*, 1968, 7, 99–108.

12   Poulos, R. W. and Davidson, E. S., Effects of a short modelling film on fearful children's attitudes towards the dental situation, unpublished manuscript, State University of New York, Stony Brook, 1971.

13   O'Connor, R. D., Modification of social withdrawal through symbolic modelling, *Journal of Applied Behaviour Analysis*, 1969, 2, 15–22; O'Connor, R. D., Relative efficacy of modelling, shaping and the combined procedures for modification of social withdrawal, *Journal of Abnormal Psychology*, 1972, 79, 327–334.

14   Stein, G. M. and Bryan, J. H., The effect of a television model upon role adoption behaviour of children, *Child Development*, 1972, 43, 268–273.

15   Ibid.

16   Wolf, T. M. and Cheyne, J. A., Persistence of effects of live behavioural, televised behavioural and live verbal models on resistance to deviation, *Child Development*, 1972, 43, 1429–1436.

17   Bryan, J. H., Model effect and children's imitative behaviour, *Child Development*, 1972, 42, 2061–2065.

18   Bryan, J. H. and, N. H., Preaching and practising self-sacrifice: children's actions and reactions, *Child Development*, 1970a, 41, 329–353; Bryan, J. H. and

Walbeck, N. H., The impact of words and deeds concerning altruism upon children, *Child Development*, 1970b, 41, 747–757.

19 Rushton, J. P. and Owen, D., Immediate and delayed effects of TV modelling and preaching on children's generosity, *British Journal of Social and Clinical Psychology*, 1975, 14, 309–310.

20 Fryrear, J. L. and Thelen, M. H., Effect of sex of model and sex of observer on the imitation of affectionate behaviour, *Developmental Psychology*, 1969, 1, 299.

21 Silverman, L. T., Effects of *Sesame Street* programming on the cooperative behaviour of pre-schoolers, unpublished doctoral dissertation, Stanford University, CA, 1977.

22 Friedrich, L. K. and Stein, A. H., Prosocial television and young children: the effects of verbal labelling and role-playing on learning and behaviour, *Child Development*, 1975, 46, 27–38.

23 Coates, B. and Pusser, H. E., Positive reinforcement and punishment in *Sesame Street* and *Mister Rogers' Neighbourhood, Journal of Broadcasting*, 1975, 19, 143–151; Coates, B., Pusser, H. E. and Goodman, I., The influence of *Sesame Street* and *Mister Rogers' Neighbourhood on children's social behaviour in the pre-school, Child Development,* 1976, 41, 138–144.

24 Lovelace, V. O. and Huston, A. C., Can television teach prosocial behaviour?, in J. Spratkin, C. Swift and R. Hess (eds), *Television: Enhancing the Preventative Impact of TV*, New York: Haworth Press, 1983 (pp. 93–106).

25 Liefer, A. D., *How to Encourage Socially-Valued Behaviour*, biennial meeting of the Society for Research in Child Development, Denver, Colorado, April 1975. (ERIC No. D 114 175); Poulson, F. L., Teaching cooperation on television: an evaluation of *Sesame Street* social programs, *AV Communication Review*, 1974, 22, 229–246.

26 Zielinska, I. E., Verbal and non-verbal sequence in an educational television production: guidelines with attention to developmental cognitive processing styles, unpublished paper, Concordia University, Montreal, 1985; Zielinska, I. E., Using group viewing of prosocial educational television for social skills training in the daycare setting, Masters thesis, Educational Technology, Concordia University, Montreal, 1992.

27 Silverman, L. T. and Sprafkin, J. N., The effects of *Sesame Street* prosocial spots on cooperative play between young children, *Journal of Broadcasting*, 1980, 24, 135–147.

28 Ahammer, I. M. and Murray, J. P., Kindness in the kindergarten: the relative influence of role playing and prosocial television for facilitating altruism, *International Journal of Behavioural Development*, 1979, 2, 133–157; Friedrich and Stein, op. cit.

29 Zielinska, I. E. and Chambers, B., Using group viewing of television to teach preschool children social skills, *Journal of Educational Television*, 1995, 21(3), 85–99.

30 Rubinstein, E. A., Liebert, R. M., Neale, J. M. and Poulos, R. W., *Assessing Television's Influence on Children's Prosocial Behaviour* (Occasional Paper 74–11), Stony Brook, New York: Brookdale International Institute, 1976; Sprafkin, J. N., Liebert, R. M. and Poulos, R. W., Effects of a prosocial televised example on children's helping, *Journal of Experimental Child Psychology*, 1975, 20, 119–126.

31 Murray, J. P. and Ahammer, I. M., *Kindness in the Kindergarten: A Multidivisional Programme for Facilitating Altruism*, paper presented to the biennial meeting of the Society for Research in Child Development, New Orleans, March 1977.

32 Baron, S. J., Chase, L. J. and Courtright, J. A., Tele-drama as a facilitator of prosocial behaviour: *The Waltons, Journal of Broadcasting*, 1979, 23, 277–284.
33 Sprafkin, J. N. and Rubinstein, E. A., Children's television viewing habits and pro-social behaviour: a field correlational study, *Journal of Broadcasting*, 1979, 23, 265–276.
34 Lee, B., Prosocial content on prime-time television, in S. Oskamp (ed.), *Television as a Social Issue*, Beverly Hills, CA: Sage, 1988.
35 Ryan, K., Television as a moral educator, in R. Adler and D. Cater (eds), *Television as a Cultural Force*, New York: Praeger, 1976 (pp. 111–127).
36 Shantz, C. U., Social cognition, in P. H. Mussen (ed.), *Handbook of Child Psychology*, New York: Wiley, 1983 (vol. 3, pp. 495–555).
37 Kohlberg, L., *The Psychology of Moral Development*, vol. 2, *Essays on Moral Development*, New York: Harper and Row, 1984.
38 Rosenketter, L. L., Huston, A. C. and Wright, J. C., Television and the moral judgement of the young child, *Journal of Applied Developmental Psychology*, 1990, 11, 123–137.

9 DOES TV ADVERTISING AFFECT CHILDREN?

1 Choate, R. B., *Petition of the Council on Children, Media and Merchandising to Issue a Trade Regulation Rule Governing the Private Regulation of Children's Television*, advertising filed before the Federal Trade Commission, Washington, DC, March 1975.
2 Choate, op. cit.
3 Brumbaugh, F., cited in L. Bogart, *The Age of Television*, New York: Frederick Ungar Publishing Co, 1958 (p. 258).
4 Packard, V., *The Hidden Persuaders*, 1957, London: Longman.
5 Brooks, R., In the dark over TV ads, *Observer*, 1987, 8 November.
6 Churchill, G. A. and Moschis, G. P., Television and interpersonal influences on adolescent consumer learning, *Journal of Consumer Research*, 1979, 691, 23–35.
7 Ward, S., Levinson, D. and Wackman, D., Children's attention to advertising, in E. A. Rubinstein, G. A. Comstock and J. P. Murray (eds), *Television and Social Behaviour*, vol. 4, *Television in Day-to-Day Life: Patterns of Use*, Washington, DC: US Government Printing Office, 1972.
8 Bechtel, R., Adelpohl, C. and Akers, R., Correlations between observed behaviour and questionnaire responses on television viewing, in Rubinstein et al., op. cit.
9 Wartella, E., Wackman, D., Ward, S., Shamir, J. and Alexander, A., The young child as consumer, in E. Wartella (ed.), *Children Communicating, Media and Development of Thought, Speech, Understanding*, Sage Annual Reviews of Communication Research, Beverly Hills, CA: Sage, 1979.
10 Zuckerman, P., Ziegler, M. and Stevenson, A., Children's viewing of television and recognition memory of commercials, *Child Development*, 1978, 49, 96–106.
11 Blatt, J., Spencer, L. and Ward, S. A., Cognitive-developmental study of children's reactions to television advertising, in Rubinstein et al., op. cit.; Ward, S., Beale, G. and Levinson, D., Children's perceptions, explanations and judgements of television advertising: a further explanation, in Rubinstein et al., op. cit.
12 Ward et al., op. cit.
13 Ward, S. and Wackman, D., Children's information processing of television advertising, in F. G. Kline and P. Clarke (eds), *New Models for Mass*

Communication Research, Sage Annual Reviews of Communication Research, Beverly Hills, CA: Sage, 1973, vol. 3.

14 Zuckerman et. al., op. cit.

15 Ward et al., op. cit.

16 Levin, S. R. and Anderson, D. R., The development of attention, *Journal of Communication*, 1976, 26(2), 126–135.

17 Wartella, E., Individual differences in children's responses to television advertising, in E. L. Palmer and A. Dorr (eds), *Children and the Faces of Television*, New York: Academic Press, 1980.

18 Greer, D., Potts, R., Wright, J. C. and Huston, A. C., The effects of television commercial form and commercial placement on children's social behaviour and attention, *Child Development*, 1982, 53, 611–619; Meyer, M., *Children and the Format Features of Television: Approaches and Findings of Experimental and Formative Research*, Munich: K. G. Saur Verlag.

19 Rolandelli, D. R., Children and television: the visual superiority effect reconsidered, *Journal of Broadcasting and Electronic Media*, 1989, 33(1), 69–81.

20 Calvert, S. L. and Scott, M. C., Sound effects for children's temporal integration of fast-paced television content, *Journal of Broadcasting and Electronic Media*, 1989, 33(3), 233–246; Scott, L. M., Understanding jingles and needledrop: a theoretical approach to music in advertising, *Journal of Consumer Research*, 1990, 17, 223–236.

21 Young, B., *Television Advertising and Children*, Oxford: Clarendon Press, 1990.

22 Ward, S., Wackman, D. and Wartella, E., *How Children Learn to Buy*, Beverly Hills, CA: Sage, 1977; Robertson, T. S. and Rossiter, J. R., Children's responsiveness to commercials, *Journal of Communication*, 1977, 27(1), 101–106.

23 Wright, P. and Barbour, F., The relevance of decision process models in structuring persuasion messages, *Communications Research*, 1975, 2, 246–259.

24 Rubin, R. S., An exploratory investigation of children's responses to commercial content of television advertising in relation to their stages of cognitive development, unpublished doctoral dissertation, University of Massachusetts, 1972.

25 Sharp, T., Dyer, R. and Divita, S., An experimental test of the harmful effects of premium-orientated commercials on children, *Journal of Advertising Research*, 1976, 3, 1–11.

26 Young, op. cit.

27 Ibid.

28 Levin and Anderson, op. cit.; Wartella, E. and Ettema, J. S., A cognitive developmental study of children's attention to television commercials, *Communication Research*, 1974, 1, 44–69.

29 Blosser, B. J. and Roberts, D. F., Age differences in children's perceptions of message intent: responses to TV news, commercials, educational spots and public service announcements, *Communication Research*, 1984, 12, 455–484; Butter, E. J., Weikel, K. B., Otto, V. and Wright, K. P., TV advertising of OTC medicines and its effects on child viewers, *Psychology and Marketing*, 1981, 8, 117–128; Young, op. cit.

30 Levin, S. R., Petros, T. V. and Petrella, F. W., Preschoolers' awareness of television advertising, *Child Development*, 1982, 53, 933–937.

31 Kunkel, D. and Roberts, D., Young minds and marketplace values: issues in children's television advertising, *Journal of Social Issues*, 1991, 47, 57–72.

32 Belk, R., Mayer, R. and Driscoll, A., Children's recognition of consumption symbolism in children's products, *Journal of Consumer Research*, 1984, 10, 386–397; Brown, D. and Bryant, J., Humour in the mass media, in P. E. McGhee

and J. H. Goldstein (eds), *Handbook of Humour Research*, vol. 2, *Applied Studies*, New York: Stringer-Verlag. 1983; Nippold, M. A., Cuyler, J. S. and Braunbeck-Price, R., Explanation of ambiguous advertisements: a developmental study with children and adolescents, *Journal of Speech and Hearing Research*, 1988, 31, 466–474; Weinberger, M. G. and Spotts, H. E., Humour in US versus UK television commercials: a comparison, *Journal of Advertising*, 1989, 18(2), 39–44.

33 Young, op. cit.

34 Kunkel, D., From a raised eyebrow to a turned back: the FCC and children's product-related programming, *Journal of Communication*, 1988, 38(4), 90–108.

35 Kunkel, D., Crafting media policy: the genesis and implications of the Children's Television Act of 1990, *American Behavioural Scientist*, 1991, 35, 181–202; Sepstrup, P., The electronic dilemma of television advertising, *European Journal of Communication*, 1986, 1, 381–405.

36 Kunkel and Roberts, op. cit.

37 Donohue, T. R., Meyer, T. P. and Hencke, L. L., Black and white children's perceptions of television commercials, *Journal of Marketing*, 1978, 42, 34–40; Meyer, T. P., Donohue, T. R. and Hencke, L. L., How black children see TV commercials, *Journal of Advertising Research*, 1978, 18(5), 51–62; Robertson, T. S. and Rossiter, J. R., *Stimulus Dispositional Variables in Children's Responses to Advertising*, paper presented at the annual meeting of the American Psychological Association, September 1975; Sheikh, A., Prasad, K. and Rao, T., Children's TV commercials: a review of research, *Journal of Communication*, 1974, 24, 126–136.

38 Greenberg, B. S., Fazal, S. and Wober, M., *Children's Views on Advertising*, London: Independent Broadcasting Authority, Research Report, February 1986.

39 Donohue, T. R., Hencke, L. L. and Donohue, W. A., Non-verbal assessment of children's understanding of television commercial content and programme market segmentation, *Journal of Advertising Research*, 1980, 20(5), 7.

40 Gaines, L. and Esserman, J. F., A quantitative study of young children's comprehension of television programmes and commercials, in J. F. Esserman (ed.), *Television Advertising and Children*, New York: Child Research Service, 1981; Rossiter and Robertson, op. cit..

41 Riecken, G. and Yavas, U., Children's general product and brand-specific attitudes towards television commercials: implications for public policy and advertising strategy, *International Journal of Advertising*, 1990, 9, 136–148.

42 Greenberg et al., op. cit.

43 Riecken and Yavas, op. cit.

44 Collins, J., Television and primary school children in Northern Ireland: the impact of advertising, *Journal of Educational Television*, 1990, 16, 31–39.

45 Isler, I., Popper, E. and Ward, S., Children's purchase requests and parental responses, *Journal of Advertising Research*, 1987, 27, 54–59; Robertson, T. S., Ward, S., Gatigon, H. and Klees, D. M., Advertising and children: a crosscultural study, *Communication Research*, 1989, 16, 459–485.

46 Adler, R. P., Lesser, G. S., Meringoff, L. K., Robertson, T. S., Rossiter, J. R. and Ward, S., *The Effects of Television Advertising on Children: Review and Recommendations*, Lexington, MA: Lexington Books, 1980.

47 Dorr, A., *Television and Children: A Special Medium for a Special Audience*, Beverly Hills, CA: Sage, 1986; Moschis, G. P. and Moore, R. L., A longitudinal study of television advertising effects, *Journal of Consumer Research*, 1982, 9(3), 279–286.

48 Galst, J. P. and White, M. A., The unhealthy persuader: the reinforcing value of television and children's purchase-influencing attempts at the supermarket, *Child Development*, 1976, 47, 1089–1096; Robertson, T. S., Parental mediation of television advertising effects, *Journal of Communication*, 1979, 29, 12–25.

49 Riem, H., *Reclame en het kind: de invioed von TV-reclame op kinderen*, Antwerp: University of Antwerp, 1987.

50 Robertson and Rossiter, Stimulus Dispositional Variables op. cit.

51 Greenberg et al., op. cit.

52 Young, op. cit.

53 Goldberg, M. E., A quasi-experiment assessing the effectiveness of TV advertising directed to children, *Journal of Marketing Research*, 1990, 27, 445–454.

54 Atkin, C. and Block, M., *Content and Effects of Alcohol Advertising*, prepared for the Bureau of Alcohol, Tobacco and Firearms, no. PB82 – 123142, Springfield, VA: National Technical Information Service, 1981.

55 Ross, A. (ed.), *Economic and Industrial Awareness in the Primary School*, London: PNL Press, 1990.

56 Moore, R., Effects of television on family consumer behaviour, in J. Bryant (ed.), *Television and the American Family*, Hillsdale, NJ: Lawrence Erlbaum Associates, 1990.

57 Smith, G. and Sweeney, E., *Children and Television Advertising: An Overview*, London: Children's Research Unit, 1984.

58 Schneider, C., *Children's Television: The Art, the Business and How it Works*, Lincolnwood, Chicago: NTC Business Books, 1987.

10 DOES TV AFFECT CHILDREN'S HEALTH ORIENTATION?

1 Harris, L. M. and Hamburg, M. A., Back to the future: television and family health-care management, in J. Bryant (ed.), *Television and the American Family*, Hillsdale, NJ: Lawrence Erlbaum Associates, 1990 (pp. 329–367).

2 Kline, F. G., Miller, P. V. and Morrison, A. J., Adolescents and family planning information: an exploration of audience needs and media effects, in J. Blumler and E. Katz (eds), *The Uses of Mass Communications*, Beverly Hills, CA: 1974; Miller, P. V. and Morrison, A. J. and Kline, F. G., *Approaches to Characterising Information Environments*, paper presented at the meeting of the International Communication Association, New Orleans, 1974.

3 Cassata, M. B., Skill, T. D. and Boadu, S. O., In sickness and in health, *Journal of Communication*, 1989, 29(4), 73–80.

4 Turow, J., *Playing Doctor: Television Storytelling and Medical Power*, Oxford: Oxford University Press, 1989.

5 Howitt, D., *Mass Media and Social Problems*, Oxford: Pergamon Press, 1982; Harris and Hamburg, op. cit.

6 Katzman, N., Television soap operas: what's been going on anyway?, *Public Opinion Quarterly*, 1972, 36, 200–212.

7 Liebman-Smith, J. and Rosen S. C., The presentation of illness on television, in C. Winick (ed.), *Deviance and Mass Media*, Beverly Hills CA: Sage, 1978.

8 Gross, L. and Jeffries-Fox, S., What do you want to be when you grow up little girl?, in G. Tuchman, A. Daniels and J. Benet (eds), *Hearth and Home: Images of Women in the Mass Media*, New York: Oxford University Press, 1978.

9 Gerbner, G., Gross, L., Morgan, M. and Signorielli, N., The 'mainstreaming' of America: violence profile no. 11., *Journal of Communication*, 1980, 30, 10–29.

10 Pearl, D., Bouthilet, L. and Lazar, J., *Television and Behaviour: Ten Years of Scientific Progress and Implications for the Eighties*, Rockville, MD: NIMH, 1982.

11 Gerbner, G., Morgan, M. and Signorielli, N., Programming health portrayals: what viewers see, say and do, in Pearl et al., op. cit.

12 Head, K., Content analysis of television drama programmes, *Quarterly of Film, Radio and Television*, 1954, 9, 175–194.

13 Smith, F. A., Trivax, G., Zuelhlke, D. A., Powinger, P., and Nghiem, T. L., Health information during a week of television, *New England Journal of Medicine*, 1972, 286, 518–520.

14 Greenberg, B. S., *Health Issues on Commercial Television Series*, Paper presented at the conference of the Institute of Medicine, Washington, DC, 1980.

15 Gerbner et al., op. cit.

16 Nunally, J. C., Jr, *Public Conceptions of Mental Health*, New York: Holt, Rinehart &Winston, 1961; Gerbner, G. and Tannenbaum, P., Mass media censorship and the portrayal of mental illness: some effects of industry-wide controls in motion pictures and television, in W. Schramm (ed.), *Studies of Innovation of Communication to the Public*, Stanford: Stanford University Press, 1962.

17 Greenberg, B. S., Pery, L. and Covet, A. M., The body human: sex education, politics and television, *Family Relations: Journal of Applied Family and Child Studies*, 1983, 32 (3), 419–425.

18 Turow, J. and Coe, L., Curing television's ills: the portrayal of health care, *Journal of Communication*, 1985, 35, 36–57.

19 Choate, R. B., *Testimony Before the Federal Trade Commission in the Matter of a Trade Regulation Rule on Food Nutrition Advertising*, Washington, DC Council on Children, Media and merchandising, 1976.

20 Barcus, F. E., *Saturday Children's Television: A Report on TV Programming and Advertising on Boston Commercial Television*, Newtonville, MA: Action for Children's Television, 1971.

21 US Senate Select Committee on Nutrition and Human Needs, *Dietary Goals for the United States*, Washington DC: US Government Printing Office, 1977.

22 'Mauro, F. J. and Feins, R. P., *Kids, Food and Television: The Compelling Case for State Action*, report for the Office of Research and Analysis Program and Committee Staff, New York State Assembly, March 1977.

23 Condry, J. C., Bence, P. and Schiebe, C., Non-program content of children's television, *Journal of Broadcasting and Electronic Media*, 1988, 32(3), 255–270.

24 Ibid.

25 Dawson, B. L., Jeffrey, D. B. and Walsh, J. A., Television food commercials effects on children's resistance to temptation, *Journal of Applied Social Psychology*, 1988, 18, 1353–1360.

26 Esserman, J., Viewing of commercials and children's understanding of the rules of nutrition, in J. Esserman (ed.), *Television Advertising and Children: Issues, Research and Findings*, New York: Child Research Service, 1981.

27 Wilman, A. R. and Newman, L. M., Television advertising exposure and children's nutritional awareness, *Journal of the Academy of Marketing Science*, 1989, 17(2), 179–188.

28 Barry, T. E. and Gunst, R. F., Children's advertising: the differential impact of appeal strategy, in J. H. Leigh and C. R. Martin Jr (eds), *Current Issues and Research in Advertising*, Ann Arbor, MI: Graduate School of Business Administration, University of Michigan, 1982 (pp. 113–125).

29 Lambo, A. M., Children's ability to evaluate television commercial messages for sugared products, *American Journal of Public Health*, 1981, 719, 1060–1062.

30 Scammon, D. L. and Christopher, C. L., Nutrition education with children via television: a review, *Journal of Advertising*, 1981, 10(2), 26–36.

31 Gerbner et al., op. cit.

32 Kaufman, L., Prime-time nutrition, *Journal of Communication*, 1980, 30(3), 37–46.

33 Golderberg, M. E., Gorn, G. J. and Gibson, W., TV messages for snacks and breakfast foods: do they influence children's preferences?, *Journal of Consumer Research*, 1978, 5, 73–81.

34 Greenberg, B. S., Fazal, S. and Wober, J. M., *Children's Views on Advertising*, research paper, London: Independent Broadcasting Authority, 1986; Aitken, P., Leathar, D. S. and Scott, A. L., Ten and sixteen-year-olds' perceptions of advertisements for alcoholic drinks, unpublished paper, University of Strathclyde, Glasgow, 1987.

35 Gerbner et al., op. cit.

36 Hanneman, G. and McEwen, V., The use and abuse of drugs: an analysis of mass media content, in R. Ostman (ed.), *Communication Research and Drug Education*, Beverly Hills, CA: Sage, 1976; Garlington, W. K., Drinking on television: a preliminary study with emphasis on method, *Journal of Studies on Alcohol*, 1977, 38, 199–205.

37 Cafiso, J., Goodstadt, M. S., Garlington, W. K. and Sheppard, M. A., Television portrayal of alcohol and other beverages, *Journal of Studies on Alcohol*, 1982, 43, 1232–1234.

38 Greenberg, op. cit.

39 Breed, W. and DeFoe, J. R., The portrayal of the drinking process on prime-time television, *Journal of Communication*, 1981, 31(1), 58–67; Lowry, B., California media way of ad bans, *Advertising Age*, 1981, 5, 66.

40 Breed and DeFoe, op. cit.

41 Breed, W., DeFoe, J. R. and Wallack, L., Drinking in the mass media: a nine-year project, *Journal of Drug Issues*, 1984, 14, 655–664.

42 Hanssen, A., Alcohol, television and young people, *Brewing Review*, 1988, Summer.

43 Tucker, L. A., Television's role regarding alcohol use among teenagers, *Adolescence*, 1985, 20(79), 593–598.

44 Rychtarik, R. G., Fairbank, J. A., Allen, C. M., Fay, D. W. and Drabman, R. S., Alcohol use in television programming: effects on children's behaviour, *Addictive Behaviour*, 1983, 8, 19–22.

45 Kotch, J. B., Coulter, M. L. and Lipsitz, A. Does television influence children's attitudes towards alcohol, *Addictive Behaviour*, 1986, 11, 67–70.

46 Austin, E. W. and Meill, H. K., Effects of interpretations of televised alcoholic portrayals on children's alcoholic beliefs, *Journal of Broadcasting and Electronic Media*, 1994, 38(3), 417–435.

47 Hanssen, op. cit.

48 Strickland, D. E., Alcohol advertising: orientations and influence, *Journal of Advertising: The Quarterly Review of Marketing Communications*, 1982, 1, 307–319.

49 Atkin, C., Hocking, J. and Block, M., Teenage drinking: does advertising make a difference?, *Journal of Communication*, 1984, 34(2) 157–167.

50 Aitken et al., op. cit.

51 Henry, H. W. and, Waterson, M., The case for advertising alcohol and tobacco products, in D. S. Leathar, *Health Education and the Media*, Oxford: Pergamon Press, 1981.

52 US Public Health Service, *The 1990 Health Objectives for the Nation: A Midcourse Review*, Washington, DC: US Government Printing Office, 1986.

53 Gerbner, G., Gross, L., Morgan, M. and Signorielli, N., Special report: health and medicine on television, *New England Journal of Medicine*, 1981, 305, 901–904.

54 Young, B., *Television Advertising and Children*, Oxford: Clarendon Press, 1990.

55 Chapman, S. and Fitzgerald, B., Brand preferences and advertising recall in adolescent smokers: some implications for health promotion, *American Journal of Public Health*, 1982, 72, 491–494.

56 Charlton, A., Children's advertisement awareness related to their views on smoking, *Health Education Journal*, 1986, 45, 75–79.

57 Levitt, E. E. and Edwards, J. A., A multivariate study of correlative factors in youthful cigarette smoking, *Development Psychology*, 1970, 2, 5–11.

58 Aitken, P. P., Leathar, D. S. and Squaire, S. I., *Young People's Perceptions of Advertisements for Cigarettes*, University of Strathclyde, Department of Marketing, November 1986.

59 O'Connell, D. L., Lloyd, D. M., Alexander, H. M., Hardes, G. R., Dobson, A. J. and Springthorpe, H. J., Cigarette smoking and drug use in school children: II. Factors associated with smoking, *International Journal of Epidemiology*, 1981, 10, 223–231.

60 Lemin, B., A study of the smoking habits of 14-year-old pupils in six schools in Aberdeen, *Medical Officer*, 1966, 116, 82–85.

61 Boddewyn, J. J., *Why do Juveniles Start Smoking?*, New York: International Advertising Association, 1986; Aaron, L. E., Wold, B., Kannas, L. and Rimpola, M., Health behaviour in school children: a WHO cross-national survey, *Health Promotion*, 1986, 1, 17–23.

62 Ledwith, F., Does tobacco sports sponsorship on television act as advertising to children?, *Health Education Journal*, 1984, 43(4), 95–98.

63 Piepe, A., Charlton, P., Morey, J., Yerrell, P. and Ledwith, F., Does sponsored sport lead to smoking among children?, *Health Education Journal*, 1984, 45(3), 145–148.

64 Breed and DeFoe, op. cit.; Breed et al., op. cit.; Fernandez-Collado, C., Greenberg, B. S., Korzenny, F. and Atkin, C. K., Sexual intimacy and drug use in TV series, *Journal of Communication*, 1978, 28, 30–37.

65 Hanneman and McEwen, op. cit.

66 Fernandez-Collado et al., op. cit.

67 Gunter, B., McAleer, J. L. and Clifford, B. R., *Children's Views About Television*, Aldershot, UK: Avebury, 1991.

68 Atkin, C. K., Effects of drug commercials on young viewers, *Journal of Communication*, 1978, 28(4), 71–79.

69 Robertson, T., Rossiter, J. and Gleason, T., Children's receptivity to proprietary medicine advertising, *Journal of Consumer Research*, 1979, 6, 247–255.

70 Milavsky, R. J., Pekowsky, B. and Stipp, H., TV drug advertising and proprietary and illicit drug use among teenage boys, *Public Opinion Quarterly*, 1975, 39, 457–481.

11 DOES TV AFFECT SCHOOL PERFORMANCE?

1 Wartella, E., The child as viewer, in M. E. Ploghoft and J. A. Anderson (eds), *Education for the Television Age*, Athens, OH: The Cooperative Centre for Science Research, 1981.

2 Elliot, N., Language and cognition in the developing child, in E. Wartella (ed.), *Children Communicating: Media and Development of Thought, Speech, Understanding*, Beverly Hills, CA: Sage, 1979.

3 Himmelweit, H. T., Oppenheim, A. N. and Vince, P., *Television and the Child: An Empirical Study of the Effects of Television on the Young*, London: Oxford University Press, 1958; Schramm, W., Lyle, J. and Parker, E. B., *Television in the Lives of Our Children*, Stanford, CA; Stanford University Press, 1961; Brown, J. R., Cramond, J. K. and Wilde, R. J., Displacement effects of television on the child's functional orientation to media, in J. Blumler and E. Katz (eds), *The Uses of Mass Communications: Current Perspectives on Gratification Research*, Beverly Hills, CA: Sage, 1974.

4 Furu, T., *Television and Children's Life: A Before–After Study*, Tokyo: Japan Broadcasting Corporation, 1962; Furu, T., *The Function of Television for Children and Adolescents*, Tokyo: Sophia University Press, 1971; Werner, A. Children and Television in Norway, *Gazette*, 1971, 16, 133–151.

5 Himmelweit et al., op. cit.

6 Schramm et al., op. cit.

7 Murray, J. P. and Kippax, S., Children's social behaviour in three towns with different television experience, *Journal of Communication*, 1978, 28, 18–29.

8 Furu, T., *Cognitive Style and Television Viewing Patterns of Children*, Tokyo, research reports, Department of Audio-Visual Education, International Christian University, 1977.

9 Zuckerman, D. M., Singer, D. L. and Singer, J. L., Children's television viewing, racial and sex-role attitudes, *Journal of Applied Psychology*, 1980, 10, 281–294.

10 Singer, J. L., The power and limitation of television: a cognitive-affective analysis, in P. H. Tannenbaum (ed.), *The Entertainment Functions of Television*, Hillsdale, NJ: Lawrence Erlbaum Associates, 1980.

11 Ibid.

12 Singer, J. L., Singer, D. G. and Rapaczynski, W. S., Children's imagination as predicted by family patterns and television viewing: a longitudinal study, *Genetic Psychology Monographs*, 1984, 110, 43–69.

13 Singer, J. L. and Singer, D. G., *Television, Imagination and Aggression: A Study of Preschoolers*, Hillsdale, NJ: Lawrence Erlbaum Associates, 1981.

14 McIlwraith, R. D., and Schallow, J. R., Television viewing and styles of children's fantasy, *Imagination, Cognition and Personality*, 1983, 2, 323–331.

15 Huesmann, L. R. and Eron, L. D. (eds), *Television and the Aggressive Child: A Cross-National Comparison*, Hillsdale, NJ: Lawrence Erlbaum Associates, 1986.

16 Klinger, E., *Daydreaming: Using Waking Fantasy and Imagery for Self-Knowledge and Creativity*, Los Angeles: Tanker, 1990.

17 Valkenberg, P. M., Vooijs, M. W., van der Voort, T. H. A. and Wiegman, O., Television's influence on children's fantasy styles: a secondary analysis, *Imagination, Cognition and Personality*, 1992, 12, 55–67; Valkenberg, P. M. and van der Voort, T. H. A., The influence of television on children's daydreaming styles: a one-year panel study, *Communication Research*, 1995, 22(3), 267–287.

18 Scott, L. F., Relationships between elementary school children and television, *Journal of Educational Research*, 1958, 52, 134–137.

19 Schramm et al., op. cit.
20 Morgan, M. and Gross, L., Television and educational achievement aspirations, in D. Pearl, L. Bouthilet and J. Lazar (eds), *Television and Behaviour: Ten Years of Scientific Progress and Implications for the Eighties*, Rockville, MD: NIMH, 1980.
21 Singer, J. L. and Singer, D. G., Implications of childhood television viewing for cognition, imagination and emotion, in J. Bryant and D. R. Anderson (eds), *Children's Understanding of Television: Research on Attention and Comprehension*, New York: Academic Press, 1983.
22 Pierce, C. (ed.), *Television and Education*, Beverly Hills, CA: Sage, 1978.
23 Armstrong, C. B. and Greenberg, B. S., Background television as an inhibitor of cognitive processing, *Human Communication Research*, 1990, 16(3), 355–386; Armstrong, C. B., Bioraskyn G. A. and Mares, M. L., Background television and reading performance, *Communication Monographs*, 1991, 58, 235–253; Furnham, A., Gunter, B. and Peterson, E., Television distraction and the performance of introverts and extraverts, *Applied Cognitive Psychology*, 1994, 8, 705–711.
24 Forsslund, T., Factors that influence the use and impact of educational television in school, *Journal of Educational Television*, 1991, 17(1), 15–30.
25 Mielke, K., Research and development at the Children's Television Workshop, *Educational Technology Research and Development*, 1990, 38(4), 7–16;
26 Forsslund, op. cit.
27 Moss, R., Jones, C. and Gunter, B., *Television in Schools*, London: John Libbey, 1991.
28 Gotthelf, C. and Peel, T., The Children's Television Workshop goes to school, *Educational Technology Research and Development*, 1990, 38(4), 25–33.
29 Choate, E., Children, television and learning in infant and nursery schools, *Educational Studies*, 1988, 14(1), 9–21.
30 Greenfield, P., *Mind and Media: The Effects of Television, Computers and Video Games*, London: Fontana, 1984.
31 Tidhar, C. E., Wohl, A. and Peri, S., *Using Television in Initial Reading Programmes: The Effects of First Grade Reading Achievement*, Tel Aviv: Israel Educational Television, 1988.
32 Moses, D. and Croll, P., *The Use of Educational Television in School Paper 1: Schools' Television and the National Curriculum*, London: BBC Research, 1989.
33 Lesser, G. S., Assumptions behind the production and writing methods in *Sesame Street*, in W. Schramm (ed.), *Quality in Instructional Television*, Honolulu: University of Hawaii Press, 1972.
34 Lesser, G. S., *Children and Television: Lessons from 'Sesame Street'*, New York: Random House, 1974.
35 Bogatz, G. A. and Ball, S., *The First Year of 'Sesame Street': An Evaluation*, Princeton, NJ: Educational Testing Service, 1970.
36 Bogatz, G. A. and Ball, S., *The Second Year of 'Sesame Street': A Continuing Evaluation*, Princeton, NJ: Educational Testing Service, 1971.
37 Bogart, J. Alexander, A. F. and Brown, D., Learning from educational television programmes, in M. J. A. Howe (ed.), *Learning from Television: Psychological and Educational Research*, London: Academic Press, 1983.
38 Bryant, J., Zillmann, D. and Brown, D., Entertainment features in children's educational television: effects on attention and information acquisition, in J. Bryant and D. R. Anderson (eds), *Children's Understanding of Television: Research on Attention and Comprehension*, New York: Academic Press, 1983 (pp. 221–240).

39 O'Bryan, K. G. and Silverman, H., *Research Report: Experimental Programme Eye Movement Study*, New York: Children's Television Workshop, 1976.

40 Chen, M., *Verbal Response to 'The Electric Company': Qualities of Programme Material and the Viewing Conditions Which Affect Verbalisation*, New York: Children's Television Workshop, 1972.

41 Ball, S. and Bogatz, G. A., *Reading with Television: An Evaluation of 'The Electric Company'* Princeton, NJ: Educational Testing Service, 1973.

42 Moss et al., op. cit.

43 McAleer, J. L. and Gunter, B., An investigation into the use and perceived value of an educational TV programme made for schools, *Journal of Educational Television*, 1988, 14(2), 123–135.

44 Hurst, P., The utilization of educational broadcasts, *Educational Broadcasting International*, 1981, 14(3), 104–107.

45 Moss et al., op. cit.

46 Gunter, B. and Moss, R., Maths teachers on maths programmes for schools, *Mathematics Teaching*, 1994, 151, 30–33.

12 HOW CAN PARENTS INFLUENCE CHILDREN'S VIEWING?

1 Bower, R. T., *Television and the Public*, New York: Holt, Rinehart & Winston, 1973.

2 Glynn, C. J., Huston, A. C. and Spera, L., Children's use of time in their everyday activities during middle childhood, in M. N. Bloch and A. D. Pellegrini (eds), *The Ecological Context of Children's Play*, Norwood, NJ: Ablex, 1989.

3 St Peters, M. and Huston, A. C., Family television use and its relation to children's cognitive skills and social behaviour, in J. Bryant (ed.), *Television and the American Family*, Hillsdale, NJ: Lawrence Erlbaum Associates, 1990 (pp. 227–251).

4 Gunter, B. and Svennevig, M., *Behind and in Front of the Screen: Television's Involvement with Family Life*, London: IBA/John Libbey, 1987.

5 Niven, H., Who in the family selects the TV programmes?, *Journalism Quarterly*, 1960, 37, 110–111.

6 Simon, D. C., The selection of television programmes, *Journal of Broadcasting*, 1961, 6, 35–44.

7 Chaffee, S. H. and Tims, A. R., Interpersonal factors in adolescent TV use, *Journal of Social Issues*, 1976, 32, 98–115.

8 Comstock, G. A., New emphases in research on the effects of television and film violence, in E. Palmer and A. Dorr (eds), *Children and the Faces of Television: Teaching, Violence, Selling*, New York: Academic Press, 1980.

9 Corporation for Public Broadcasting, *Proceedings of the 1980 Technical Conference on Qualitative Television Ratings: Final Report*, Washington, DC: US Government Printing Office, 1980.

10 Ward, B., Television viewing and family differences, *Public Opinion Quarterly*, 1968, 32, 84–94.

11 Lull, J., How families select television programmes: a mass observational study, *Journal of Broadcasting*, 1982, 26, 801–811.

12 Lull, op. cit.

13 Schramm, W., Lyle, J. and Parker, E. B., *Television in the Lives of our Children*, Stanford, CA: Stanford University Press, 1960.

14 McLeod, J. and Brown, J. D., The family environment and adolescent television use, in R. Brown (ed.), *Children and Television* London: Collier Macmillan, 1976.

15 Chaffee, S. H., McLeod, J. M. and Atkin, C. K., Parental influences on adolescent media use, *American Behavioural Scientist*, 1971, 14, 323–340.

16 Chaffee, S. H., McLeod, J. M. and Wackman, D., Family communication patterns and adolescent political participation, in J. Dennis (ed.), *Socialisation to Politics*, New York: John Wiley, 1973.

17 Wade, S. E., Interpersonal discussions: a critical predictor of leisure activity, *Journal of Communication*, 1973, 23, 426–445.

18 Chaffee et al., op. cit.

19 McLeod and Brown, op. cit.

20 Chaffee et al., op. cit.

21 Hedinsson, E., *TV, Family and Society: The Social Origins and Effects of Adolescents' TV Use*, Stockholm: Almquist and Wiksell International, 1981.

22 Lull, J., The social uses of television, *Human Communication Research*, 1980, 6, 97–109.

23 Olwers, D., *Aggression in the Schools: Bullies and Whipping Boys*, Washington, DC: Hemisphere, 1978; Singer, J. L. and Singer, D. G., *Television, Imagination and Aggression: A Study of Preschoolers*, Hillsdale, NJ: Lawrence Erlbaum Associates, 1981.

24 Desmond, R. J., Hirsch, B., Singer, D. and Singer, J., Gender differences, mediation, and disciplinary styles in children's responses to television, *Sex Roles*, 1987, 16(7/8), 375–389.

25 Ibid.

26 Gunter, B., Sancho-Aldridge, J. and Winstone, P., *Television: The Public's View – 1993*, London: John Libbey, 1994.

27 Greenberg, B. S., Ericson, P. M. and Vlahos, M., Children's television behaviour as perceived by mother and child, in E. A. Rubinstein, G. A. Comstock and J. P. Murray (eds), *Television and Social Behaviour*, vol. 4, *Television in Day-to-Day Life: Patterns of Use*, Washington, DC: US Government Printing Office, 1972.

28 Abel, J. D. and Bennison, M. E., Perceptions of TV programme violence by children and mothers, *Journal of Broadcasting*, 1976, 20, 355–363.

29 Cantor, J. and Reilly, S., Adolescents' fright reactions to television and films, *Journal of Communication*, 1982, 32, 87–99.

30 Steiner, G. A., *The People Look at Television*, New York: Knopf, 1963.

31 Lyle, J. and Hoffmann, H. R., Children's use of television and other media, in Rubinstein et al., op. cit.

32 McLeod, J. M., Bybee, C. R. and Durrell, J. A., Decision-making by adolescent children and their mothers, unpublished manuscript, Mass Communication Research Centre, University of Wisconsin, Madison, 1978.

33 Streicher, L. and Bonney, N., Children talk about television, *Journal of Communication*, 1974, 24, 54–61.

34 Mohr, P. J., Parental guidance of children's viewing of evening television programmes, *Journal of Broadcasting*, 1979, 23, 213–228.

35 Holman, J. and Braithwaite, V., Parental lifestyles and children's television viewing, *Australian Journal of Psychology*, 1982, 34, 375–382.

36 Dorr, A., Kovaric, P. and Doubleday, C., Parent–child coviewing of television, *Journal of Broadcasting and Electronic Media*, 1989, 33, 35–51.

37 Messaris, P. and Sarett, C., On the consequences of television-related parent–child interactions, *Human Communication Research*, 1981, 7(3), 226–244.

38 Messaris, P. and Kerr, D., Others' comments about TV: relation to family communication patterns, *Communication Research*, 1983, 10(2), 175–194.

39 Abel, J. D., The family and children's television viewing, *Journal of Marriage and the Family*, 1976, 38, 331–353; Collins, W. A. and Westby, S., *Moral Judgements*

of Television Characters as a Function of Programme Comprehension, paper presented at the Society for Research in Child Development biennial meeting, Boston, MA, April 1981.

40 Reid, L. N. and Frazier, C., Children's use of television commercials to initiate social interaction in family viewing situations, *Journal of Broadcasting*, 24, 149–158.

41 Messaris, P., Family conversations about television, *Journal of Family Issues*, 1983, 4(8), 293–308.

42 Heald, G. R., Television viewing guides and parental recommendations, *Journalism Quarterly*, 1980, 37, 141–144.

43 Cohen, A., Abelman, R. and Greenberg, B. S., The impact of child- and adult-oriented TV literacy information on high and moderate conscience, unpublished manuscript, Department of Telecommunication, Michigan State University, East Lansing, 1988.

44 Abelman, R., *Sex Differences in Parental Disciplining Practices: An Antecedent of Television's Impact on Children*, paper presented at the annual International Communications Association conference, Honolulu, Hawaii, May 1985.

45 Korzenny, F., Greenberg, B. S. and Atkin, C. K., Styles of parental disciplining practices as a medium of children's learning from antisocial television portrayals, unpublished manuscript, Department of Telecommunications, University of Michigan, East Lansing, 1978.

46 Abelman, op. cit.

47 Ibid.

48 Desmond, R. J., Singer, J. L., Singer, D. G., Calam, R. and Colimore, K., Family mediation patterns and television viewing: young children's use and grasp of the medium, *Human Communication Research*, 1985, 11(4), 461–480.

49 Bybee, C., Robinson, D. and Turow, J., Determinants of parental guidance of children's television viewing for a special subgroup: mass media scholars, *Journal of Broadcasting*, 1982, 26, 697–710.

50 Van der Voort, T. H. A., Nikken, P. and van Lil, J. E., Determinants of parental guidance of children's television viewing: a Dutch replication study, *Journal of Broadcasting and Electronic Media*, 1992, 36(1), 61–74.

51 Kelley, M. R., *A Parent's Guide to Television: Making the Most of it*, New York: Wiley, 1983.

52 Brown, L. K., *Taking Advantage of Media: A Manual for Parents and Teachers*, London: Routledge & Kegan Paul, 1986.

13 HOW CAN SCHOOLS INFLUENCE CHILDREN'S VIEWING?

1 Moss, R., Jones, C. and Gunter, B., *Television in Schools*, London: John Libbey, 1991.

2 Masterman, L., *Teaching About Television*, London: Macmillan, 1980.

3 Langham, J., *Teachers and Television: A History of the IBA's Educational Fellowship Scheme*, London: John Libbey, 1990.

4 ibid.

5 Moss et al., op. cit.

6 Moss et al., op. cit.

7 Buckingham, D., Media education and the media industries: bridging the gaps?, *Journal of Educational Television*, 1995, 21(1), 7–22.

8 Bates, I., Clarke, J., Finn, D., Moore, R. and Willis, P., *Schooling for the Dole: The New Vocationalism*, London: Macmillan, 1984; Stafford, R., Media studies

or manpower services?, *Screen*, 1983, 24(3), 74–76; Wollen, T., The new vocationalism, in Society for Education in Film and Television, *Papers from the Bradford Media Education Conference*, London: SEFT, 1986.

9   Bazalgette, C. (ed.), *Primary Education: A Curriculum Statement*, London: British Film Institute, 1989.

10   Blanchard, T., *Media Studies at 16+*, London: British Film Institute, 1989; Burton, G. and Dimbleby, R., *Teaching Communication*, London: Routledge, 1990.

11   Stafford, R., Redefining creativity: extended project work in GCSE media studies, in D. Buckingham (ed.), *Watching Media Learning*, London: Falmer Press, 1990.

12   Dowmunt, T., *Video with Young People*, London: Interaction Imprint, 1980.

13   Lorac, C. and Weiss, M., *Communication and Social Skills*, Exeter: Wheaton, 1981.

14   Ferguson, B., Practical work and pedagogy, *Screen Education*, 1981, 38, 42–55; Masterman, L., *Teaching about Television*, London: Macmillan, 1980.

15   Anderson, J. A., Television literacy and the critical viewer, in J. Bryant and D. R. Anderson (eds), *Children's Understanding of Television: Research on Attention and Comprehension*, New York: Academic Press, 1983.

16   Ibid.

17   Blessington, J., What the TV industry is doing to help youth, in M. E. Ploghoft and J. A. Anderson (eds), *Education for the Television Age*, Athens, OH: The Cooperative Centre for Social Science Education, 1981; Columbia Broadcasting System, Office of Social Research, *A Study of the CBS Television Reading Program*, New York: CBS, 1979; Warford, P., Educational projects at ABC television, in Ploghoft and Anderson, op. cit.; Young, M. R., The PTA Project, in Ploghoft and Anderson, op. cit.

18   Buerkel-Rothfuss, N., Mediating effects of television violence through curriculum education, University of Pennsylvania, unpublished doctoral dissertation, 1978.

19   Anderson, op. cit.

20   Ibid.

21   Fransecky, R. B. and Ferguson, R., New ways of seeing: the Milford visual communication project, *Audiovisual Instruction*, 1973, 18, April, 44–49.

22   Singer, D. G. and Singer, J. L., Television and the developing imagination of the child, *Journal of Broadcasting*, 1981, 25(4), 373–387; Singer, D. G., Zuckerman, D. M. and Singer, J. L., Helping elementary school children learn about TV, *Journal of Communication*, 1980, 30(3), 84–93.

23   Dorr, A., Graves, S. B. and Phelps, E., Television literacy for young children, *Journal of Communication*, 1980, 30(3), 71–83

24   Christenson, P. G., Children's perceptions of TV commercials and products: the effects of PSAs, *Communication Research*, 1982, 9(4), 491–524.

25   Singer, D. G. and Singer, J. L., Learning how to be intelligent consumers of television, in M. J. A. Howe (ed.), *Learning from Television: Psychological and Educational Research*, London: Academic Press, 1983.

26   Dorr, A., When social scientists cooperate with broadcasting, in S. Oskamp (ed.), *Television as a Social Issue*, Beverly Hills, CA: Sage, 1980.

27   Abelman, R. and Courtright, J., Television literacy: Amplifying the cognitive level effects of television's prosocial fare through curriculum intervention, *Journal of Research and Development in Education*, 1983, 17(1), 46–57.

28 Abelman, R., TV literacy II: amplifying the affective level effects of television's prosocial fare through curriculum intervention, *Journal of Research and Development in Education*, 1987, 20(2), 40–49.

29 Masterman, op. cit.

30 Buscombe, E., *Television in Schools and Colleges*, London: Independent Broadcasting Authority, Educational Fellowship Report, 1977.

31 Kelley, P., Buckle, L. and Gunter, B., The television literacy project, *Secondary Education Journal*, 1986, 15, 21–22; Kelley, P. and Gunter, B., Television literacy, *Times Educational Supplement*, 1984, 12 October; Kelley, P., Gunter, B. and Kelley, C., Teaching television in the classroom: results of a preliminary study, *Journal of Educational Television*, 1985, 11, 57–63.

32 Kelley, P., Failing our children? The comprehension of younger viewers, *Journal of Educational Television*, 1991, 17(3), 149–157.

33 Vooijs, M. W. and van der Voort, T. H. A., Teaching children to evaluate television violence critically: the impact of a Dutch schools television project, *Journal of Educational Television*, 1993, 19(3), 139–152.

34 Vooijs, M. W., van der Voort, T. H. A. and Hoogeweij, J., Critical viewing of television news: the impact of a Dutch schools television project, *Journal of Educational Television*, 1995, 21(1), 23–36.

14 MAKING THE BEST OF TELEVISION

1 Biocca, F. and Levy, M. R. (eds), *Communication in the Age of Virtual Reality*, Hillsdale, NJ: Lawrence Erlbaum Associates, 1995.

2 Davies, M. M., *Television is Good for your Kids*, London: Hilary Shipman, 1989.

3 Okagaki, L. and Frensch, P. A., Effects of video game playing on measures of spatial performance: gender effects in late adolescence, *Journal of Applied Developmental Psychology*, 1994, 15, 33–58; Subrahmanyam, K. and Greenfield, P. M., Effect of video game practice on spatial skills in girls and boys, *Journal of Applied Developmental Psychology*, 1994, 15, 13–32.

4 Mandinach, E. B. and Corno, L., Cognitive engagement variations among students of different ability level and sex in a computer problem-solving game, *Sex Roles*, 1985, 13, 241–251.

5 Subrahmanyam and Greenfield, op. cit.

6 Bryant, J. and Anderson, D. R. (eds), *Children's Understanding of Television: Research on Attention and Comprehension*, New York: Academic Press, 1983.

7 Clifford, B., Gunter, B. and McAleer, J., *Television and Children: Programme Evaluation, Comprehension and Impact*, Hillsdale, NJ: Lawrence Erlbaum Associates, 1995.

8 Ibid.

9 Federman, J., *Executive Summary: National Television Violence Study*, Los Angeles, CA: Mediascope, Inc, 1996.

10 Gunter, B., *Dimensions of Television Violence*, Aldershot, UK: Gower, 1985; van der Voort, T. H. A., *Television Violence: A Child's Eye View*, Amsterdam, The Netherlands: Elsevier, 1986; Hodge, B. and Tripp, D., *Children and Television*, Cambridge, UK: Polity Press, 1986.

11 Gunter, B., McAleer, J., and Clifford, B., *Children's Views About Television*, Aldershot, UK: Avebury, 1991.

12 Griffiths, M. D., Amusement machine playing in childhood and adolescence: a comparative analysis of video games and fruit machines, *Journal of Adolescence*, 1991, 14(1), 53–73.

Index

Abelman, R. 193–4
actors on television 47, 48, 86
adolescents: alcohol 148, 159–61; delinquent/non-delinquent 49–50; horror movies 26; occupations 80–1; opportunity costs 13; smoking 162; viewing rates 187
advertising: age factors 136–9, 143; alcohol 147–8, 156–7, 160–1; children's reactions 133–7, 144–8; cognitive overload 68–9; controls 132–3, 134; failures 148; immorality used in 134; nutrition 153–5; pharmaceuticals 153, 163–5; and programmes 43, 47, 132–3, 135–7, 140–4; recall 139–40; selling purpose 140, 142; sex differences 142, 143, 145–6; sponsorship 141, 163; tobacco 161–3; understanding 135–44, 207
advice, from television 19, 20–1
age factors: advertising 136–9, 143; attention while viewing 31–2, 36–8, 136–9; factual recall 59, 65–6; form/content of programmes 41; moral judgements 53–5, 129–30; parental pestering 145; reality/fantasy distinctions 46–52; understanding of programmes 34, 44–6; viewing time 4, 6–7, 168, 187
aggressive behaviour: perpetrator-action-target 95–6; pre-existing 103–4, 109–10, 112–14; violence on television xii, 4–5, 24–5, 92–4, 201, 221
AIDS 150, 151
alcohol advertising 147–8, 156–7, 160–1
alcohol consumption 156, 157, 159–61, 166

All in the Family 87, 89
American Psychological Association 93
Anderson, Dan 3, 35, 36
Anderson, James 201
Andison, Scott 116
animation 48; *see also* cartoons
arousal, from violence portrayed 102
Aston University Communication Research Group 98
Atkin, Charles 88, 89–90
attention to viewing 3, 4, 29–32, 36–8, 135–9
attentional inertia 35
Australian television 12, 114, 126, 162, 169

Bandura, Albert 106–7
BBC, television research 96–8
behavioural influences 114, 121–7, 145–8
Belson, William 112
Berkowitz, Leonard 107
bias, television 72–3
The Big Blue Marble 86
The Bill 50
Birth of a Nation 84
black people portrayed 83–6, 88–91
black viewers 90–1
Blue Peter 175
The Brady Bunch 125–6
brand loyalty 162
brand names 137, 139
brand switching 144, 161
Britain: educational television 174–5, 179–81; reading/television studies 168–9; sex-role influences 79–80; television literacy 209–16; violence on television 93–4, 96–9, 111–12